Public versus Private Power during the Truman Administration

Modern American History
The United States since 1865

Frank Ninkovich
General Editor

Vol. 1

PETER LANG
New York • Washington, D.C./Baltimore • Boston
Bern • Frankfurt am Main • Berlin • Vienna • Paris

Phyllis Komarek de Luna

Public versus Private Power during the Truman Administration

A Study of Fair Deal Liberalism

PETER LANG
New York • Washington, D.C./Baltimore • Boston
Bern • Frankfurt am Main • Berlin • Vienna • Paris

333.7932
D 36 p

Library of Congress Cataloging-in-Publication Data

de Luna, Phyllis Komarek.
Public versus private power during the Truman administration:
a study of fair deal liberalism / Phyllis Komarek de Luna.
p. cm. — (Modern American history; v. 1)
Includes bibliographical references and index.
1. Electric utilities—Government ownership—United States—History.
2. Hydroelectric power plants—Government ownership—United States—
History. 3. Truman, Harry S., 1884–1972. 4. United States—Politics and
government—1945–1953. I. Title. II. Series: Modern American history
(Peter Lang Publishing); v. 1.
HD9685.U5D4   333.79'32'0973—DC20   96-19238
ISBN 0-8204-3144-3
ISSN 1085-066X

Die Deutsche Bibliothek-CIP-Einheitsaufnahme

de Luna, Phyllis Komarek:
Public versus private power during the Truman administration:
a study of fair deal liberalism / Phyllis K. de Luna.
– New York; Washington, D.C./Baltimore; Boston; Bern;
Frankfurt am Main; Berlin; Vienna; Paris: Lang.
(Modern American history; Vol. 1)
ISBN 0-8204-3144-3
NE: GT

Cover design by James F. Brisson.

The paper in this book meets the guidelines for permanence and durability
of the Committee on Production Guidelines for Book Longevity
of the Council of Library Resources.

∞

Printed in the United States of America.

For my daughters,
Cindy, Chris and Susan,
who have filled my life with love
and my heart with pride.

Acknowledgments

The assistance of many persons over a number of years made this study possible.

First of all, I want to thank staff members who facilitated my research at the Washington National Archives, the Library of Congress, the Federal Power Commission and the Harry S. Truman Library.

The help of Richard S. Maxwell and Joseph Schwarz at the Archives, Lawrence Byrd at the old Washington National Records Center in Suitland, Maryland and William L. Webb at the FPC was invaluable.

I am especially grateful to Director Benedict K. Zobrist and the staff of the Harry S. Truman Library. In particular, librarian Elizabeth Safly and archivists Dennis E. Bilger, Harry Clark, Raymond Geselbracht, Philip D. Lagerquist, Warren Ohrvall, Sam Rushay, and Randy Sowell provided me with friendly, efficient assistance.

Special thanks must go to my sister and brother-in-law, Pat and Charles Ferris, who extended me their warm hospitality during my research trips to Independence, Missouri.

I benefited from the advice of Lang Publishing's anonymous reader and that of Professors Burton M. Smith of the University of Alberta (Canada) and Roland L. De Lorme of Western Washington University, both of whom read an earlier version of this book. My thanks to Lang managing director, Christopher S. Myers, to the other Lang staff members who assisted me, and to Modern American History editor, Professor Frank Ninkovich.

The conscientious work of word-processors Ginny Elliott and Vivian Wenger made my task much easier than it otherwise would have been.

Finally, I am particularly grateful to my late father, Pat Komarek, who instilled in me a love for learning, and to my husband, French historian Frederick A. de Luna, whose support and encouragement were vital to the completion of this project.

Contents

Preface

In characteristic fashion, Harry S. Truman wrote in his memoirs that throughout his public service he had acted on the belief that government should be run "for the benefit of all the people and not for just the special crew who has the inside track." This rather simplistic "people versus the interests" ideal guided him and members of his administration as they fought to expand public power, particularly after 1948, when Truman was elected president in his own right.

The story of this effort, which pitted the government against a determined and powerful private power industry, provides a fascinating study of liberalism under the Fair Deal. Spirited battles were fought out amidst a torrent of ideological rhetoric. Espousing a form of economic democracy, Truman and certain administration officials put themselves forward as defending the country's natural resources against monopolization by special interests and ensuring that they were developed for the good of the whole citizenry.

Arrayed against these champions of public power and their supporters both inside and outside government, were those who fought in an equally dedicated manner for the right of private companies to develop certain water power sites and to prevent further government involvement in the generation and transmission of electrical energy. They hurled such epithets as "socialistic" and "super-government" when denouncing their opponents' program.

During more than three decades of historical debate, scholars have disagreed considerably on the political significance of the Truman presidency. Some have argued that it continued and in some respects expanded on New Deal liberalism, or that at the very least, it set an agenda for reform down the road. Others have suggested that twentieth century liberalism itself was flawed and that Truman accomplished very little real reform. A more recent trend has been to step back from the practice of judging the Fair Deal in relation to the New Deal. In doing so, some historians have viewed the Truman years as a transition to a new conservative order.

Although they have disagreed on both its nature and extent, scholars have cited the Truman Administration's public power record to support their various interpretations. They have given it only superficial attention, however, essentially because a detailed analysis of this issue has been lacking.

This book attempts to fill that void. Based on extensive archival research, it examines, in all their complexity, the many and diverse forms of this contest between public and private power interests. These range from the great battle over the administration's efforts to establish a Columbia Valley Authority to the conflicts sparked by its attempts to save four choice water power sites for federal development.

Because part of understanding this issue involves motivation, this study evaluates the Truman Administration's commitment to the New Deal heritage and to electric power liberalism in particular. It assesses the government's record in implementing its public power policies, examines the reasons behind its successes and failures and appraises the political implications of its performance. The results of this study offer valuable insights into the nature of Fair Deal liberalism and contribute to an overall understanding of the political significance of the Truman years.

The study focuses on the period 1949 to 1952, since during most of his first term Truman was indecisive about adopting a reform program. Elected by the people in 1948, he pledged to support the liberal proposals he had put before the Eightieth Congress and to renew the New Deal as he had promised in the campaign. At this point, following Truman's surprising victory at the polls, most liberals of the day agreed that liberalism went on the offensive.

1

The Progressive-New Deal
Legacy

When Harry S. Truman assumed the presidency upon the death of Franklin D. Roosevelt in April 1945, his administration inherited from the New Deal a stand on hydroelectric power that was a key component of contemporary American liberalism. This position grew out of the liberal belief that the natural resources of the country must be developed for the greatest good of the greatest number; therefore, the federal government had the responsibility to protect these resources against monopolization by special interests for private gain. Consonant with this view was the conviction that the government must ensure that electric power be developed and transmitted for the general welfare of the people.

Efforts to implement these ideas began with progressive movements in the late nineteenth century when a newly developed private power industry, aware of possibilities of long-distance transmission of electric power, began to perceive the potential advantages from building dams in navigable rivers. To ensure that private enterprise would not exploit a resource that belonged to the people, reformers urged government participation in the development and control of hydroelectric power. The conflict with private power that resulted from growing government responsibility became part of the Truman Administration's progressive-New Deal heritage. The legacy from this half-century struggle to work out the nature and extent of federal involvement also included a maze of confusing policies, laws, administrative methods and attitudes concerning public power.

Federal control of electrical energy grew out of the government's concern that privately built dams at potential power sites would impede navigation. Based on its constitutional authority to regulate interstate commerce, Congress, in acts passed in the 1890s, assumed the right to regulate these structures, declared its control over all navigable rivers and required that private companies obtain special approval from Congress to build such dams.[1]

In 1903, President Theodore Roosevelt vetoed authorization for a private group to develop water power at Muscle Shoals in Alabama. In so doing, he referred for the first time to a principle being advocated by some proponents of multipurpose development: by selling power, the government could finance river improvements. Roosevelt also urged that granting privileges to develop such sites be "considered in a comprehensive way" and that a policy be formulated to ensure that similar rights be disposed of in a manner that would "best conserve the public interest."[2]

Under the General Dam Act of 1906, Roosevelt approved a number of applications for private water power development in navigable streams. However, perhaps influenced by the conservationist leader, Chief Forester Gifford Pinchot, he came to oppose the practice of granting such permits on a "forever and for nothing" basis. Progressives argued that time limits and charges must be set in order to prevent exploitation of a natural resource that belonged to the people. The president vetoed bills in 1908 and 1909 because they contained no such provisions.[3]

Roosevelt supported the principle of multipurpose river development, as did the Inland Waterways Commission he appointed in 1908 to investigate the development of water power on navigable streams. Most progressives believed that efficiency and economics demanded that a river be developed not for just one purpose but several, such as flood control, navigation, irrigation and electric power, so as to produce the maximum benefit. Roosevelt also agreed with a recommendation of the commission, favored by reformers, that a single executive should coordinate the entire administration of water resource development. Efforts to enact the commission's recommendations failed in Congress, partly due to the opposition of the Army Corps of Engineers and the chairman of the commission himself.[4]

During Theodore Roosevelt's administration, the government became involved in the development and sale of hydroelectric power. This second entry into the electrical energy field came about incidentally, through some of the single-purpose irrigation projects in the arid and semi-arid states of the West. In 1906, Congress authorized the secretary of the interior to sell surplus power or lease power privileges from these projects. Preference was to be given to municipal bodies, and the proceeds would help irrigators with their repayment charges. Although reclamation officials saw the possibility of exercising this authority to help pay for multipurpose projects, it was little used over the next two decades. The small hydroelectric projects that were built were mainly used for pumping water at the site, and the revenues helped decrease the amounts payable by irrigation users.[5]

The federal government became involved with hydroelectric energy in a third way through its assumption of responsibility for flood control. Congressional recognition that flood control was a proper federal, rather than an essentially local, matter developed slowly, however. A turning point came in 1916 when Congress appointed a committee to study flood control in the Mississippi Valley. By 1927, when a disastrous flood hit that area, Congress established federal responsibility with a large appropriation. Dams built for this single purpose led to government generation of power. The Flood Control Act of 1936 authorized the installation of facilities for electric power development at any dam if recommended by the chief of engineers of the Army and approved by the secretary of war.[6]

An important public power principle set forth in the progressive period was contained in the preference clause of the Reclamation Act of 1906. To be repeated in a number of later acts, it granted preference in selling power generated at federal projects to municipalities and other publicly-owned bodies.

Uncertainty as to whether private enterprise could lawfully build dams and locks and be granted power rights in perpetuity continued until 1920 when key legislation was passed. The Water Power Act of that year affirmed the principle of ownership rights and jurisdiction of the federal government over water power sites in all navigable rivers; limited licenses to a maximum period of fifty years and affirmed the right of the government to charge for this privilege; granted preference to public bodies in cases of conflict with private companies; and authorized the federal government to build hydroelectric projects on the recommendation of a Federal Power Commission, which was created to administer the act.[7]

II

Truman's inheritance from the progressive and New Deal periods included three different approaches to the electric power question: government regulation, complete federal ownership and control, and partnership or other cooperative arrangements with private industry. A number of progressives, like Pinchot and Roosevelt, wanted government to set rules for the development of electric power resources in the public interest. They held that state and federal governments had the right, under common law and because of the special nature of the electric power business, to regulate electric companies. Intended to insure acceptable standards of service as well as reasonable charges, regulation was to substitute for competition.[8]

Unsatisfactory local regulation by statutes that set maximum rates, term limitations and other conditions to monopolistic franchises gave way during the Progressive Era to state commissions intended to scientifically ascertain the facts and make regulations. In general, these systems failed, mainly because of contradictory and inconsistent court decisions. In addition, private utilities

4

formed great holding companies, which effectively put them beyond the reach of state government interference.[9]

A second approach, actively promoted by Senator George Norris of Nebraska beginning in the mid-1920s, was government ownership and operation of the industry. Norris argued that this solution was required because electric power was by its nature a monopoly and because the private power industry was a "gigantic octopus" that could not be contained by regulation.[10]

A middle course between tightening regulation and complete public ownership involved partnership or other cooperative arrangements between the public and private sectors. Most progressives, however, opposed this approach because it gave corporations the opportunity to profit from government development of resources, which they said belonged to the people. In 1914 and 1916, for example, they defeated proposals in Congress to provide government aid to a private company that proposed building dams to make Muscle Shoals on the Tennessee River navigable and to generate electric power. Another version of the cooperative approach called for the government to sell federally generated power to private companies at wholesale for distribution to consumers. The government followed this practice generally in its reclamation program and, to a certain extent, at the Boulder Dam project on the Colorado River. The 1928 Boulder Dam Act allowed the government to use power revenues to finance repayment of its building costs, but failed to provide for government transmission lines or to exclude giving preference to private corporations. President Herbert Hoover later boasted that this law, which he had helped draft during the Coolidge Administration, "kept the Federal government out of the business of generating and distributing power," but because public agencies contracted to buy over 90 percent of the firm power, progressives did not agitate to change the law.[11]

Proponents of both public ownership and stricter government regulation, who usually regarded their positions as mutually exclusive, as well as advocates of other or additional measures, such as the "public yardstick" idea (comparative rate performance), conservation, and comprehensive river development, joined forces in the Muscle Shoals fight during the 1920s. Led by Senator Norris, progressives successfully fended off efforts by conservative members of Congress and Republican administrations to turn a project at Muscle Shoals over to private enterprise. The federal government had authorized the building of Wilson Dam in 1916 (unfinished until 1926) to provide electric power for producing nitrogen for explosives at two plants. It also owned two steam plants and a transmission line in the area. When Henry Ford and other private interests proposed taking over these facilities in the early 1920s, opponents charged that their doing so would preclude unified development of the Tennessee Valley in the interests of the people.[12]

The defeat in Congress of these schemes improved chances of success for Norris's plan for federal multipurpose development of the Tennessee Valley. The Norris plan called for improvement of navigation on the Tennessee River, development of power from a series of dams and production of cheap fertilizer on a trial basis. It envisioned government-owned transmission lines and an independent governmental body whose electric power operations would serve as a yardstick and prove that private companies were charging exorbitant rates. Although versions of it passed Congress, they were vetoed by conservative presidents Calvin Coolidge and Herbert Hoover. It took the election of Franklin D. Roosevelt by a huge electoral margin in the midst of a paralyzing depression to bring Norris's plan to fruition.

III

As governor of New York, Roosevelt had built up a liberal record on public power. He had successfully backed a bill in the legislature to create the New York Power Authority, which was authorized to develop hydroelectric power in the Niagara and St. Lawrence river sites. The law gave priority to municipal distributors over private ones and to rural and household consumers over industrial ones. The legislature also granted the state the right to build transmission lines. No activity occurred, however, because of strong opposition from vested interests to both the hydroelectric and Great Lakes-St. Lawrence Seaway navigation plans of the authority and because the plans required agreement between the chief executives of the United States and Canada. Both issues persisted into the Truman years and constituted an important public power problem.[13]

Roosevelt campaigned in 1932 on keeping electric power generally in the hands of private business, but with strict government regulation that would provide a yardstick for rates to prevent abuse of the public. Muscle Shoals was one of four huge government power development sites that he said could be used as such a measure. Moving swiftly once elected, Roosevelt won from Congress the Tennessee Valley Authority Act during the First Hundred Days. An important victory for the concepts of multipurpose resource development and regional planning, the act represented a significant element of the New Deal public power legacy. Production of electric power was not its main objective, but was important because it could help defray the costs to the taxpayer necessary for meeting the goals of the TVA. The major goals were maximum flood control and navigability of the Tennessee River, but generation of the greatest amount of electrical power consistent with these goals was included, along with a number of other objectives, such as national defense, reforestation, proper use of marginal lands, the agricultural and industrial development of the area, and improvement of the social and economic welfare of the valley's residents.[14]

The concept of multiple-purpose development was applied to other rivers during the 1930s, including the Bonneville Dam on the Columbia and Fort Peck Dam on the Missouri, built by the Army Corps of Engineers; and the Grand Coulee on the Columbia, built by the Bureau of Reclamation, an agency of the Department of the Interior.[15]

None of these dams was built with power generation as a major purpose, but the government saw that, in addition to helping to finance a project, the cheap and abundant power that resulted would be important in reviving the economy and in maintaining long-term economic development. This "cheap and abundant use" doctrine was based on the belief that electric power could help save the farmers, rural communities and democracy itself. Prodigal use was rationalized by the belief that if the power were not developed and used, water resources would be wasted. Private power companies opposed this theory, arguing that competitive fuels, like coal, were being put at a disadvantage because taxpayers subsidized the electric power.[16]

The unanswered question of whether the federal government should or constitutionally could build steam plants fired by coal to generate electricity was another public power legacy of the New Deal that began with the TVA. Defense production required the authority to make full use of the plants it had acquired in purchasing private systems in the area and to begin building a new plant at Watts Bar dam in 1940. Private power objections, silenced during the war, resumed once peace was restored.

The TVA also provided Truman with the first successful example of a unified administrative approach to river development. In this case, the administration was decentralized. Instead of the usual pattern in which the Department of Agriculture dealt with the problems of farmers, the Corps of Engineers worked on flood control and navigation, and the Department of the Interior concerned itself with reclamation and power, the Tennessee Valley Authority, as an autonomous public agency headquartered in the local area, administered all aspects of the improvement and use of the region's natural resources.[17]

The Roosevelt Administration pursued the cooperative approach with private industry in connection with the TVA, but it discarded the idea when the two sides reached an impasse. An interim agreement with the Commonwealth and Southern Company that carved out respective market territories lapsed in 1936. A subsequent effort to agree on a jointly owned transmission network failed after nineteen southern power companies filed a constitutional suit against the TVA, angering president Roosevelt and causing the government to break off negotiations.

After the Supreme Court upheld the constitutionality of the Tennessee Valley Authority Act in 1939, the Commonwealth and Southern Company sold its ten-firm system to the federal government, ridding the TVA of competition. Thereafter the TVA became an undeniable success. By 1943, it had built twenty-one dams, doubled consumption of electric power in the valley and demonstrated that rates could be lowered with increased use of electricity. In addition, the authority increased navigability of the Tennessee River; stimulated the production and use of new, more effective fertilizer; carried out a large reforestation program; and helped bring to the area industrial development, improved recreation facilities, road construction and increased educational facilities.

Although Roosevelt favored additional valley authorities, none were developed during his administration, partly because of a strong propaganda campaign by private utilities, often supported by national business organizations, against the TVA and public power generally. Another factor was a lack of agreement among administration and other advocates of reform as to the proper solution to the whole organizational problem. The Department of the Interior, under Harold Ickes, favored additional valley authorities, while the Department of Agriculture and the Army Corps of Engineers opposed any extension of the TVA model. Even among liberals who supported additional authorities there was disagreement. Ickes wanted the TVA and any new authorities placed in the Interior Department, while TVA Director David Lilienthal and Senator Norris believed they should be independent.[18] The disagreements on organizational structures for river basin development were handed down to Truman and would make it difficult for the new president to extend the TVA model, if he should decide to do so.

Also contributing to the failure to create more valley authorities was Roosevelt's lack of commitment to a specific plan. In 1937, FDR directed the drafting of legislation that would set up TVA-type agencies in seven regions in accordance with a plan he had discussed with Norris. He sent a message to Congress asking for such regional authorities, but he failed to push for Norris's "seven sisters" plan, which became buried in Congress.[19]

Interagency rivalry also played a role. New Deal liberals favored an authority for the Missouri Valley to reduce duplication of effort in the area by the Corps of Engineers and the Bureau of Reclamation. Roosevelt had been considering an MVA in 1944 when conflict erupted between the two agencies over their respective comprehensive development plans. Reclamation's "Sloan Plan" emphasized "upstream development with irrigation and hydroelectric power," while the engineers' "Pick Plan" stressed "down-stream, mainstem works aimed at flood control and navigation." This rivalry and lack of program coordination lent support to liberals' cry for a Missouri Valley Authority and led Roosevelt to ask Congress to create such an organization. After Congress rejected his request, the president ordered the two agencies to combine their reports, and Congress then authorized the offspring of this "shotgun marriage," the Pick-Sloan Plan, in the Flood Control Act of 1944. Roosevelt again asked Congress for a Missouri Valley Authority early in 1945, but at the time of his death in April, it had taken no action.[20]

IV

As early as 1934, officials in the Roosevelt Administration realized that when the time came to dispose of the power from the dams being built or planned, the government would have to consider establishing a clearly formulated general power policy. Efforts to do so failed, but the Roosevelt Administration did work out a policy of sorts in piecemeal fashion.

With no national broad power policy in place, one of the first important tasks of the Tennessee Valley Authority had been to formulate a policy of its own. Announced on August 25, 1933, the statement would influence policy decisions by administration officials regarding electric power elsewhere in the country. It contained eleven points. The first stated the philosophy of those who advocated public ownership: "The business of generating and distributing electric power is a public business." The next three points and point six attested to the superiority of the public interest over private in the use of this power and stated that where conflict between the two arose, the public interest must prevail, but added that the two should be reconciled if that could be done without injuring the public interest. Point five declared the right of communities to own and run their own power plants—a weapon that could be used to obtain reasonable rates either by taking over the existing plant or setting up a competing one. Points seven and eight set forth the geographical area which the TVA intended to serve to produce its "yardstick" for rates and stated that it would consider going outside this area to serve the public interest. The final three points said that the authority would try to avoid duplication when it was wasteful and in competition with private utilities, and would conduct open accounting that would allow comparisons with private utility charges.[21]

Rural Electrification Administrator Morris L. Cooke recommended to Secretary Ickes in 1934 that a broad power policy be established. Without one, he said, it was not surprising that some of the government's actions in the power field might seem "opportunistic if not illogical."[22] Ickes agreed, and at his urging, President Roosevelt appointed a National Power Policy Committee, made up of representatives of relevant government agencies and departments, to develop a general policy for both public and private power. He wanted the group to work out a plan "whereby national policy in power matters may be unified and electricity made more broadly available at cheaper rates to industry, to domestic and, particularly, to agricultural consumers." Roosevelt also asked the committee to consider the problem of federal regulation of holding companies.[23]

The NPPC came up with a power trust control measure, but failed to develop a broad power policy. Among the reasons were the concern of many of its members for protecting the prerogatives of their own agencies and their inability or unwillingness to view the power question as a whole.

The War Department's Corps of Engineers was the agency most often opposed to the liberal power policy proposals of the president and interagency committees like the National Power Policy Committee. In 1937, it opposed legislation recommended by the NPPC, which Roosevelt had charged with drawing up a federal power program that would fit in with his executive reorganization plan and deal with the problem of disposing of electric power from the Bonneville Dam project. Corps of Engineers spokesmen argued against setting low, uniform rates for the Pacific Northwest, opposed building what they termed a superpower network of transmission lines, and agreed with private power interests that there was no market for this power in the Northwest.[24]

Measures had been introduced in Congress authorizing the Corps of Engineers to run Bonneville and dispose of the power. Public power liberals believed that passage would have been tantamount to selling the power to private companies at the bus bar (where the transmission system connects to the powerhouse). The Bonneville Project Act of 1937, however, called for the engineers to be involved only in the operation of the navigation facilities. The secretary of the interior was directed to appoint an administrator to build up a grid system connecting Bonneville with Grand Coulee and to dispose of the electric power, granting preference to public bodies and cooperatives.[25]

By the Reclamation Project Act of 1939, these policies for distribution of power at Bonneville Dam were applied generally to Bureau of Reclamation projects (although many of them had been followed on such projects for a number of years).

In the same year, Roosevelt directed a reactivated and reconstituted National Power Policy Committee to work out a national power policy appropriate for the needs of both war and peace. But with the emphasis on producing electricity for a defense program, the problem of enunciating a broad power policy was again evaded.[26]

Through the efforts of the president and the Department of the Interior, the policies for Bonneville power distribution were made to apply generally to projects constructed by the Corps of Engineers under Section 5 of the Flood Control Act of 1944.

This act authorized an extensive postwar program of multipurpose projects, spelled out federal policy for the construction of Army flood control and multipurpose river basin projects, and authorized the secretary of the interior to dispose of electric power generated at reservoir projects controlled by the War Department. The power was to be marketed according to the principles of encouraging the most widespread use at the lowest possible rates consistent with sound business practices and granting preference to public bodies and cooperatives. Rate schedules were to be determined with the aim of recovering the production and transmission costs of the electric power, including the "amortization of the capital investment allocated to power over a reasonable period of years." The Corps of Engineers did not support Roosevelt in this move nor in his decision to designate the Department of the Interior as the marketing agency for power; in fact, it made recommendations to Congress that were at variance with the president's wishes.[27]

During congressional consideration of the 1944 Flood Control bill, debate became heated over the question of whether the government had the right and responsibility to build transmission lines or whether federally generated electric power should be sold to private companies at the bus bar. Private power proponents tried unsuccessfully to require that hydroelectric power from Corps of Engineers projects be sold at the dams, which would have meant private power would have gotten most of the power. The final version granted the secretary of the interior the right, with funds to be appropriated by Congress, "to construct or acquire . . . only such transmission lines and related facilities as may be necessary to make the power and energy . . . available in wholesale quantities . . . to facilities owned by the Federal Government, public bodies, cooperatives and privately owned companies."[28]

The 1944 act contained the basis for much of the government's power policy when Truman became president. One of the important issues it left unresolved was whether the federal government had the responsibility to ensure that the American people would be provided with sufficient power or whether its role was merely to generate electrical energy secondary to its other activities and to make it available at wholesale.

V

More unfinished public power business when Truman entered the Oval Office was completion of the task of bringing electricity to the nation's farmers. Liberals regarded the establishment of the Rural Electrification Administration as an important New Deal achievement, for its programs had resulted in reduced control of private industry over the basic needs of society and had opened new markets by stimulating increased use of electricity.

A 1934 report by Morris L. Cooke, who had fought for public power in Pennsylvania, showed that only about 650,000 farmers out of 6 million in the country had electric service, and presented evidence that farm electrification was economically feasible. This report helped spawn the REA, which was created by executive order in 1935.[29]

The agency began as a part of the New Deal's works relief program, but Cooke, as its administrator, won the right to operate the REA as a lending agency.[30] Rejecting the idea of private utilities as recipients of the loans, Cooke embarked on a program of encouraging farmer-established, non-profit cooperatives to carry out the rural electrification program.[31]

The utility companies fought back, opposing bills introduced in Congress to make the REA an independent agency and resisting efforts to make private companies ineligible for REA loans. The Rural Electrification Act, passed in May 1936, which established the REA as a permanent federal agency, represented a compromise. Private companies could apply for loans, but nonprofit agencies would receive preference. The act also stipulated that the REA could not make grants but only loans to "self-liquidating" rural electrification projects that could assure a repayment of the loan with interest within twenty-five years.

Despite opposition from the private utility companies, which used "flying squads" of public relations men to dissuade farmers from setting up cooperatives, the REA continued to grow, particularly after it became a part of the Department of Agriculture in 1939. By 1942, nearly 40 percent of the farms in the United States had electricity as compared with 10.9 percent just before the REA was established. The agency's success was demonstrated in 1944 when Congress extended its loan authority for an indefinite period.[32]

VI

The Truman Administration also inherited from the New Deal a lessening of control by holding companies over the distribution and sale of electric power. Although not as liberal as some other New Deal public power measures, the Public Utility Act of 1935 represented an attack on bigness in favor of individual enterprise. The measure provided for immediate dissolution of holding companies containing more than three tiers of companies and the limitation of smaller systems to single utility systems. In addition, the Securities and Exchange Commission (SEC) was granted power, after 1940, to force the dissolution of all holding companies that could not justify their existence economically. Under this act, the Federal Power Commission could regulate mergers, issues of securities, and property sales of companies that transmitted electricity across state lines. The FPC also was granted the power to "integrate the operating companies into regional systems on the basis of technical efficiency."[33]

VII

When Harry Truman took office, much of the program advocated by various progressives and liberals over the past half century had been sanctioned in law and successfully tested. A number of federal multipurpose projects that included generation of power had been built, and more had been approved by the Flood Control Act of 1944. The concepts of federal comprehensive river basin development and unified, decentralized administration were realized in the Tennessee Valley Authority. And the forty-year old preference principle had been confirmed in the 1944 act.

Elements of the two major progressive approaches to the public versus private power problem formed the basis of liberal policy. Government regulation of the private power industry had been strengthened by the 1920 Water Power Act and the holding company legislation of 1935, while government ownership and control of electric power had been strengthened by the success of the TVA and by the endorsement of additional valley authorities by President Roosevelt and other prominent liberals.

The idea of forging partnership arrangements with private power as a means of advancing public power policies was tried in the New Deal period but lost ground with its rejection in the TVA experience. However, most New Deal liberals did not advocate public ownership of the entire electric power industry. To ensure that this natural monopoly would serve the best interests of the people, they wanted a federal power program large enough to compete with private industry and bring down its rates. Meeting this goal would require the federal government not only to build more hydroelectric projects but also to grant preference to public bodies and cooperatives in marketing its power. It also would require the government to encourage the formation of cooperatives and to build transmission lines to get the power to them and other preference customers.

If the Truman Administration decided to promote such ends, it was sure to face many problems inherent in the New Deal electric power legacy. These included a lack of a broad and consistent public power policy; a complex set of government units responsible for electric power that had entrenched interests and varying motives; and, with peace at hand, a private power industry ready to resume the battle to halt the expansion of public power.

2

Public Power Liberalism, 1945-1948

When World War II ended a few months after Truman became president, public power proponents hoped that the administration would turn its attention to the advancement of liberal electric power policies. At the same time, they expected private power to resume its opposition with renewed vigor.

The public versus private power conflict had been muted during the war when the private power industry had been called upon to supply much of the nation's defense needs. Both private and federal ownership of generating capacity grew considerably, but federal ownership increased at a faster rate. At the end of the war, the government's percentage of the nation's total capacity had nearly doubled, while private power's share had decreased by about 5 percent. Private companies controlled 80.4 percent of the nation's generating capacity, as compared with 85 percent in 1941; the federal government's portion stood at 10.2 percent, up from 5.5 percent in 1941. The remaining 9.4 percent rested with state and local public bodies.[1] With peace restored, each of the two sides prepared to protect and extend its own position.

Liberals in 1945 agreed that the resources of the major river basins of the country belonged to all the people and that the federal government had a responsibility to develop them for the social and economic welfare of the people. The success of the Tennessee Valley Authority experiment had demonstrated that the amount of hydroelectric energy offered was related directly to the support of a larger population with a high standard of living; therefore, low cost federal power should be made available to as many citizens as possible. For this reason and because a shortage of power was anticipated as home and industrial use increased and because some multiple-purpose projects were so large, additional direct government involvement in the generation and sale of electrical energy would be required.[2]

Seymour Harris, the prominent Keynesian economist who edited and introduced the significant economic manifesto of liberalism entitled *Saving American Capitalism*, perceived an economic advantage in government development of resources in cases when private industry could or should not be involved. He argued that such federal involvement could create a "significant outlet for the country's excess savings and a means of pushing the nation's income upward."[3]

To achieve their aims, public power advocates wanted the federal government to take a number of steps: First, in addition to building more water development projects that would include generation of hydroelectric power, it should create effective organizational and administrative machinery for bringing about comprehensive planning, development and use of the resources in the major river basins.[4] For many liberals, this meant establishing valley authorities on the TVA model; to others, it called for consolidating functions of various federal agencies responsible for water resource activities. Second, the government should maintain and expand federal power marketing policy, including strict adherence to the preference clause, through agencies like the Bonneville Power Administration. Third, it should build transmission lines to carry power generated at federal plants to preference customers, build steam plants where necessary to meet increased demand for electricity, interconnect the great dams of the country in the interest of efficiency, and encourage the formation of public utility systems and cooperatives. Fourth, the government should complete the task of rural electrification and extending REA cooperatives. Finally, it should incorporate the power policies set forth in federal statutes into a broad, national power policy.[5]

A number of statements regarding the objectives of federal generation and marketing of electric energy had already been set down in various acts of Congress. Taken together, they constituted an informal policy that most liberals wanted to maintain. Interior Secretary Harold Ickes summarized these principles in a memorandum to his staff on January 3, 1946: (1) "Federal dams shall where feasible include facilities for generating electrical energy," (2) "Preference in power sales shall be given to public agencies and cooperatives," (3) "Power disposal shall be for the particular benefit of domestic and rural consumers," (4) "Power shall be sold at the lowest possible rates consistent with sound business principles," and (5) "Power disposal shall be such as to encourage widespread use and to prevent monopolization."[6]

The major citizen groups that advocated this program were the American Public Power Association, whose members were local, publicly owned electric utilities; and the National Rural Electric Cooperative Association, which represented politically the REA-financed rural electric cooperatives.[7]

II

Private power interests objected strenuously to the liberal electric power philosophy and program. They wanted to consolidate their gains made during the war and to prevent further government encroachment. Only a minority held out the hope of recouping private power's position prior to the New Deal when it had enjoyed monopolistic control along with the ability to exact high rates. Most private power proponents, too, no longer argued that it was impossible to have flood control and hydroelectric power in the same project; instead, they accepted the Tennessee Valley Authority and projects like Bonneville on the Columbia River and Fort Peck on the Missouri River as irreversible. And they resigned themselves to the sale by the federal government of surplus power from these projects. On the other hand, they opposed the establishment of further valley authorities on the ground that they represented super-government and socialistic trends.

Private power spokesmen held strongly to the principle that government should not do what private industry could. They argued, first, that private companies should be allowed to develop individual water power sites when capital was available and the job not too large and, second, that government should not be involved in the business aspects of the electric power field. An earlier significant position of private power advocates held that power should be sold at federal dams as falling water. This course, which required private industry to build the power plant, would have meant the elimination of the government from both generation and transmission of hydroelectric power. However, efforts to achieve this goal had largely failed by 1945; private power companies now concentrated on gaining control of the federally generated power at the bus bar, which would remove the federal government from the transmission business.[8]

Private power adherents objected to the federal government's policy of selling power at the bus bar to preferred customers on the ground that it discriminated against private electric utilities. They also disagreed with the government's policy of building transmission lines as a justification for reaching those preferred customers and assuring low rates, arguing that in claiming the right of the government to take such steps, Ickes' memorandum went far beyond the intent of Congress. Private power proponents further maintained that government rates were unfair because public power enjoyed a hidden subsidy.[9]

When Senator James E. Murray introduced a bill to create a Missouri Valley Authority in 1944 and President Roosevelt recommended the plan to Congress, private utility representatives had reopened their public relations campaign against the extension of public power. The old National Electric Light Association, whose reputation had been tarnished in the early thirties, was gone, but the industry soon had four organizations to help advance its message.[10] Created in 1945, and the only one that worked openly as a lobby, was the National Association of Electric Companies. Operating with a large staff from the nation's capital, by 1949 it was one of the largest organizations registered under the Lobby Act. The other groups were the Edison Electric Institute, the national trade association of the electric power industry; the Council of Electric Operating Companies, which sponsored Nelson Eddy and the Electric Hour on radio and conducted an extensive advertising campaign in newspapers and magazines; and the Public Information Program, which devoted itself to enhancing the industry's image.[11]

Also effective in this lobbying and propaganda effort were such organizations as the National Resources Department of the Chamber of Commerce of the United States, the Mississippi Valley Association and the National Reclamation Association. The last group, which operated mainly in the Northwestern states, vigorously opposed valley authorities in the Missouri and Columbia basins.[12]

With its campaign, private power interests hoped to influence the public, as well as the Truman Administration and Congress.

III

In the executive branch of government, it was the president, of course, who had the most authority to change federal electric power policies. But in April 1945, neither side of the public versus private power fight could be sure what Harry S. Truman would do.

Liberals noted that on at least two occasions before becoming president, Truman had intimated that he opposed the extension of valley authorities. As an initiator of the Pick portion of the Pick-Sloan Plan in the Missouri Valley, a supporter of the scheme in its entirety and a friend of the Army Corps of Engineers, the new president could be regarded as an opponent of a Missouri Valley Authority since, if the Pick-Sloan Plan succeeded, the need for an authority would be lessened. Furthermore, during his vice-presidency, as president of the Senate, he had referred a bill for a Missouri Valley Authority to the Commerce Committee, which was known for its hostility to the authority, when he could have chosen another committee.[13]

Adding to the uncertainty about Truman's attitude was his ambiguous reply when asked at a press conference shortly after he assumed office if he was going to continue "the public power ambitions" of his predecessor. The president said, "Whenever it is possible and necessary, I am."[14]

Truman's actions on public power issues in his first two years in the Oval Office generally mirrored those he took on most liberal issues. Vacillating between a moderate, sometimes fairly conservative, approach and a strong liberal one, he spoke out in general terms for liberal programs pending before congress, but rarely backed specific legislation.[15]

The president also sent mixed signals by the appointments he made. At first, he encouraged liberals by retaining a number of Roosevelt men who favored expanding the New Deal, most notably Harold Ickes at interior and Henry A. Wallace at commerce; by reappointing the New Dealer David E. Lilienthal as chairman of the Tennessee Valley Authority and appointing a few progressives, like Lew Schwellenbach as secretary of labor and Fred M. Vinson as secretary of the treasury. Counterbalancing those choices was the appointment of a number of conservatives and inept cronies. Liberals were particularly critical of the president's selection of his old friend John Snyder to replace Vinson, whom Truman sent to the Supreme Court. Leader of the conservative faction in the administration and a former banker, Snyder favored big business and opposed revival of the New Deal.

Truman appeared ready to assume leadership of the liberal movement, however, with his Special Message to Congress on September 6, 1945. He fired off 21 proposals for a wide range of reforms, including an expansion of social security, a permanent Fair Employment Practices Committee and legislation to ensure full employment. Expressly based on FDR's Economic Bill of Rights as set forth in his 1944 State of the Union Message, Truman saw the speech in retrospect as marking the "beginning of the 'Fair Deal'" and as symbolizing his becoming president in his own right.[16]

Included in the list of reforms was a call for "regional development of the natural resources of our great river valleys." Although he did not specifically urge valley authorities as a means of carrying out this work, Truman did praise the TVA as an inspirational example. As if to dispel any doubts he might have raised with his remarks, the President told reporters on October 8 that he was "not retreating at all" on his idea of large, federal, regional power authorities.[17]

Despite these hopeful signs, the president's follow-up disappointed liberals. Just two days later, when dedicating a dam at Gilbertsville, Kentucky, Truman said the TVA, which was "no longer an experiment but a demonstration," could serve as guide for development other river valleys. But at the same time, he backed away from a strong valley authority stand when he added that "the details of administration and control" for each valley "may have to be different." He continued in 1945 and 1946 to praise the TVA experiment but rather than exhorting Congress to extend the model, he merely spoke generally about the importance of developing the Missouri, Columbia and other major river valleys. Nor did Truman enunciate liberal goals in pushing for federally built steam plants and transmission lines. In his 1946 State of the Union Message he justified these facilities as necessary to provide the maximum amount of power needed at wholesale markets, which are often a long distance from dams.[18]

Truman's approach to the rest of his liberal agenda was similar. He compromised again on such items as a strong unemployment compensation bill and opposed labor's resort to strikes in an attempt to protect its purchasing power. These actions, as well as the exit from the cabinet of New Dealers Harold Ickes and Henry Wallace were among the factors that led to the disastrous defeat of the Democrats in the 1946 election, when, for the first time in nearly twenty years, they lost control of Congress.[19]

Understandably, many liberals, including public power proponents, questioned whether the new president was really one of them. But those who considered the broader picture, saw that the president could not be guided in his decision making solely by ideology. Influencing his actions were many pressing domestic and foreign problems, as well as a recalcitrant congress.

A major reason for Truman's failure to push strongly for liberal domestic measures was his decision to give top priority to foreign policy. Once peace came, the most pressing problem was the growing tension between the Soviet Union and the United States. Spilling over from that conflict, which by 1947 became known as the Cold War, was the perceived threat of communism at home, which became the dominant issue in domestic affairs.

Other important domestic problems, including those associated with reconversion to a peacetime economy, also demanded the president's attention. Truman had to find a way to keep the reins on an economy that tended toward inflation in the short run and at the same time try to prevent another depression. As he struggled with price controls and demands for wage increases, Americans demanded consumer goods amidst a dramatic rise in expectations.

Contributing significantly to his difficulties with Congress was an inherited split in the Democratic Party, which had helped create a deadlock between the executive and Congress. A conservative, anti-New Deal coalition had been unleashed over Roosevelt's Supreme Court-packing plan in 1937, and by 1945, a southern and western rural group, which fought urban New Deal liberalism, had allied with Republicans in Congress.[20]

Truman understood from the beginning many of the problems he would face. Although he "believed firmly and without reservation" in Roosevelt's program and prided himself on having supported it in the Senate, he told Senator Claude Pepper of Florida in 1945 that as president he would probably have to be "middle of the road" on most issues. But he urged Pepper to continue backing liberal causes, adding, "I'll be with you whenever I can."[21]

In early 1947, however, the president decided to take the offensive against the newly-elected Republican Congress. No longer inhibited by expectations of results, he began demanding reform measures and taking increasingly liberal stands. Truman nominated the prominent New Dealer, David Lilienthal, to head the Atomic Energy Commission and stood solidly behind him when Republicans in the Senate tried to block the appointment. In May, he urged Congress to consider his national health insurance program, and in June scored highly with union leaders and many liberals with his veto of the Taft-Hartley Act. During the year, he vetoed Republican tax cut measures, which he called inflationary and designed to help the rich, and pressed for such reforms as extended social security, federal aid to education, adequate housing, and a higher minimum wage.[22]

Believing that the second session of the Eightieth Congress would "do nothing but wrangle," Truman resolved to use its recalcitrance to build a record for the 1948 campaign. As he prepared to present his state of the union message, he eagerly embraced Administrative Assistant George M. Elsey's proposal: The message must "be controversial as hell, must state the issues of the election, must draw the line sharply between Republicans and Democrats. The Democratic platform will stem from it, and the election will be fought on the issues it presents."[23]

The opening salvo for the 1948 campaign, this message outlined a large-scale, liberal social and economic program. Truman and his liberal advisors knew there was no chance the Congress would approve his proposals, which were intended mainly to win votes in the fall election.[24]

As part of his new approach, the president took a more positive stand on public power. Devoting a large part of a June 7, 1947 speech at Kansas City to the topic, he demanded that Congress restore cuts in electric power programs. Later in the year, he informed Secretary of the Interior Julius Krug that he did not wish to see any federal programs blocked because of private utility company transmission systems.[25]

In his 1948 State of the Union Message, the president called for immediate action on "applying the lessons" of the TVA experience in the other great river basins, and he stressed that to avoid private power monopoly and encourage broad use at reasonable rates, the government should transmit its power directly to it markets. His budget message called for more transmission lines to be built by the Department of the Interior in the Bonneville and Southwestern Power Administration areas. On May 26, he urged Senate Appropriations Committee Chairman Styles Bridges to restore the House cut of funds for a TVA steam plant at New Johnsonville, Tennessee. After the Senate followed the president's wishes but the House refused to go along, Truman publicly took the Congress to task, calling the decision "bad" for "the welfare of the people," and "reckless" because "the security of the nation may be adversely affected." In June, when he signed the Interior Department Appropriations Act for 1949, the president again lashed out at Congress for making "a broad attack 'on the national public power policy" by failing to authorize funds for building previously authorized transmission lines and power facilities at various government-built dams outside the Tennessee Valley Authority area.[26]

After he was nominated for the presidency, Truman called a special session of Congress for July 26, 1948. As a political tactic, the president defiantly called on the Republican Congress to pass every liberal proposal he had suggested since early 1947. He included his long-standing request for approval of the 1941 agreement with Canada for development of the St. Lawrence waterway and power project, and he recommended immediate reconsideration of appropriation requests for public hydroelectric projects.[27]

"That 80th Congress was dumb enough not to do it," he wrote later. "If they'd passed only two bills I would have been up against real trouble." Its failure to comply with his requests lent credibility to the "do-nothing Congress" epithet Truman used so effectively in his election campaign.[28]

Delivering 275 speeches on a phenomenal "whistle-stop" campaign that covered nearly 22,000 miles, Truman carried his liberal message directly to the people.[29] Water resource development, reclamation and public power were enormously important in the campaign since they were major concerns in the West, the area of the country that was assigned top priority. Throughout this region, Truman repeatedly charged that the Republicans, whom he tagged "gluttons of privilege" working in the interests of private power, were trying to reverse New Deal gains by failing to adequately fund projects in the West.[30]

"This 'do-nothing' 80th Congress tried to choke you to death in this valley by cutting off appropriations that would have provided for public power lines," Truman told citizens of Roseville, California. When the government doesn't build the transmission lines, "Who benefits? The private power interests benefit, of course, at your expense," he said in Salt Lake City. And he warned, "You have been crudely and wickedly cheated by the power lobby in Washington, operating through the Republican 80th Congress."[31]

Although his message was enthusiastically received in many places, especially after he began speaking off-the cuff, journalists, pollsters and most politicians were convinced Truman would lose to the Republican nominee, Thomas Dewey. The Democratic Party failed to attract sufficient campaign funds, and its left and right wings had split off from it. Henry Wallace, who led the bolted communist infiltrated extreme left, was running on a Progressive ticket, and South Carolina Governor J. Strom Thurmond was heading a States' Rights ("Dixicrat") party. Furthermore, many liberals, believing that Truman's recent vigorous support of their cause had been merely a political ploy, remained unconvinced of his sincerity.

Truman's surprising victory in 1948 was in many respects a personal one. But it also demonstrated that the Roosevelt coalition of farmers, unionized workers, urban immigrants and northern blacks still endured and that the New Deal would be preserved. Liberals exulted that it represented a triumph not only for Harry Truman but also for progressivism, the New Deal and the Franklin Roosevelt heritage. "Nothing less than a new era of reform has been demanded by America and nothing less will Americans accept," proclaimed the *New Republic*.[32]

Many liberals thought the president had at last come over to their point of view, but he had been there all along. Harry Truman was a man who fit well in the progressive-New Deal tradition.

IV

Truman and other mid-century liberals were descended from late nineteenth and early twentieth century reformers who had chosen a center path within the capitalist system that involved government power acting positively to promote the general welfare.

Far from monolithic regarding the amount and methods of using this governmental power, these early reformers included some who sought efficient management of business and government, and others who stressed strengthening democracy and protecting individual rights. Furthermore, three methods of effecting corporate reform had emerged. One would use legislation to break up trusts and force business back to a more competitive position; a second would rely on government regulation to control corporations in the interests of protecting underprivileged sectors of society; and a third called for business self-regulation through trade associations, rationalization of business and voluntary upgrading of business ethics.

Building on this progressive base, liberalism during the New Deal developed the idea of a social welfare state with the government supplying a social security system, promoting education and acting as a broker between such groups as business, agriculture and labor. New Deal liberalism also included a concern for small farmers and laborers, a program to redistribute wealth through progressive taxation, compensatory government spending, partial government planning, occasional encouragement of competition, and the idea of counter-organization.

When Harry Truman took office as president, most liberals advocated using the later New Deal methods of limited intervention of government and regulated welfare capitalism. The government should adhere to the broker state theory of countervailing powers and concentrate on economic growth, which would be tempered by Keynesian fiscal and monetary methods, and an enlarged social assistance program.[33]

Other government programs also would preserve capitalism, as well as strengthen the country and enrich the lives of the people. Examples included low-cost housing, urban renewal, a federal highway system, public health facilities, sufficient old-age benefits, flood control and electric power programs.

Truman agreed with most of these aims and programs, but his liberalism was not a coherent philosophy or creed. A professional politician who was abidingly loyal to his party and friends, Truman held to a common sense, instinctual kind of liberalism that derived from his midwestern Populist values.

Although not completely comfortable with it, he accepted the label "liberal," along with "progressive" and "New Dealer," as applicable to him. He thought that a "liberal" president was simply one who tried to "accomplish things for the good of the people," and he once defined the term "liberal" as basically "a person who believes in the interest and welfare of all the people." Soon after finding himself president he vowed privately that he would do the job in precisely that way—"in the interest and welfare of all the people," adding, "No pressure group need apply."[34]

A man with Missouri farm roots who spoke plainly, without any "double talk," and who had no formal education beyond high school, Truman felt ill at ease in the company of many of the Eastern establishment New Deal theorists and intellectuals. These "professional liberals" were to him "the lowest form of politician," and he often referred to many people close to Roosevelt as "crackpots and the lunatic fringe."[35]

Like many New Dealers, Truman felt comfortable with the Populist heritage, which featured a hostility toward big business, Wall Street and the railroads because they threatened the very existence of the farmer and small business. He felt an affinity for the Populist-progressive concept of government acting for the "people against the interests" to deal with an over concentration of corporate power. This legacy included "trust-busting" to protect the "toiling multitude" and to restore economic individualism. After he became president, Truman wrote proudly to a friend about his membership on the Senate committee that in 1935 investigated the utilities and "broke up the holding companies' strangle hold on the gas and power utilities."[36]

His speeches often included the "people versus private interests" theme. Running for the presidency in 1948, Truman said there was just one issue in the campaign: "It's the issue of whether the people will rule the country or whether the special interests will." And he warned that big business was working through the Republican Party. "Wall Street reactionaries," he said in Dexter, Iowa, "want to increase their power and their privileges," by spending "fabulous sums of money" to elect the Republican candidate. "Republican reactionaries want an administration that will assure privilege for big business, regardless of what may happen to the rest of the Nation."[37]

The "people" Truman wanted the government to defend against "special interests" included all ordinary citizens, but he talked most about farmers, housewives and the common man (sometimes called workers or laboring men but seldom union workers). He said rural electrification would liberate the farmer and his wife; declared that more public electric power and federal development of water basins would raise the living standards of farmers, workers and housewives; and railed against "special interests" for opposing subsidies for farmers and minimum wages for workers, as well as improvements in housing, health and education for all the people.

Truman's belief in the theory of countervailing powers was grounded in his own experience. As a former farmer and small businessman who had known bankruptcy, he was concerned that big business would gain excessive power. That had happened in the 1920s, he told a group of Iowa voters in 1948, when "agriculture, labor, and small business played second fiddle, while big business called the tune." [38]

The president saw that, unlike the New Deal years when economic recovery from a depression was the primary goal, the postwar world offered hope of an economy of abundance. It could provide "equal opportunity for all Americans," one of his "consuming goals." Unversed in economic theory but guided by instinct, Truman embraced the ideas, including the theory of a "constantly expanding economy," advocated by Leon Keyserling, a member of the New Council of Economic Advisers. [39]

Asking Congress after 1946 for what he knew it would not grant did not indicate insincerity. As Clark Clifford, his special counsel, has pointed out, he "really believed in the programs he proposed, such as housing, conservation and public power." [40]

Truman's style of administration was to gather around him people with contrasting viewpoints. This approach explains why he appointed conservatives as well as liberals to his cabinet and to the independent regulatory commissions. "I wanted to be exposed to opposite poles of opinion in forming my own conclusions and making my own decisions on basic policy matters," he wrote later. [41]

Those decisions usually reflected a left-of-center, moderate-liberal approach. Clifford and Charles F. Murphy, who succeeded Clifford as special counsel in 1950, agreed that most of the president's policies were liberal, although, as Murphy observed, Truman didn't always "go all the way" with liberals. Clifford maintained later that when given a clear choice between a conservative or liberal path, Truman usually went with the New Deal, liberal one. [42]

Clifford was part of a group of mainly sub-cabinet officials who met secretly during 1947 and 1948 to promote liberal principles within the administration because they felt that a progressive president was being pressured by conservative insiders. Clifford believed that in the struggle between administration liberals and conservatives to win the heart and mind of the president, the liberal view won out by "a very substantial margin." [43]

The liberal "Monday Night Group," as its members dubbed the coterie, did help persuade Truman to swing to the left and played a significant role in developing the successful 1948 campaign strategy, but Truman was inclined to move in that direction in any case. The president likely was aware of the liberal-conservative struggle to influence him. In retrospect, Murphy said, "I think he

not only knew what was going on, he was calling the shots for both sides."
Once Truman made up his mind, the liberal group strengthened that resolve and
became an important source of ideas.[44]

V

With Truman elected in his own right and with the Democrats back in control
of both houses of Congress, the outlook for advancing liberalism in general and
public power in particular appeared bright in January 1949. But whether a
liberal public power program would be carried out during Truman's second term
would depend not only on the president's performance but also on the
cooperation of powerful and often entrenched interests in both the executive
branch and Congress.

While he was familiar with the workings of Congress, Truman had little
knowledge of how to run a huge bureaucracy. He hoped to reorganize the
executive branch but soon realized how difficult a task that was. One attempt
was the reforms he sought through the Commission on Organization of the
Executive Branch of Government, which Congress set up in 1948 and which
Truman chose former president Herbert Hoover to head. One of its adopted
recommendations that affected public power authorized the president to name the
chairmen of some of the independent regulatory agencies, including the Federal
Power Commission. The FPC chairman, who was made directly responsible to
the president, was also given increased powers that enabled him to make
important personnel and budgetary decisions. Truman had sought this change in
furtherance of his desire to put his "finger on the people directly responsible in
every situation."[45]

Truman began his presidency with the idea that he could clearly lay out
lines of authority from him at the top, in somewhat the way he had run Jackson
County during his days as a Missouri county judge. He told his cabinet members
that they were "simply a board of directors appointed by the president to help
him carry out policies of the government." He encouraged them to offer him
advice "whether he liked it or not," but he emphasized that when he gave them
"an order they should carry it out."[46]

A man who liked to make decisions, Truman believed that cabinet meetings
were not a place for cooperative decision-making. If decisions were made there,
he made them, without calling for a vote. Although he came to realize that
cabinet members could not be treated as staff but rather had to be allowed to run
their own departments, Truman kept control of issues that were of importance
to him.[47]

Truman also maintained command of his staff. He organized the White
House Staff on the traditional model of secretaries for press, correspondence and

appointments, along with some special assistants. Except for the special counsels, who were usually generalists, he gave most of the assistants distinct areas within which to work. Although he increased the staff to about 285 people, including clerical workers, it was still small enough for him to maintain definite lines of authority. Certain staff members could influence the president's decisions since in many cases they determined the information he would receive and the people he would see, but Truman never relinquished control. He refused to appoint a chief of staff, and he often met with congressional leaders and others without any staff attending.[48]

In addition to structure and efficiency, Truman created an environment of "informality, enthusiasm, and camaraderie," in the White House. Partly to reinforce personal relations with his staff, every morning at 8:30, he held meetings where "anyone could speak up." Years later, Murphy rated his ex-boss as "tops" among presidents since Hoover in administrative ability, as well as "tops as a man."[49]

Truman's ability to lead Congress cannot be so highly rated. Part of the reason was his limited conception of the president's role as a legislator. Truman believed that as president, he was obliged only to recommend legislation, not to cajole the Congress into passing it: "What the country needed in every field . . . was up to me to say . . . and if Congress wouldn't respond, well, I'd have done all I could in a straightforward way."[50]

As a former senator, Truman abhorred the arm twisting techniques that Roosevelt had used with Congress. During most of his own presidency, Truman maintained no formal legislative liaison mechanism, but preferred allowing departments and agencies to work directly with Congress. When the White House did get involved in legislation, the president liked to deal personally with one or a few members of Congress. Charles Murphy, whose major job was handling legislative matters, found that the "best, quickest and most effective way" to get results was to ask Truman to make a call to the hill: "I could typically go in and get him to do this and get the whole transaction completed within three or four, not more than five minutes."[51]

Truman probably should have used this technique more often, but even if he had, he still would have encountered serious obstacles to implementing the liberal electric power agenda not only from Congress but also from an array of federal agencies that had overlapping authority, entrenched interests and long held animosities.

VI

In 1945, the federal agencies responsible for the planning and building of power plants were the Tennessee Valley Authority, the Army Corps of Engineers and the Bureau of Reclamation. Those charged with marketing power were the TVA and the Department of the Interior. The Rural Electrification Administration was responsible for financing and providing services to bring electricity to farm areas.

Building dams and marketing power had become the Tennessee Valley Authority's largest commercial and revenue producing activity through its power granted by Congress to produce and sell electric power incidentally to its other river basin development responsibilities. All of the TVA's facilities operated as a single, integrated power system interconnected with other systems, with transmission lines and substations located in the six states of Tennessee, Alabama, Kentucky, North Carolina, Georgia and Mississippi. According to law, the authority followed the general policy of selling power at wholesale to municipalities and cooperatives in the area it served. It also sold power to a few large, industrial users and neighboring utility systems. The TVA obtained funds not only from congressional appropriations but also from the sale of bonds, its own operations and properties transferred from other government agencies. As a federal agency itself, it was subject to neither state nor federal regulatory commissions.

The Army Corps of Engineers, in its civil functions (which were entirely separate from its military functions), was an agency primarily responsible for the design, building and operation of flood control and navigation improvement projects on rivers and other waterways. It was granted flood control as a major-purpose responsibility by the Flood Control Act of 1936, with hydroelectric power production as a purpose incidental to that responsibility. Power, along with recreational facility development and irrigation water provision, was made a major purpose of engineers' projects in the 1944 Flood Control Act.[52]

By assigning flood control as a general purpose to the engineers and allowing the Bureau of Reclamation to keep its responsibility for irrigation (granted in 1902), the 1936 legislation engendered competition between the two agencies over the right to build and operate projects in the same river; led to duplication of effort; and meant that the Corps of Engineers worked upstream while the bureau worked downstream. As a result, the two agencies often operated at cross purposes with the principle of unified river basin management.

Historically, the Corps of Engineers had opposed most liberal public power objectives. It resisted multiple-resource development and optimum power development for two reasons. First, it wanted to protect its authority, which related mainly to navigation and flood control. These major purposes conflicted with the concept of building dams for the primary purpose of generating electricity since flood control requires empty storage space prior to high-water season, storage during flood season and release of water during dry spells, while power generation needs as even a flow of water as possible. Secondly, the corps tended to view each project according to the benefits likely to accrue to the local area represented by a congressman advocating the development. Rarely did these benefits involve the liberal aim of improving the social and economic lives of the people.[53]

The Corps of Engineers was officially answerable to the president through the secretary of war until 1947 and then through the secretary of the army after the military establishment was unified in the Department of Defense.[54] The secretaries, however, rarely intervened to insist that the corps follow administration liberal power policies. During Franklin D. Roosevelt's presidency, for example, Secretary of War Henry L. Stimson had ignored the president's directive that he wanted the Bureau of Reclamation, rather than the corps, to build the California Kings River project, and actively opposed FDR's efforts to develop a national power policy. As a member of the Hoover Commission, James Forrestal, Truman's secretary of defense from 1947 to 1949, refused to vote on a majority recommendation to consolidate the civil functions of the Corps of Engineers and the functions of the Interior Department into one agency that would administer the country's water resources. The secretaries of the army during Truman's second administration, Kenneth C. Royall, Gordon Gray and Frank Pace, Jr., continued this tradition.[55]

Even if these heads of the army had tried to change the engineers' electric power policies, they probably would have had little success because the corps traditionally bore little responsibility to the executive branch. Rather, as the executor of policy formulated by the legislative branch, the agency in effect was responsible to Congress, particularly to certain of its committees and individual members.[56]

Rendering this relationship with Congress even stronger was the involvement of certain members of Congress and officers of the corps in the National Rivers and Harbors Congress, one of the most powerful water lobby groups in the nation. Believing that only through plans developed by the corps could the country "obtain a consistent and coordinated improvement of . . . water resources," the group's policy was to push for those projects that the Corps of Engineers recommended.[57] The pressure group opposed most of the liberal public power program, including valley authorities, executive reorganization that would remove civil functions from the army, and all federal steam plants.

The Corps of Engineers' assumption that the agency was directly responsible to the Congress rather than the president could be attributed not only to the corps' special relationship with members of Congress but also to the manner in which its projects were approved. These projects usually grew out of pressure from local interest groups who went to their congressman, who, in turn, went to the Public Works Committees of the House and Senate and to Congress to get a survey for the project authorized. After the survey was completed, the chief of engineers would send his report on the plan to Congress, after it was cleared by the Executive Office of the President. The report was usually referred to the House Subcommittee on Public Works, which generally considered for authorization only those projects that had received a favorable report from the engineers. If, after hearings, it agreed that the project should be carried out, the subcommittee would draw up a provision for it as part of an omnibus rivers and harbors authorization bill.[58]

The primary concern of the Bureau of Reclamation lay in the area of irrigation since it was charged with the task of administering federal reclamation laws in the seventeen states west of the one-hundredth meridian. However, the bureau program included not only single-purpose irrigation projects but also complete multipurpose projects and single-purpose power projects, as well as both power and irrigation projects that obtained their water supply from reservoirs built by the Corps of Engineers. This picture contrasted with most of the engineers' projects, which normally consisted of one structure such as a dam, with perhaps an incidental one such as a power plant.[59]

The Bureau of Reclamation was responsible for marketing the power it produced as a part of its multipurpose projects, except for the area in which the Bonneville Power Administration operated. It also marketed surplus power from projects built by the Corps of Engineers.

Like the corps, the bureau was jealous of its powers; it therefore opposed any system of river basin organization that would do away with its functions and properties. For example, in 1945, it carried out a public relations campaign to discourage acceptance of the authority idea after President Truman had endorsed the method for river basin planning.[60]

However, unlike that of the Corps of Engineers, the bureau's philosophy of river basin development and public power coincided with liberal objectives on some issues. As an important part of comprehensive river basin development in the West, the bureau planned, at the end of the war, to develop further sources of electric power and build transmission lines for bringing this power to market.[61]

In marked contrast to the Corps of Engineers, the Bureau of Reclamation also had a history of striving for social goals. After Truman appointed Michael Straus commissioner in 1945, it began to reemphasize those goals, which had been gradually played down over the bureau's forty-year history. "You are a lot of social planners if we are following the Reclamation laws," Straus told his regional directors in 1946. Straus believed it was the bureau's mission to spread the benefits of natural resource development to as many people as possible.[62]

The variation in philosophies of the two agencies was largely attributable to the different laws under which they operated. Reclamation law, for example, stipulated that the power generated at bureau projects be sold at the lowest practical price with preference to public bodies, required that water users repay a good portion of the government's cost of building the project, and forbade speculation on the government's investment. The laws that governed corps operations offered no protection of public monies, and the agency favored selling its power at the bus bar where only big private companies could afford it.[63]

Furthermore, the Bureau of Reclamation did not enjoy the close relationship with committees and members of Congress that the engineers did. One reason was related to the procedure for authorizing bureau projects. The bureau planned and initiated its own projects and then went to the secretary of the interior for approval. The secretary transmitted the project report, together with the Bureau of the Budget's recommendations, to the House of Representatives, where it commonly was sent to the Committee on Interior and Insular Affairs, which held hearings on the proposal. Unlike those of the Corps of Engineers, interior projects were usually authorized by Congress in separate bills.[64]

Because the Department of the Interior enjoyed less consistent backing from Congress than did the engineers, it tried to seek the support of the Oval Office. Arthur A. Maass, a Harvard political scientist, wrote in 1950 that the conflict could be illustrated this way: "Corps of Engineers + Congress v. Secretary of the Interior + Executive Office of the President."[65]

While the Tennessee Valley Authority marketed its own electric power, the Department of the Interior was responsible for virtually all of the rest of the federally generated power in the country. The secretary was authorized in law to market power from projects built by the Bureau of Reclamation and to transmit and dispose of power generated by dams built by the Corps of Engineers. In addition to the Bureau of Reclamation, the interior agencies responsible for marketing of power in 1949 were the Bonneville Power Administration, which marketed power produced on federal projects in the Pacific Northwest, and the Southwestern Power Administration, created in 1945 to market hydroelectric energy from the engineers' multipurpose projects in the Arkansas-White-Red Rivers system in the Southwest.

The administrators of these power agencies were appointed by and responsible to the secretary of the interior. Dr. Paul Raver, BPA administrator since 1939, could hardly be matched in his reputation as a public power liberal. Firmly committed to comprehensive river development in the Northwest, he had testified before Congress in 1945 in support of a Missouri Valley Authority. Douglas G. Wright, the SWPA head, had worked on New Deal public works and power agencies since 1937 and was an outspoken advocate of the farmer and the common man. But he also was willing to cooperate with private power under the right circumstances. In 1949, he said his agency had three options for delivering its power to cooperatives and public bodies: build its own lines, interchange power with hydroelectric plants owned by public bodies, or make contracts with private utilities, as long as they did not "try to 'mouse trap'" the SWPA.[66]

The Department of the Interior was by no means monolithic in its support of liberal power policies. In 1945, Secretary Ickes had favored valley authorities but wanted to retain administrative responsibility in the Department of the

Interior. He agreed with Straus that the Bureau of Reclamation should handle river basin development in the West, while the Bonneville Power Administration backed a valley authority for the Columbia basin. Intradepartmental conflict increased after Ickes resigned in March 1946.[67]

Truman's appointment of Julius Krug to succeed Ickes seemed to signal a turn toward increased cooperation between public and private power because of Krug's pro-business leanings as head of the War Production Board and because he had steered a middle course between public and private power in his job as director of the Office of War Utilities.[68]

Krug, however, soon revealed that he was a public power supporter. At his confirmation hearing, he said he believed in public ownership of most electric utilities, and a few months later came out in favor of valley authorities. In October, Krug criticized the Pick-Sloan Plan because under it no single agency was empowered to develop projects in the Missouri Valley, and he endorsed the Columbia Valley Authority concept as contained in a bill that had been introduced in January by Washington Senator Hugh B. Mitchell.[69]

Toward the end of his presidency, Truman reflected that Krug "had made a great secretary for some time," but then Truman had "had to ask for his resignation" toward the end of 1949. Speculations were that the secretary had been too fainthearted in his support of the president in the 1948 campaign, that he had pressed too much for reclamation projects, and that he had made an "end run" directly to Congress for appropriations. Truman never revealed the reasons, and Krug refused to comment.[70]

Krug's replacement was Under Secretary Oscar L. Chapman, a man with impeccable liberal credentials. Chapman had long been associated with progressive causes, going back to his work in Colorado with Judge Ben Lindsey's Juvenile Court in the 1920s and as chairman of the State Child Welfare Committee in the early 1930s. In 1933, he accepted a job as assistant secretary in the Department of the Interior because he saw it as a good way to further the rights of minorities. The president would later say he considered Chapman to be "as fine and efficient [a] Secretary of the Interior" the country had ever had.[71]

Chapman was one of the leading liberals in the administration and one of Truman's most indefatigable supporters in the months leading up to the 1948 election. While Krug made some speeches on behalf of the president, Chapman took leave from his job and traveled 26,000 miles as Truman's advance man. "I did it," he told reporters, "because for me, politics means fighting for a program."[72]

The new secretary, whose nomination the Senate confirmed without a dissenting vote, promised to continue the policies of his predecessor and to "carry forward with vigor" the president's program of multiple-purpose river development, which would "provide low cost power to farm homes, industries and city dwellers."[73] Though the new secretary did not differ greatly from his predecessor in philosophy, he did in demeanor. While Krug was reserved and rather brusque, Chapman was known as a smiling and even-tempered man.

Chapman remained true to his New Deal heritage. Asked shortly after he took office if he was as much a New Dealer as he had been in 1933, he replied that "the Fair Deal is just an extension of the New Deal." And *The Nation* called him "one of the few surviving authentic New Dealers in the Truman Administration." Marquis Childs, the columnist, believed him to be "such a rarity" in this regard that "it would not be surprising one day to find him under glass in the Smithsonian Institution."[74]

Instead of relying on an under secretary, Chapman increased the responsibilities of the two assistant secretaries already on the job. William E. Warne had been with the department since 1937. As a reporter for the Associated Press who got his start covering water problems in the West, Warne had caught the attention of Harold Ickes and his assistant, Michael Straus, after being sent to Washington in 1933. When Straus became director of the Bureau, Ickes asked for "the young fellow who asks all those questions about reclamation," to take the job of chief of information. Warne's public power record was not devoid of blemishes, however. As assistant commissioner, Warne had worked with Straus in the campaign to discourage valley authorities even though Truman had endorsed them in his twenty-one-point message.[75]

C. Girard "Jebby" Davidson, the other assistant secretary, was a well-known liberal and enthusiastic public power advocate. He had been general counsel to the BPA, and then assistant secretary since 1946. A regular in the "Monday Night group," Davidson had urged Truman to take on the 80th Congress in the election campaign and provided Clifford with material for the president's speeches on natural resources.[76]

Davidson had a reputation, going back to his BPA days, for needling his bosses into taking liberal positions, so public power advocates were counting on him in 1949 to promote liberal policies within the administration.[77]

The Rural Electrification Administration granted loans to farmers and rural residents who were not receiving central station service for building and operating generating plants and constructing transmission and distribution lines. Claude Wickard, who became administrator in 1945, was determined to finish the job of rural electrification, which then was only about 55 per cent complete. Although he understood the difficulties of the job that lay ahead and may also have sensed Truman's rather low opinion of him as cabinet material, Wickard had asked Truman for the REA job after the new president replaced him as secretary of agriculture.[78]

Wickard reported to Clinton P. Anderson, the secretary of agriculture, who succeeded him, and then to Charles Brannan when Anderson left his post in 1948 to run for the Senate. Brannan was known as a militant liberal, and

Truman regarded him as the best secretary of agriculture since he had come to Washington in 1935 and one of his two best cabinet members.[79]

The Bureau of the Budget, part of the executive office of the president, played a role in electric power activities through its responsibility for recommending and overseeing executive branch budgets. It acted as a clearing house for all agency legislative proposals to determine whether they harmonized with the president's program. Although Truman would see a cabinet member who insisted on a meeting, normally the department head had to submit his proposals through the bureau, which would relay the president's opinions back to the cabinet member.[80]

In August 1946, the president replaced FDR holdover Harold D. Smith with James E. Webb as his budget director. Truman had a good relationship with him and his two successors, Frank Pace, Jr. and Frederick Lawton, all of whom enjoyed regular consultations with the president.[81]

In practice, none of the duties assigned to the Budget Bureau added up to much authority over public power. Reductions it made in executive agency requests could be appealed by the official involved before the congressional appropriations committees. If the president forbade this approach or if the official thought it unwise to so testify, interest groups could help persuade Congress to restore the cuts. While it provided valuable information, the clearing function likewise produced little effect, particularly on an agency like the Corps of Engineers, whose supporters on the Public Works Committees could insist that an engineers' project report disapproved by budget be sent to Congress. In fact, from 1941 through 1948, Congress approved all but eight of forty-two Corps of Engineers projects that the Bureau of the Budget had rejected in whole or part. Another factor that limited the Budget Bureau's powers was its inability to secure sufficient funds from Congress to adequately carry out its resources and public works coordination function.[82]

The Budget Bureau had more power over the Federal Power Commission and the other independent regulatory commissions because they had less staff and were not represented on the cabinet as executive agencies were. Thus, these agencies were less likely to get bureau cuts in their budgets restored.[83]

The Federal Power Commission, which Congress created in 1920, had considerable authority over electric power. By 1945, its jurisdiction included the right to issue licenses to private companies for the development and operation of hydroelectric power projects affecting interstate or foreign commerce and to regulate interstate, wholesale rates of such power. By law, the Corps of Engineers had to obtain the FPC's recommendation before installing penstocks for power development at army dams, and the commission had the authority to make investigations and studies of comprehensive river basin development and to advise other federal agencies regarding installation of power facilities.[84]

Although the commission had been established as an independent body, Congress sought to make the FPC its effective instrument, free of executive control. To accomplish this aim, Congress provided that no more than three of the five commissioners be of the same political party and set the terms of the members at five years with expiration to occur in successive years.[85]

When Truman became president, the FPC had a liberal and pro-public power bent, and when two commissioners resigned before the year was out, the new president made appointments that retained that viewpoint.

The chairman was Leland Olds, whom Roosevelt had appointed to the commission in 1939 in an effort to change the FPC to a more public minded body. Long known for his support of public power, Olds had been named chairman of the New York Power Authority by FDR as governor. During hearings in 1944 to consider Roosevelt's nomination of Olds to serve a second term on the Federal Power Commission, some senators accused the nominee of being a Communist, citing excerpts from his speeches in the 1920s and the fact that the *Daily Worker* was among the newspapers that had bought his press service columns. Olds vigorously denied the accusations, retained the support of the president and stayed on the commission.[86]

When the other two Democrats on the commission resigned, Truman appointed Richard Sachse, a Democrat who had been president of the California Railroad Commission, and Harrington Wimberly, a fairly liberal Oklahoma Democrat who had been a newspaper editor and publisher. The two members held over from the Roosevelt Administration were Nelson L. Smith, an Independent who had been a member of the New Hampshire Public Service Commission from 1933 to 1941, and Claude Draper, a Republican who had been on the FPC since 1930 and before that a member of Wyoming's Public Service Commission. With the election of the Republican Eightieth Congress in 1946, the other commissioners persuaded Smith to take over as chairman from Olds, arguing that the commission would be better off with an Independent in that job. When Sachse's term expired in 1948, Truman nominated Thomas C. Buchanan, a member of the Pennsylvania Public Utility Commission known for his liberal views.[87]

Because of its obligations, the FPC could be expected to seek optimum development of power resources in comprehensive river basin work and act as a public control on special interests. However, its freedom from executive control made it susceptible to pressures from the interests it was supposed to regulate. One student of the independent regulatory agencies has concluded that the commissioners often would begin with a strong concern for the public welfare but would become "increasingly attached to the viewpoint of the interests under their regulation."[88]

VII

Both Congresses in Truman's first administration proved to be unenthusiastic about the expansion of federal power. Although they made large appropriations for building dams and hydroelectric facilities, they rejected proposals for comprehensive development of river valley resources and, for the most part, refused requests for money for federally-built transmission lines and steam plants.

In the Democratically controlled Seventy-ninth Congress, a public versus private power fight erupted over federal transmission lines. Friends of public power, like House Speaker Sam Rayburn of Texas and Senator Carl Hayden of Arizona, managed to beat back attempts to block appropriations for transmission lines for federal dams in California, the Arkansas-Texas-Oklahoma area, and in several northwestern and midwestern states. But with the Republicans in control in the Eightieth Congress, legislators refused funds for transmission lines to the Southwestern Power Administration and approved funds for only one small BPA line. Private power advocates agreed with Representative Ben F. Jensen of Iowa that interior wanted to "drive the private utilities to the wall by giving them so much competition at below-cost rates that they could not exist."[89]

The Eightieth Congress refused to authorize a steam plant for the Tennessee Valley Authority, and the Senate failed to act on the St. Lawrence Seaway and Power Project bill. The House, with a sizable Republican majority, was particularly reluctant to approve measures favored by public power advocates. The Senate, with a smaller Republican majority (51 to 45), however, generally befriended public power as it had for several years. In 1947, it restored most of the House cuts in funds for the Department of the Interior's reclamation and power program and in 1948 removed most of the restrictions the House had placed on the interior appropriations bill.[90]

In 1949, public power adherents expected a dramatic change as a result of a newly elected Democratic majority. Although a conservative coalition of senior Republicans and southern Democrats still controlled Congress, Truman's campaign against the "do-nothing" Eightieth had helped send more progressives to Congress. And presumably, Democrats would be anxious to cooperate with Truman since by equating the Eightieth Congress with Republicanism, he had helped create that Democratic majority.

The new Congress also appeared promising for public power liberalism because Democrats had a better record on that issue than did the Republicans. While the Republican platform was silent on federal power, the Democratic one called for federal "development of hydroelectric power and its widespread distribution over publicly owned transmission lines . . . with preference to public agencies and REA cooperatives" and "continued expansion of the Rural Electrification Program."[91]

A number of long-time public power supporters gained important positions when the chairmanship and majority control of the relevant committees passed into the hands of the Democrats.[92] And with more Democrats as members, the likelihood of getting western power programs through Congress increased. Unlike their Republican counterparts, non-Western Democrats had a record of voting with their Western party members.[93]

A closer look, however, revealed that clear sailing for public power measures was not assured. Although Truman's 1948 victory, with slightly less than 50 percent of the popular vote, indicated that the FDR coalition had held, many members of the groups comprising it, such as blacks, organized labor and farmers, had diverse, short-term interests rather than a desire for broad change. This situation was reflected in Congress. Although Democrats campaigned on Truman's liberal agenda, after the election, many of them turned to protecting interests based on urban, agricultural or regional differences.

The conservative coalition, which had grown even stronger with the 1946 Republican victory and Truman's liberal civil rights efforts, continued to present a problem for the president in the Eighty-first and Eighty-second Congresses. Truman recognized that "only on the surface" was the Eighty-first a Democratic Congress, even with its substantial majorities in both Houses. "The majority is made up of Republicans and recalcitrant Southern 'Democrats' who are not Democrats. So I get the responsibility and the blame," he confided to his diary. Fighting a Republican Congress was easy, but it was impolitic to fight his own Congress: "Trying to make the Eighty-first Congress perform is and has been worse than cussing the Eightieth," he wrote. "I've kissed and petted more consarned SOB so-called Democrats and left-wing Republicans than all the presidents put together. I have very few people fighting my battles in Congress as I fought FDR's."[94]

Even if a majority did support a piece of Fair Deal legislation, the restrictive House rules, the Senate filibuster and the seniority system (which usually meant southern Democrats and midwestern Republicans headed the committees) made it possible for a minority to block it.

Despite their rather promising new leadership, the committees concerned with public power contained a number of anti-public power men. Notable were Democrat Elmer Thomas of Oklahoma and Republican Guy Cordon of Oregon on the Senate Interior Subcommittee of the Committee on Appropriations, and Republican Ben F. Jensen of Iowa and Democrat W.L. Norrell of Arkansas on the corresponding House subcommittee. Another key figure was Republican George A. Dondero of Michigan, a member of the House Public Works Committee, who prided himself on his long battle "to combat the socialistic trends of the New Deal and Fair Deal Administrations." Furthermore, many congressmen, including some serving on these key committees, supported the Corps of Engineers in its competition with the Bureau of Reclamation because the engineers' single-purpose, pork-barrel projects were good vote getters.[95]

The National Rivers and Harbors Congress, which lobbied for projects the corps wanted, promised continued influence in the Eighty-first Congress. In fact, some congressmen involved in making key public power decisions held offices in the very group that was lobbying them. In 1949, Arkansas Senator John McClellan, a member of the Public Works Committee and the subcommittee of the Committee on Appropriations, was president of the lobby group. Serving as vice-presidents were Nebraska Senator Kenneth S. Wherry, also a member of the appropriations subcommittee; Mississippi Congressman William M. Whittington, chairman of the Committee on Public Works; and South Dakota Representative Francis H. Case, a member of the House subcommittee that considered corps appropriations.[96]

VIII

In its efforts to advance public power, the Truman Administration also faced other complicating situations over which it had little control. The ideological bent of Congress, which contained a majority to the right of the Fair Deal, reflected the mood of the country. Eager to enjoy postwar prosperity after a depression, war and reconversion and a drastic change in foreign policy, voters were growing more conservative.

Fighting the cold war at home and abroad continued to demand a good deal of attention from the president after 1948. Thanks in large part to that often-maligned Eightieth Congress, the Truman Administration had launched Marshall's European recovery program, granted military aid to Greece and Turkey to fight off Communism and enjoyed relative success in containing Communism in Europe. During Truman's second administration, foreign policy, now more concerned with Asia, remained burdensome, as did the anti-communist hysteria at home that often stemmed from it. In 1949, China "fell" to the Communists, and the Soviet Union exploded its first atomic bomb; in January 1950, Alger Hiss was convicted of perjury; and in February, Senator Joseph R. McCarthy opened his campaign to uncover supposed Communists in government. McCarthy's accusations made it difficult for the president to persuade citizens and Congress to take an interest in public power measures, which were often tagged as "socialistic."

The Korean War, which began in June, 1950, gave added momentum to McCarthyism. Anti-Communist hysteria reached its height in September 1950 with the passage of the McCarran Internal Security Act, which required Communist organizations to register with the attorney general. In that same month, Secretary of the Interior Chapman and Bureau of Reclamation Commissioner Straus had to fend off personal attacks by Senator Andrew Schoeppel of Kansas, who questioned their loyalty because they had struck out loyalty oath sections when signing their oaths of office. Schoeppel backed down after Chapman presented a vigorous defense, but the hearings and attendant publicity hurt the public power cause.[97]

The Korean War itself turned the nation's attention away from the Fair Deal and toward defense measures, as the United States approached a war-time mobilization of its economy. The Truman administration was forced to put many of its reform proposals aside, but on defense grounds urged Congress to approve new power projects, speed up work on others and build transmission lines. The administration argued that anything close to full mobilization would bring a critical electrical power shortage.[98] In some areas, the emergency would serve to lessen the public versus private power strife, but in others it would have little effect.

Most of these problems, however, were unforeseen at the beginning of 1949. Then, public power proponents had reasons to be optimistic. Truman had been elected in his own right on a program of New Deal liberalism, and he had obviously done so by excoriating the Eightieth Congress, which had put public power on the defensive. Furthermore, the president seemed determined to deliver on his campaign promises. Four days after his victory, he told his cabinet that he expected the full cooperation of the executive departments in making these assurances a reality. Then, declaring in his 1949 State of the Union Message that "every segment of our population and every individual has a right to expect from our Government a fair deal," Truman included among his liberal goals resource development, expansion of public power programs and river basin organization based on the TVA experience.[99]

3

The Opening Battle:
The Valley Authority Question

In 1949, with Truman president in his own right and facing a Democratic Congress, the chances for winning acceptance of new valley authorities seemed better than they had at any time since the end of the war. The extension of the TVA model to other great river basins in the country would fulfill a major New Deal promise.

Since the president had carried ten out of the eleven Western states, some public power advocates argued that voters had handed Truman a mandate to carry out federal river valley development in the West. However, despite the fact that he had used resources policy as a major campaign issue, Truman had generally avoided the controversial topic of water resource management, concentrating instead on such other Western issues as Republican appropriation cuts in reclamation and power projects. In one of his few references to the issue in a Seattle speech, he refrained from advocating the authority as the specific method he would choose and merely repeated his admiration of the TVA as showing the direction to move in the other large river valleys.[1]

Truman's sole reference to river basin management reform in his 1949 State of the Union Message was similarly vague and brief: "We should apply the lessons of our Tennessee Valley experience to our great river basins." So it was still by no means clear whether or not the president would push for more TVA-type organizational structures.[2]

II

At the same time, alternative organizational arrangements were being advanced, particularly by opponents of the TVA model. One of these was the inter-agency committee approach, which had evolved as federal agencies moved in to fill organizational vacuums. In 1939 President Roosevelt and the National Resources Planning Board had secured a tripartite agreement among the Department of the Interior, the Department of Agriculture and the Army Corps of Engineers to coordinate preparation of water resource reports on multiple resource projects. In 1943, when the president lost his fight with Congress to keep the Planning Board for postwar planning, coordination had ended; the corps refused to continue the agreement; and the Bureau of the Budget attempted to fill a coordinating role. Thereupon, to head off the Budget Bureau, the Corps of Engineers announced a new agreement, which differed little from the old one except that the Federal Power Commission was added to the participating agencies. Out of this arrangement the Federal Inter-Agency River Basin Committee was born. In 1946, the Department of Commerce was added to the membership. Representatives of these agencies and departments met monthly in Washington to coordinate their respective river basin planning activities.[3]

In March 1945, the federal body created the Missouri Basin Inter-Agency Committee as its first regional subcommittee, after Congress approved the Pick-Sloan plan for development of the Missouri Valley. The regional committee was intended to supply some administrative machinery for implementation of the Pick-Sloan Plan, which was only a schedule of planned works that depended upon separate Congressional appropriations. By 1947, its membership included representatives of the same agencies represented on the federal committee, as well as five persons chosen by the governors of the ten basin states.[4]

The federal committee established the Columbia Basin Inter-Agency Committee in February 1946 to coordinate "planning, construction and administration" for the basin's development program. Membership included one representative from each of the Department of the Interior, Corps of Engineers, Department of Commerce, Department of Agriculture, Federal Power Commission and Bonneville Power Administration. Governors of the seven states lying wholly or in part in the Columbia Basin, or their representatives, could participate in the committee meetings.[5]

In 1948, the Pacific Southwest Federal Inter-Agency Technical Committee, composed of representatives of each of the agencies represented on its parent federal committee, was created to coordinate the technical and field work and interchange data among the federal agencies working in the Southwest.[6]

Many New Deal liberals opposed these inter-agency committees as an answer to the river basin organization problem because of their obvious weaknesses. The committees were voluntary, carried out most of their work through technical subcommittees, and could resolve no important policy matters. Because they operated under the rule of unanimity and had no neutral leadership, not even those set up to coordinate work of federal agencies in the area could settle such basic matters as whether the Bureau of Reclamation or the Corps of Engineers should plan and develop particular works in a river valley.

The Hoover Commission Task Force on Natural Resources in 1948 noted the inadequacies of this approach to comprehensive river valley planning: "The committees have failed to solve any important aspects of the [coordination] problem . . . because the dominant members, the Corps and the Bureau, have been unwilling to permit inter-agency committees to settle their differences."[7]

Despite its shortcomings, the inter-agency approach was widely supported, partly as a means of blocking the creation of further valley authorities. Concerned about protecting their respective vested interests, the corps and the bureau had been pushing the device for several years. Commissioner Michael Straus had helped establish the Columbia Basin Inter-Agency Committee and served on it as the Interior Department's representative.[8] In a 1946 speech to Western state engineers, he warned that if the inter-agency system failed, there would be an increased demand for valley authorities, a "punishment that fits our crime."[9]

In December 1947, the division engineer in the region, Colonel Theron D. Weaver, recommended that the Columbia Basin Inter-Agency Committee be strengthened as a way to combat a Columbia Valley Authority. The chief of engineers agreed and urged Weaver to do everything possible to make the area governors aware "of the 'Authority' threat" so as to win their support for the committee.[10]

Congressional representatives and governors of the river basin states involved, as well as business and other local groups, backed the inter-agency approach as a means of forestalling valley authorities. Governor Val Peterson of Nebraska and Governor George T. Mickelson of South Dakota were among those who praised the Missouri Basin Inter-agency Committee in testimony before Congress in 1949 and 1950. They claimed that a spirit of cooperation prevailed between the corps and the bureau in the basin, and asserted that the citizens of their states were well satisfied with the mechanism.[11]

A report prepared in the Office of the Bureau of the Budget revealed that the Truman Administration was well aware of this strategy: "These committees . . . have been put forth as the answer to the demand for valley authorities. In the Missouri Valley the participating agencies were able to get the governors . . . and certain local organizations to block President Roosevelt's and Senator Murray's proposal for a valley authority."[12]

III

By 1949, Truman, who considered himself "committed politically and on the record to river valley authorities," had decided to act. Although he said he was also interested in the development of the Missouri and Red River valleys and the Central Valley of California, it was the Columbia the president chose for his first effort because he believed that an authority there stood the best chance of winning acceptance.[13]

A few days after his inauguration, Truman directed the secretaries of interior, agriculture and commerce, the director of the Bureau of the Budget and the chairman of the Council of Economic Advisers to prepare a bill that would create a Columbia Valley Authority. He chose Administrative Assistant Charles S. Murphy to coordinate the work and gave Secretary Krug the responsibility of presenting the legislative proposals to Congress. Krug delegated the department's assignment to Assistant Secretary Davidson, a staunch CVA supporter.[14]

With the announcement of these moves, the private utility industry prepared to battle what it considered the greatest ideological threat since the creation of the Tennessee Valley Authority. Purcell L. Smith, president of the National Association of Electric Companies, attacked the plan as a costly effort to create a "superstate," and Colonel H. S. Bennion, managing director of the Edison Electric Institute, warned that a Columbia Valley Authority would jeopardize state water rights.[15]

In the Northwest, private utilities and other business representatives lined up in opposition to a CVA. These groups argued that the inter-agency program provided adequate management; all that was needed was for Congress to adopt a long-range plan and set aside funds for each of its phases. Many of these opponents considered the existing system of federal-state cooperation a democratic device, while an authority represented a "corporate-state, centralized-control administration method."[16]

Opposition to an authority also came from other quarters in the area. The governors of Oregon, Idaho, Wyoming and Washington told Truman they were against it because the states did not want to give up their autonomy and their natural resources. Republicans generally opposed an authority, as did the Farm Bureau Federation, reclamation groups and a large portion of the press.[17]

Joining their ranks were many Northwest Granges, public utility districts and private citizens who favored some kind of coordinating body, but feared loss of local control to a powerful autonomous agency with responsibility only to the president and Congress. Even a majority of federal officials in the field seemed inclined to compromise. Some favored coordination of federal agency activities either through the Bonneville Power Administration or the Executive Office of the President.[18]

Truman refused to be discouraged by these early warning signs. He wrote to a friend that he would ignore the comments of the Republican governors, adding, "I think the people in those two states are entitled to the development of this great river valley and I am going to try and get it done."[19]

Liberals generally were optimistic. Declaring prospects for a CVA brighter than at any other time, *The Nation* pointed out that the long-time sponsor of a

Missouri Valley Authority, Senator James Murray of Montana, had been "overwhelmingly reelected"; Hugh B. Mitchell of Washington, author of the original CVA bill, had been returned to Congress as a representative; and Murray, with Representative Henry Jackson of Washington, had already prepared a CVA bill for the new session. Furthermore, Davidson, the main administration advocate of the valley authority approach, was assigned to handle CVA matters for interior.[20]

Expressions of approval from the Northwest poured into the Oval Office in January and February. Included were messages from labor organizations, Farmers' Union Granges (except the Idaho Grange), the Washington State House of Representatives, and fifteen Oregon state legislators. Davidson wrote Murphy that he liked the way the fight was shaping up: "So far the Republicans and private utilities are against it and the Democrats, labor and farmers are for it. What more could we ask?"[21]

In accordance with the president's instructions, the committee to draft the legislation was expanded to include representatives from the Department of the Army and the Tennessee Valley Authority as well as liaison delegates from the Federal Power Commission and other concerned agencies and departments. Disagreement among several of the agencies soon developed, mainly over "how the Columbia Valley Authority should be related to the 'functional' agencies of Government" and whether operational powers should be vested in the authority.[22]

Both the Corps of Engineers and the Bureau of Reclamation informed the president of their continued opposition to a TVA-type arrangement for the Columbia Valley. For nearly a decade they had quietly fought the establishment of further valley authorities. In 1941, after he had helped draft bills to create regional authorities in the Southwest and in the Columbia Valley and had seen them die in committee, David Lilienthal observed: "It has been impossible to get a bill through Congress . . . because the Bureau of Reclamation and the Corps of Engineers have more political influence than the People themselves are able to express."[23]

If a CVA were created, these agencies' water resources responsibilities would be transferred to the new authority. The army recommended as an alternative that the Columbia Basin Inter-Agency Committee be granted power "to formulate programs and submit recommendations to the President and to the Congress."[24] Smarting because the Bureau of Reclamation had not been invited to take part in the drafting, Commissioner Straus objected that the bill being developed seemed to require the bureau to abdicate its "responsibility for the nation's water-resources conservation and use program in the West." He suggested instead the old Ickes idea of placing the CVA in the Department of the Interior.[25]

Fearing that its property and land functions would be transferred to a Columbia Valley Authority, the Department of Agriculture advised that existing agencies retain operational authority and the new body be granted only coordinating and supervisory responsibilities.[26]

The Department of Commerce, which was chiefly interested in the production of cheap and abundant power to enhance economic development of the Northwest, favored a weak CVA authorized only to plan and build dams, control the flow of water through them, and run a strong power distribution program.[27]

Representative Mitchell understood the danger of the opposition from various executive branch agencies. In a letter to the president, he charged that the BPA, the engineers and the bureau were the real foes of the CVA plan because they feared it would replace them in the region.[28]

Despite this disagreement among members of the drafting committee, the proposal that went to Congress differed little in substance from the TVA model and the original Mitchell bill. It called for a Columbia Valley Administration, set up as a government corporation with a general manager appointed by the directors and responsible for operations. The head office would be located in the region, and two of the three directors were required to be area residents. The powers of the CVA would include construction and operation of projects for improving navigation; preventing and controlling floods; producing, transmitting and selling electric power at wholesale; and conserving and reclaiming lands, wildlife, fish and mineral resources.[29]

The new body would take over all projects and properties of the Bonneville Power Administration, the Corps of Engineers and the Bureau of Reclamation in the basin and would be responsible for preparing unified plans and programs, which it would recommend to the president. These proposals would then go to Congress for approval.[30]

Anxious to avoid the charges of "super-government" and loss of local control that had been leveled at the Mitchell plan, the Truman Administration emphasized that under its proposal no new powers would be granted the federal government; instead, powers it already had would merely be relocated in the Columbia Valley area, thus providing more, rather than less, local control. The substitution of the word "Administration," for "Authority" in the title undoubtedly was meant to reflect this idea and to increase the likelihood of the plan's acceptance.[31]

Truman was careful to stress this aspect of local control in his request to Congress on April 13, 1949. Noting that the coordination of activities of federal agencies that had long participated in the resource development of the Northwest presented "a difficult organizational problem," he asked for legislation that would allow the federal government to deal more effectively with development and conservation of the resources of the area. He further requested the Congress to be guided by two principal objectives: (1) "unified treatment of the related resources within each natural area of the country" and (2) the "greatest decentralization of federal powers and the greatest possible local participation in their exercise."[32]

The four identical Columbia Valley Administration bills that were subsequently introduced into Congress differed from the president's proposed legislation in only one minor respect.[33] Another measure that pertained to the administration of Columbia Valley development was intended to put the Newell-Weaver plan into effect. Sponsored by Republican Senator Harry P. Cain, of Washington, a long-time foe of a Columbia Valley Authority, this bill was regarded as a serious threat to the administration's proposal. The Newell-Weaver plan, which was an agreement between the Corps of Engineers and the Bureau of Reclamation on the principles and responsibilities for carrying out comprehensive development of the Columbia River Basin, had been presented to the president just two days before he sent his message to Congress recommending a Columbia Valley Administration.[34]

With this agreement to divide areas of predominant interest in the basin, the two erstwhile antagonists had joined forces in the face of a common threat. The corps and the bureau had been working on separate reports for Columbia Valley development for some time, and the corps had twice refused to come to terms on a combined program. But as Truman's intention to propose a CVA to Congress became likely in December 1948, the agencies agreed to correlate their respective plans.[35]

Assistant Secretary Davidson first heard of the agreement through the newspapers. Livid, because he feared it would thwart the administration's CVA efforts, he reprimanded Straus for the leak and for intimating that interior had already approved the joint plan. Warning the commissioner to refrain from publicizing this Newell-Weaver report until the department could study it, Davidson ordered Straus to remind his employees that the department's policy was to support a Columbia Valley Authority.[36]

Straus insisted that the agreement concerned only technical and minor matters. Going over Davidson's head, he complained to Secretary Krug that he had feared he would one day be placed in just such a dilemma. The commissioner reminded Krug that he had earlier assured Straus that the bureau "would not be expected either to oppose or support Authority legislation." The reply came from Davidson. Repeating his original instructions to the commissioner, the assistant secretary added curtly that he knew "of no statement of the secretary's or anyone else" that exempted Straus from taking such orders.[37]

Although Truman himself had directed the corps and the bureau to review their plans after the 1948 floods in the Pacific Northwest and had later ordered them to correlate their studies after the bureau submitted a plan unilaterally, he realized that compliance now could endanger his proposal for a Columbia Valley Administration. Congressional authorization of the combined report would destroy one of the main arguments for a CVA since it would end the conflict between the two agencies over how and by whom the Columbia Valley should be developed.[38]

In light of this threat, the president wrote Secretary Krug on April 12, 1949 that since the Newell-Weaver plan in several ways bore upon his Columbia Valley Administration proposal, he believed "that nothing should be done with the Agreement" until he had a chance to study it further. He informed both Krug and Secretary of the Army Kenneth C. Royall that since he viewed this plan as "merely an interim step in the preparation of reports," he felt it unnecessary to approve it at that time.[39]

Krug and Davidson energetically promoted the president's bill to create a CVA. Krug had publicly endorsed the plan in early March, and on May 12, he told the American Public Power Association that Truman's recommendation for a Columbia Valley Administration was "the most important public power move of the decade."[40]

At the congressional hearings that opened on May 27, Krug based his arguments on the need for integration of "planning, budgeting, and operation" of the many federal agencies involved in the development of land and water resources in the Pacific Northwest and for decentralization of authority in carrying out these functions.[41]

Assistant Secretary Davidson testified for several days before both the Senate and House committees on Public works on behalf of the administration's proposal. While he agreed that the multiple-purpose projects recommended in the Newell-Weaver report were needed, Davidson said the combined plan failed to provide either a "single unified comprehensive balanced development program" for the region or a method for "relating the resources of all the agencies concerned."[42]

Krug enlisted other department or agency heads to testify in favor of the proposal. These included Secretary of Agriculture Brannan, Assistant Secretary of Commerce Thomas C. Blaisdell, Secretary of the Army Gordon Gray and Edward Falek of the National Security Resources Board.[43]

Support for the President's proposal also came from outside the government. Several state officials from Washington and Oregon testified or sent letters to the two committees, and the Washington State Legislature passed a resolution endorsing the plan by a majority of nearly three to one. Others who expressed approval of a Columbia Valley Administration included Northwest farm and public utility groups.[44]

Despite these promising beginnings, real problems lay ahead for the CVA proposal. One of the difficulties for the committees was determining whether or not a majority of the people in the Northwest wanted a Columbia Valley Administration. Both supporters and opponents insisted that the people were on their side. Washington Governor Arthur Langlie told the House Public Works Committee that if given the opportunity, the people would overwhelmingly turn down a CVA. Senator Cain agreed and advocated holding a referendum on the issue in the states involved, but Congress ignored his suggestion.[45]

Opposition from governors of the basin states carried weight with many Congressmen. In addition to Langlie, the governors of Idaho, Utah, Oregon and Nevada testified against the proposal, arguing that it would mean loss of local control and water rights, would create a super government and was unnecessary since the Corps of Engineers and Bureau of Reclamation were already doing a good job.[46]

Perhaps more serious for Truman was the lack of unanimous support within his own administration. Only the Office of the Secretary of the Interior vigorously backed his CVA plan. The Corps of Engineers and the Bureau of Reclamation were the most definite and effective in their opposition, but the lukewarm support of other agencies and departments also hurt the proposal's chances.

Although they testified on behalf of the bill as requested, the secretaries of commerce and the army expressed no enthusiasm. Secretary of the Army Gray was placed in an awkward position since the proposal would transfer the responsibilities, property and personnel of the Corps of Engineers to the new organization. Under sharp questioning by loyal corps supporters, Gray left the impression that he supported the plan only because, as a member of the administration team, he was expected to do so. In their written opinions, both Gray and Secretary of Commerce Charles Sawyer praised some aspects of the bill but failed to recommend its adoption.[47]

The secretary of agriculture was more positive, but just prior to his appearance, Brannan's new Northwest representative, Herbert M. Peet, stated publicly that he was neutral on the CVA issue.[48]

Other federal officials worked at cross purposes to the president's policy, in particular those who sat on the Columbia Basin Inter-Agency Committee and the Federal Inter-Agency River Basin Committee. For example, in a statement on its background and accomplishments for use by the congressional committees considering the CVA bills, the federal committee credited inter-agency committees with success as arbiters of jurisdictional conflicts that they did not deserve. Fearing that opponents would exploit the document, the administration decided not to send it on to the Senate Public Works Committee.[49] The congressional committees thus had available to them no unbiased description with which to judge the advantages and disadvantages of the Columbia Valley Administration as compared with the inter-agency approach.

However, it was the Corps of Engineers and the Bureau of Reclamation that worked most effectively to defeat the proposed Columbia Valley Administration. Their best weapon was the Newell-Weaver report, which they used to fight a rear guard action while the CVA bills were before Congress. By making their joint plan public, they in effect offered it as a counter proposal, thus forcing the administration to go on the defensive.

By July 1, five bills to put the Newell-Weaver plan into effect had been introduced in Congress, even though the executive branch still had not transmitted the two reports. Publicly, Truman explained that they had not yet been fully studied. In fact, the president and the Interior Department were delaying action because they realized that in recommending the reports to Congress, they would be asking for approval of the Newell-Weaver agreement. And that, they feared, would seriously jeopardize the CVA's chances.[50]

Krug had held off approving the army's plan for transmittal to the president until June 16, explaining to Chief of the Corps of Engineers Lewis A. Pick that although he endorsed both reports as based on the agencies' agreement, he believed they did not present as effective a plan as did the one calling for a Columbia Valley Administration. Emphasizing to Commissioner Straus that his approval of the Bureau of Reclamation's plan did not mean it was a "satisfactory substitute" for a CVA, Krug finally sent that report to the president on July 20. He advised Truman to transmit the two reports to Congress "at an early date" but to include the same point that he had made to Pick and Straus.[51]

Still hoping to win authorization for his Columbia Valley Administration, the president, however, continued to postpone approval. Administrative Assistant David Bell recommended that the Budget Bureau should be allowed to "go slowly and submit the reports next session" since "those in Congress who are unfriendly to the bill will try to force these reports out of the executive branch."[52]

With the reports bottled up in the White House, friends of the Corps of Engineers in Congress worked for authorization of just the corps-proposed projects in the Columbia Basin. The House approved $108 million in the Omnibus Rivers, Harbors and Flood Control Bill, which it passed on August 22. In the Senate, the Public Works Committee added another $142 million for this purpose and explained that it was still considering a separate Columbia Valley Administration bill.[53]

Doubting that the CVA bill, which he had introduced, would be passed and fearing that only individual projects would be authorized, Senator Warren G. Magnuson of Washington tried to get the committee to approve the Newell-Weaver plan. The president, however, asked Chairman Dennis Chavez to wait until the two reports could be reviewed in the normal way, and no action was taken.[54]

In October, the Senate approved the committee's recommendation for increasing funds for Corps of Engineers projects, causing CVA proponents to fear that, as a member of the Washington State Columbia Basin Commission put it, the army engineers were "so darned powerful they could shove her on through as is and leave the Interior's part of the plan stranded high and dry."[55] Senator Magnuson was able to get final action on the omnibus bill delayed, but the session ended soon thereafter, and with it went any real chance for a Columbia Valley Administration.

When the second session of the Eighty-First Congress opened in 1950, President Truman again asked for authorization of the CVA. Realizing, however, that Congress was unlikely to comply, he decided that adoption of the Newell-Weaver plan would be better than passage of legislation that slighted or omitted Interior Department projects and that provided for no coordination of operations of the two agencies involved. Truman therefore approved the joint report on February 2, 1950.[56]

Also sensing that the Columbia Valley Administration proposal was doomed, public power proponents in the Senate tried to salvage what they could from the Omnibus Rivers, Harbors and Flood Control Bill. An amendment, introduced by Democrat Joseph C. O'Mahoney of Wyoming and recommended by the Interior and Insular Affairs Committee, authorized $412.7 million for Bureau of Reclamation projects in the Columbia Valley and established an administration-approved Columbia Basin Account. This fund was intended to pool all revenues from federal Columbia River Basin projects to pay for area project reimbursements. Assisted by Republican Guy Cordon of Oregon and Democrat Spessard L. Holland of Florida, who charged that the basin account was a first step toward a Columbia Valley Authority, opponents succeeded in tabling the amendment.[57]

The Omnibus Rivers, Harbors and Flood Control Bill that Congress passed in 1950 represented a resounding defeat for public power liberals. After signing the bill into law on May 17, Truman vigorously criticized its piecemeal approach to river basin development in a special message to Congress. He pointed out that instead of authorizing the joint plan of the Departments of the Army and Interior, which recommended an "integrated schedule of projects," the act merely approved the army's projects, and he urged Congress to "authorize the missing pieces" at its earliest opportunity.[58]

The Truman Administration continued to pay lip-service to the CVA plan. When dedicating the Grand Coulee Dam on May 11, 1950, the president reaffirmed his belief that the Columbia Valley Administration was a "necessary step in the sensible, democratic development of the resources of the Northwest." And Secretary of the Interior Oscar L. Chapman, who had succeeded Krug in December 1949, reassured Senator Glen Taylor of Idaho, who planned to campaign for the proposal in the 1950 elections, that the "creation of a CVA is part of the President's program and of the program of the Democratic Party."[59]

But the plan was rapidly losing all chance of approval. In May, the *New York Times* reported that the CVA proposal was no longer the subject of lively discussion in the Northwest and that even Secretary Chapman had said it probably would be defeated if put to a vote of the people in the area. Glen Taylor's defeat in his race for the Democratic nomination for the United States Senate symbolized the failure of the Truman Administration's one major effort to establish a valley authority.[60]

IV

No other serious attempt was made during Truman's second term to extend the Tennessee Valley Authority idea to other major river basins. Although bills were introduced into Congress to create valley authorities in the Merrimack, Connecticut and Missouri river basins during this period, none got out of committee.

The Missouri had seemed a likely target since an authority for that river basin had received considerable attention near the end of World War II. President Roosevelt had recommended a Missouri Valley Authority in both 1944 and 1945, and the leader of the effort in Congress, Senator James Murray of Montana, had introduced bills for an MVA every year since 1944.

Since his vice-presidential days, Truman had been ambiguous on a Missouri Valley Authority. He had advocated it in the 1944 campaign, but his referral of Murray's bill to a hostile committee when he was vice-president had created suspicion that he intended to sabotage the plan. Truman protested that he was simply following the rules: "If a bill cannot get a fair hearing from any Senate committee, then the Senate is not the great legislative body I think it is."[61]

Shortly after Truman became president, Murray asked him to support this same bill, but the president only made general statements favoring an authority for the basin. After two committees failed to report the bill, it was finally sent to the Agriculture and Forestry Committee, which set hearings for early 1946. Judging that its chances were slim with the 79th Congress, Murray asked that hearings be postponed. Ironically, on January 19, 1946, just two days after the committee announced that hearings were being delayed indefinitely, Truman told reporters, "I plan to do everything I can to get MVA in 1946."[62]

With devastating floods occurring in the Missouri River Valley, Truman encouraged Murray on July 2, 1947 to push the bill in Congress and told the press that he had always supported an MVA. But on July 12, he asked Congress to increase the budget of the Corps of Engineers and the Bureau of Reclamation under the Pick-Sloan Plan, prompting critics again to charge that Truman was undermining chances for an MVA. Assistant to the President John Steelman wrote MVA supporters that the president felt flood control was "so urgent that immediate steps must be taken without waiting" for MVA legislation.[63]

The president continued to express interest in seeing additional valley authorities established, but he never wholeheartedly supported one for the Missouri. He often said that whereas the Columbia and the Tennessee Valleys were similar, the Missouri Valley required special consideration. Truman spoke of the conflict of interests between downstream and upriver residents, explaining that whereas Missourians were most concerned with flood control and navigation, people living in areas on the upper reaches of the river were interested in reclamation; and some in certain parts of Montana, the Dakotas and Missouri were concerned primarily with electric power.[64]

An astute politician, Truman also knew that nearly all of the governors of the nine affected states, as well as many other residents in the area, were strongly opposed to a Missouri Valley Authority and that the plan stood little chance of passing in Congress. He could appease liberals by giving Murray nominal support without pushing hard enough to risk defeat. Some critics charged that Truman actually opposed an MVA, preferring instead the Pick-Sloan Plan, with which he was closely associated. His friendship for Lewis Pick, whom President Truman had recommended for promotion to deputy chief of engineers in 1945, was well known. While in the Senate, Truman had worked with Pick on the Corps of Engineers plan, which Murphy recalled later was "one of his pets." In 1944 he had claimed that he was "more responsible for the general over-all Pick plan than anyone else except Colonel Pick himself." [65]

Following several official visits with the president after the 1948 election, Murray reintroduced his MVA bill into the Senate on March 2, 1949, and indicated that it had Truman's complete support. However, when asked at a press conference in April about a Missouri Valley Authority, Truman said he had no plans for one at present, and he did nothing to help the Murray bill, which failed to get out of committee. During the next year the president alluded to the development of the river basin in several speeches but never specified that he wanted an authority.[66]

In the summer of 1951, serious flooding in the Missouri Valley forced Truman to face head-on the question of a Missouri Valley Authority. In a letter to the president, which he made public, Philip Murray, president of the Congress of Industrial Organizations, blamed the Pick-Sloan Plan for the immense damage done by the flooding of the Kansas and Missouri Rivers, pronounced the plan "discredited, wrong in purpose and wrong in method" and called upon the President to "throw the weight of the administration behind the establishment of a Missouri Valley Authority."[67]

The labor leader in effect demanded that Truman stop talking and act. In a calm and friendly tone, the president replied that the Missouri basin did not necessarily need a replica of the Tennessee Valley Authority, but a single agency, based in the area, with responsibility for devising a comprehensive plan and "for seeing that plan is put into effect efficiently."[68]

Actually, Truman was angered and frustrated by the Murray letter; he believed, as he wrote in his reply, that his position on a Missouri Valley Authority had remained constant. The problem lay with conservative representatives of the people involved. In a notation he placed on a preliminary draft of his answer, the president suggested that if Murray really wanted a Missouri Valley Authority he should help elect Democratic congressmen and senators. This unsent version continued,

When you talk of any plan—Pick-Sloan or any other—being to blame for the flood, I fear you've forgotten your history. Backward looking governors, State Legislatures and Congressmen caused the present state of affairs in the Missouri Valley.[69]

Among Philip Murray's recommendations was a proposal that the president set up a commission to devise a program for development of the Missouri Valley to be submitted to Congress by January 15, 1952. Acting on the suggestion, Senator Thomas C. Hennings of Missouri, on August 20, 1951, introduced a bill to establish a Missouri Basin Commission no later than June 30, 1952. He then wrote Special Counsel Charles Murphy asking for advice on the plan.[70]

The White House was receptive to the idea. Here was an opportunity for the administration to appear to be taking action on the Missouri Valley and at the same time avoid a defeat in Congress. The president's advisors recommended that the commission be established for the following reasons: (1) Strong sentiment "based largely on misleading propaganda" against a Missouri Valley Authority canceled out any hopes for such an agency in the near future; (2) if the right appointments were made to the commission, it would perhaps at least point out that the "present administrative hodge-podge" was far from adequate and (3) it would aid the chief executive politically to put the question of the Missouri Valley in the hands of a commission rather than campaigning on it.[71]

On January 3, 1952, Truman signed an executive order creating such a commission, composed of private citizens and members of Congress, to study land and water resources of the Missouri River Basin and make recommendations for their development, use and protection within one year.[72] With this step, the President disappointed liberals by effectively burying the Missouri Valley Authority idea. Some disenchanted liberals even saw his appointment of Senator Murray to the commission as an act of appeasement.[73]

After holding public hearings in all of the basin states and receiving the testimony of 400 witnesses, the Missouri Basin Survey Commission reported in January 1953. It found, as had the Hoover Commission Task Force on Natural Resources and the President's Water Resources Policy Commission before it, that the Pick-Sloan Plan and the inter-agency committee approach were inadequate, but it did not recommend a Missouri Valley Authority.[74]

V

The Hoover Commission, which made its report in early 1949, suggested another alternative for solving the problem of water development organization and administration. Based on a proposal of its Task Force on Natural Resources, it called for consolidating nationally all water resource functions performed by the various government agencies in a Water Development and Use Service. The commission also advised that a board be established in the Executive Office of the President to review and coordinate river basin and project proposals and report to the president and Congress on their "public and economic value."[75]

The task force and a minority of three commission members wanted this Water Development and Use Service placed in a new Department of Natural Resources, which would combine most of the responsibilities of the Department of the Interior and those of the Forest Service (an agency in the Department of Agriculture). The Interior Department would cease to exist. The majority of the commission members, however, recommended putting the Water Development Service in the Department of the Interior and leaving the Forest Service in the Department of Agriculture.[76]

The task force unanimously advised removing all water functions from the army. Secretary of Defense James Forrestal, one of the commissioners, disqualified himself on this issue, but the majority of the main body, led by Hoover, went along with it. The commission's Task Force on Public Works reported that it was "absurd" to say that only the corps could carry out river and harbor work when fewer than 200 army engineers were involved and the rest were civilians "who supply most of the detailed knowledge and continuing direction."[77]

The Department of the Interior favored the approach of the Task Force on Natural Resources; it recommended that interior serve as the nucleus of the new Department of Natural Resources. Secretary Krug argued that by adding the forest functions of the Forest Service and the rivers and harbor functions of the Corps of Engineers to the Interior Department's present functions, "there would be established under one management the inter-related responsibilities for multi-purpose water resource development and multi-use public land control."[78]

During 1949 and 1950, opposition to the commission's plan for reorganizing federal water resources functions was strong and effective. The same people who opposed additional valley authorities fought the reorganization proposal for the same reasons. Among the opponents were western and mid-western governors. Governor Mickelson of South Dakota told a Senate subcommittee:

> We have had fine cooperation from the Federal agencies and we do not want anything like that recommendation of that task-force committee or the Hoover Commission report to come in here and interfere with this program [the inter-agency approach in the Missouri Valley].[79]

Supporters of the army engineers in Congress, many of whom were southern Democrats, also fought the proposal. Two of these opponents also were members of the commission. Senator John L. McClellan of Arkansas and former Congressman Carter Manasco of Alabama, both Democrats, argued that the water resources reorganization plan would create inefficiency, additional expense and divided responsibility and would "completely emasculate" the corps and render a "crippling blow" to the national defense.[80]

Under the general reorganization act of June 20, 1949, plans submitted to Congress would become law within sixty days unless voted down. Defenders of the corps in Congress helped get included the proviso that a negative vote of just one of the houses would kill a plan. This stipulation meant that any reorganization plan that would tamper with the civil functions of the army held little chance of becoming law. House Majority Leader John W. McCormack blamed the Corps of Engineers for the failure of Congress to enact a "clean bill":

> Some of the friends of the Army Engineers are . . . putting the Army Engineers in a position of being more powerful than Congress, more powerful than the President, more powerful than everybody, more powerful than the Government itself.[81]

Truman sent twenty-one plans for reorganization of the executive branch to Congress under this act. He had earlier urged that all of the commission's recommendations be carried out, warning that other reorganization proposals had failed because of a piecemeal approach. But he failed to include the natural resources plan among his proposals, probably because he knew it would be voted down.[82]

Not until 1952 did Truman resurrect, and then only briefly, the Hoover Commission plan. To determine if there was any support for it in Congress, administration sources leaked a story to the press that the president was planning to submit a proposal that all water resource development activities be consolidated in a new agency located in the Interior Department. The Reclamation Bureau would be abolished, and its functions, as well as the civil duties of the Army Corps of Engineers, would be transferred to the new agency. At a news conference on April 17, Truman said he had been considering such a plan ever since the Task Force had recommended it and added that when a bill was ready, it would be sent up to Congress.[83]

Opponents of the plan feared Congress might adopt it. The *Electrical World*, a private power journal, commented that because it was an election year and because the army engineers had been under attack for their management of air bases abroad, trying to defeat the plan would "be uphill work." Truman decided, however, to abandon the plan, perhaps influenced by the negative reaction from the same group of southern Democrats who had been quick to condemn it in 1949. As a strong party man, Truman also may have decided that he should not risk splitting the Democrats in an election year. In any case, by April 1952 Truman had cast aside this plan for consolidating governmental water resource activities.[84]

VI

At the end of 1950, when prospects for solving the organizational problems in comprehensive river valley development looked especially bleak, the President's Water Resources Policy Commission (PWRPC) offered some unsolicited suggestions. Out of them would emerge a fourth alternative called "river basin commissions." Truman had established this body in January to study the whole problem of major policy questions in administering federal water resource programs. Nearly a year later, on December 11, the commission presented to the president the main portion (Volume 1) of its report.

Although it was authorized to consider only questions of policy, the PWRPC also included recommendations on organizational matters. It applauded the Tennessee Valley Authority, but concluded that the best structure for handling comprehensive water resource development of a river basin would be a single department like that recommended by a minority of the Hoover Commission and by its Task Force on Natural Resources. The Water Resources Policy Commission went on to say that if these changes were not effected, then, as an "absolute minimum," the present inter-agency committee approach could be satisfactory if the following changes were made: (1) Each river basin "commission," created by Congress on an inter-agency basis, should be "presided over by an independent chairman appointed by and responsible to the President"; (2) a Board of Review should be set up in the executive branch; (3) congressional authorizations and appropriations for river basin planning and development should be changed to "fit the new approach" and (4) the states should provide a procedure for cooperating with this organization.[85]

As an alternative to both plans, the commission suggested establishing "regional or valley administrations to manage water and related land resources of the several basins in cooperation with state and local agencies." It did not say if this approach would be preferable to the second option.[86]

The new idea of river basin commissions created confusion. No one was sure whether they were to be authority-type organizations, as anti-public power forces feared, or groups with only coordinating and advisory functions. Hearings were held before a subcommittee on Irrigation and Reclamation of the House Committee on Interior and Insular Affairs just to try to interpret the meaning of the PWRPC recommendations. When asked by a committee member if the report contemplated an authority in each basin, Melvin Scheidt, of the Bureau of the Budget, revealed that he, too was confused. He replied that it was difficult from reading the document to determine "the precise line of demarcation in the assignment of authority."[87]

When the commission submitted the rest of its report in February 1951, it included a draft of legislation that would put its recommendations into law. Included was a provision to establish fifteen river basin commissions to coordinate activities of federal agencies in water and land resources work. The basin commission idea appeared to be an effort to compromise the argument of "regional authority *versus* controlling Federal bureaus." Top control boards would be placed over the existing federal agencies, which would carry on their old functions under a new direction. Six of the nine members of each commission would be appointees of federal agencies, the seventh would be appointed by the president, and the other two would be named by people in the area.[88]

Truman had been reluctant to receive any legislative proposals from his Water Resources Policy Commission because Volume 1 of its report had indicated that such suggestions would include measures for organizational solutions, the topic he had wanted the group to avoid. Acting on the advice of both the Bureau of the Budget and the Department of the Interior, the president refused to release this portion of the report. Interior opposed the river basin commission plan, favoring instead a Department of Natural Resources to consolidate natural resources functions, and the Budget Bureau argued that statutory river basin commissions "would be highly controversial" and probably could not "be favorably considered at this time." The president wrote an old Kansas City friend that he was holding back the plan because it "was not a good one," but he also apparently wanted to avoid the controversy he knew it would engender.[89]

Increasingly embarrassed by the unsatisfactory answers of White House office personnel to the House subcommittee studying the report, commission chairman Morris L. Cooke several times asked Truman to release the draft legislation. Not until August 1, 1951, nearly six months after the proposal was first submitted to the Oval Office, did Truman get around to explaining to Cooke why he had held back the draft legislation. The president wrote that some of the organizational recommendations "might stir up such controversy and feeling" that it would be difficult to get a "fair hearing" of the commission's policy suggestions. Agreeing that reform was needed, Truman said the river basin commission idea deserved "careful consideration," but he cited "the difficulties" with which he was concerned. The president added that he would not object to the release of the draft if the organizational issue were omitted.[90]

Cooke replied that because the commission had disbanded, it would be impossible to release just part of the draft legislation, but, since the commission was anxious to cooperate with Truman, it would withdraw its request for release.[91] However, the matter was not yet closed. With the publication a few days later of the correspondence between Philip Murray and the president relative to the establishment of a Missouri Valley Authority, Cooke suggested to Truman that he might want to change his mind:

Now that you have again expressed your views rather fully as to multiple-purpose river basin development, perhaps the fact that you disagree with some features of our legislative recommendations may make it easier for you to release the document without endorsement of any kind or perhaps you would prefer that I give it out.[92]

Truman decided to grant the commission permission to release the draft entirely on its own. At the same time, the president warned Cooke that the proposals he would make to Congress would differ "in several significant ways" from those of the commission. On February 18, 1952, almost exactly one year after he first submitted it, Cooke released the draft legislation.[93]

Meanwhile, Truman had a special Inter-Agency Review Committee under the leadership of the Bureau of the Budget working on its own draft of legislation based on the recommendations of the President's Water Resources Policy Commission, which he hoped to transmit to Congress before his term of office expired. This committee's draft differed in several respects from the commission's recommendations. For example, it omitted the plan for a Board of Review in the Executive Office of the President, and it proposed increasing participation of states and local groups in water resources work.[94]

The Bureau of the Budget tried to work out a compromise. Its draft provided for river basin commissions but called for only one representative from each river basin state. Budget hoped to win the support of not only states and local groups but also the Departments of Commerce and Agriculture and others who wanted to correct the main weaknesses of the inter-agency approach—the lack of an independent chairman and of clear responsibility for coordinating water resources activities on a regional basis.[95]

While this compromise plan was being developed, the Missouri Basin Survey Commission was working on a similar plan for organization in that particular river valley. In its official report, presented to President Truman just a few days before he left office in January 1953, the majority of the commission recommended the establishment of a Missouri Basin Commission, which it described as a "middle ground" between the two "extremes of thought." The commission would be a federal body, composed of five members appointed by the president, that would "direct and supervise the federal agencies" carrying out water resource functions in the Missouri Basin, thus providing unified direction while permitting local and state participation.[96]

As the Truman Administration was nearing its end, states' rights and anti-valley authority sentiments appeared to prevail in the Columbia and Missouri Valleys as the states there moved toward the establishment of basin compacts, the antithesis of valley authorities.[97] BPA Administrator Paul Raver shocked public power proponents with a proposal in December 1952 to remove the federal government from the business of power sales and distribution in the Northwest. His plan involved giving over the functions of the Bonneville Power Administration to a locally controlled interstate power commission.[98]

Truman left office without having sent Congress any further recommendations for achieving efficient organization and administration of regional river basin planning and development.

In a special message to Congress on the day before his successor was inaugurated, Truman outlined what he considered his accomplishments in the field of land and water resources. At the head of this list was a review of the special study commissions and committees he had appointed. Truman announced that he was officially transmitting to Congress the report of his Water Resources Policy Commission, and the recommendations of the Missouri Basin Survey Commission would be made available "within a few weeks." The outgoing president again praised federal multipurpose development, particularly the Tennessee Valley Authority, and comprehensive river basin development in general. Reiterating the need for more efficient "regional river basin planning and management," Truman mentioned the recommendations of the PWRPC and the Hoover Commission, as well as the legislative proposals that the Budget Bureau was preparing for presentation to the new administration. There he left the matter hanging.[99]

The President's attitude toward solving the problem of river basin organization had gone full circle. From his determined effort to establish a Columbia Valley Authority in 1949, he had retreated to his uncertain and ambiguous position of the 1945-47 period. On the day before he left the presidency, Truman told Congress that a better means of organizing river development was needed, but he declined to say what kind, only that it "need not be the same for all regions."[100]

4

Major Campaigns:
Steam Plants and Transmission Lines

While they were struggling over water resources organization, public and private proponents also were fighting new battles in the old conflict over whether the government should build steam plants and transmission lines.

The government sought congressional appropriations for fuel-burning steam-electric generating plants mainly for three reasons: (1) to meet an anticipated shortage of hydro power when demand would outrun supply; (2) to serve peaking purposes since steam, unlike hydro, power is constant; and (3) to augment hydro power in times of droughts or national emergencies. The administration based its case for building transmission lines on its legal responsibility to provide low-cost energy to wholesale customers, with preference to public bodies.

Many private power advocates saw these activities, along with the Interior Department's power marketing agencies, as part of an elaborate scheme to win government control of private utilities and eventually of the national economy. Active in promoting it, they maintained, was a former socialist, Carl D. Thompson, who had published a book, *Public Ownership*, in 1925. This book contained a map outlining a vast, public power network of municipally and federally owned plants, along with future steam and hydroelectric plants that the government might build.[1]

Involved in the movement to nationalize the utility industry, so the theory went, were organizations that conducted vigorous campaigns in the twenties on behalf of public ownership. Among these groups were the League for Industrial Democracy, which claimed both Thompson and the Socialist leader Norman Thomas as active members, and the National Popular Government League. Private power advocates saw a connection between this effort and the government power structure. They pointed out that Senator George Norris and other members of Congress had been active in several of these organizations;

Thompson had been appointed to a review board set up by Secretary of the Interior Ickes in 1935 to speed up federal grants to municipalities so they could enter the power business, and in 1938 Thompson was employed by the Bonneville Power Administration.[2]

Private power sympathizers also argued that the Interior Department in its annual reports of 1946 and 1947 had presented an agenda for putting the whole Thompson program into effect. In these reports, interior projected a power program that within twenty years would double the 1936 federal hydroelectric capacity. To carry out such a program, steam plants would have to be built in such areas as the Arkansas-White-Red Rivers systems, California and the Southeast, where rivers were not "miracles" like the Columbia but rather were "flashy and irregular" and produced "little firm energy."[3] Interior's plan also included the building of transmission lines by the marketing agencies and the interconnecting of various government hydroelectric plants.[4]

Therefore, it seemed to private power proponents in 1949 and 1950 that this "master plan" would soon become a reality. The entire Interior Department program, they charged, constituted an effort to socialize and eventually eliminate the private electric power industry. According to the *Electrical World*, no significant change in the law would be necessary; socialization could be achieved merely by installing "a vast transmission network coupled with steam and hydro generating stations subsidized by the federal government. The takeover of local distribution systems would logically and inevitably be the next step."[5]

It was with this fear in mind that private power advocates during Truman's second term worked to keep public power expansion at bay. They sought to block appropriations for Southwestern Power Administration while it was young, in the hope of destroying it, and to prevent the establishment of new power marketing agencies. They opposed appropriations for federal steam plants and transmission lines and the interconnecting of federal plants. They fought against the Rural Electrification Administration's practice of making loans to federations of rural electric cooperatives for building transmission lines and steam plants. And, where government dams were already generating electrical power, the private power industry sought to buy power at the bus bar and thus break down the government's preference policy.

The struggles that took place in the Northwest, the Central Valley of California, the Southwest and the Southeast illustrate the intensity of the controversy surrounding these issues.

II

The steam plant issue had its origins in the Tennessee Valley Authority area in the 1930s. Then, private power proponents argued that it would be unconstitutional for the TVA to build steam standby plants because the only purposes contemplated under the act that established the authority were navigation and flood control. Although recognizing that it was constitutional for the TVA to sell surplus power generated at dams that were built primarily for water control purposes, they held that to generate power by steam would constitute an intention to produce power without this "incidentalness."[6]

The pressing needs of national defense, however, soon silenced such opposition. The TVA found it necessary to make full use of the four steam plants it had acquired in purchasing private systems in the area as well as one it had gained in 1933 from the War Department. Further demands placed on the authority by the growing needs of the Atomic Energy Commission plant at Oak Ridge, Tennessee, made additional steam plants seem necessary. Congress, therefore, in 1940, authorized the construction of a new plant at Watts Bar dam.[7]

Although few private power advocates found fault with this program when it involved national defense, once the war was over, they again began to raise objections on constitutional grounds.

In 1948, TVA spokesmen argued that the authority had exhausted the potential for hydroelectric development and would therefore need additional steam plants in order to supply the increasing demand for electricity in the area. They believed steam plants were the logical answer since great quantities of coal nearby were available at reasonable prices. A trend already could be discerned toward greater use of steam generation, which had risen from 0.5 per cent of TVA power production in fiscal 1939 to 8 percent in 1947.[8]

The administration's request for $4 million in 1948 for the Tennessee Valley Authority to build a steam generating plant at New Johnsonville, Tennessee aroused heated debate in the Republican Eightieth Congress. The House Appropriations Committee on Government Corporations denied the request on the grounds that it was illegal, was not essential to meet the needs of priority customers, and would set a precedent for future expansion of power-generating facilities by methods that were unrelated to navigation and flood control. The majority report also mentioned opposition by Chambers of Commerce and private power companies.[9]

Similar arguments were advanced on the House floor prior to failure of an amendment to restore the item. They included debate on the degree to which Purcell L. Smith of the National Association of Electric Companies, one of the highest paid lobbyists in the capital, had influenced the committee.[10]

While hearings were being held before the Interior Subcommittee of the Senate Appropriations Committee, Truman wrote Chairman Styles Bridges that the steam plant was needed to meet the normal, peacetime increase in demand for electric power, as well as for possible future defense needs. After the Senate approved $3.6 million for the facility but the House conferees refused to go along, Truman berated Congress for rejecting the steam plant, calling the decision "reckless and irresponsible."[11]

In 1949, the chances for approval of funds for the New Johnsonville steam plant appeared much brighter because the 1948 elections had sent a good number of public power sympathizers to Congress and put out of office many friends of private power. Even the *Electrical World* predicted success for the government.[12]

Truman asked for an immediate appropriation to get the project started and additional funds for 1950 to speed up its construction. The First Deficiency Appropriations Bill contained $2.5 million for the steam plant, and although this amount represented only a fraction of one per cent of the total bill, it engendered as spirited a debate as the issue had in the Eightieth Congress.[13]

The ranking Republican member of the House Appropriations Committee, John Taber of New York, opposed the steam plant on the ground that it represented another step toward socialization of the electric power industry. He and other Republicans also argued that, to take advantage of cheap power, several large corporations had moved to the Tennessee Valley from the Northeast, causing economic harm to that area.[14]

Democratic Representative Joe Evins of Tennessee countered that although some branch plants had located in the Tennessee Valley, not a single industry had moved there from the North, and Democrat George H. Christopher of Missouri declared that the Republican argument against forward-looking, ostensibly "socialistic" legislation was "so old that its whiskers drag on the floor of this chamber every time they drag it out."[15]

Arguing against the steam plant on constitutional grounds, Democratic Senator Willis Robertson of Virginia called the measure the first real test of congressional attitudes on government competition with private power. He warned that following closely on this decision would be one on the proposed Delta plant at Antioch in the Central Valley of California.[16]

Among senators who spoke in favor of the plant were Democrats Kenneth McKellar of Tennessee and Lister Hill of Alabama, who based its constitutionality on the commerce clause and on national defense.[17] The steam plant proponents were victorious, with both houses defeating every effort to delete the item, and the appropriations bill became law on May 24, 1949.

When the president asked Congress early the next year for $7 million (as part of a supplemental appropriations bill for fiscal 1950) to immediately begin construction of a $37 million TVA steam plant on Widow's Creek in Alabama, scarcely a murmur of protest was heard from private power advocates. The marked contrast to their vociferous opposition to the New Johnsonville proposal was clearly attributable to cold war arguments made more persuasive by the USSR's first successful test of an atomic bomb a few months earlier. Truman justified his request as necessary to fill the growing needs of the Atomic Energy

Commission's plant at Oak Ridge, as well as to supply reliable service to aluminum, ferro-alloy and other industries.[18]

Although it had called the New Johnsonville plant "an unnecessary going-out-of the way by government to help people who don't need help," the *Electrical World* found the Widow's Creek item acceptable:

> The industry has never opposed—and never could—a federal power development seriously tagged by responsible federal officials as "emergency, for national security."[19]

Congress again cooperated when President Truman and Chairman Gordon Clapp justified in terms of national defense items for continuing work on the New Johnsonville and Widow's Creek steam plants for fiscal year 1951.[20]

The opening of the Korean War in June 1950 further reduced opposition to budget requests for steam plant construction by the Tennessee Valley Authority. But with peace negotiations underway, a request in 1952 for eight new plants revived some of the old arguments. Calling the TVA "the platinum-coated, sacred cow of the government," Republican Representative Frederic R. Coudert of New York offered an amendment to reduce funds for the authority by $4 million. The House approved the amendment, which would have eliminated two of the steam plants, in addition to two removed by the Appropriations Committee in its nearly $15 million cut. The Senate Appropriations Committee reinstated the higher House committee figure, but a big battle ensued over the issue on the Senate floor.[21]

An amendment introduced by Republican Senator Homer Ferguson of Michigan would have cut out four of the steam units. Calling the TVA a government monopoly, Ferguson complained that Congress had been "feeding the calf" with its appropriations and that it was now time "to wean this calf." Senator McKellar countered that the TVA was "one of the most successful calves of its kind" ever raised in the United States. In the end, the Senate voted to accept its appropriations committee's figure of $186 million, and this amount went into the final bill. However, the vote that rejected the Ferguson amendment was a close 31 to 36.[22]

When a Supplemental Appropriations bill for fiscal 1953 came before it in June 1952, the House accepted an amendment by Representative Coudert to cut $65 million from Tennessee Valley Authority funds, leaving only $85 million to build steam plants, transmission lines and other power facilities for the expansion of the Atomic Energy Commission program. The request was justified on national defense grounds, but Coudert's argument that private companies could easily supply this power carried weight. However, senators sympathetic to public power again won out in the upper house, and the original $150 million request was granted.[23]

Public power could claim success on the TVA steam plant issue because of the ground-breaking approval of the New Johnsonville plant. Before Truman left office, Congress authorized several more steam plants, which by 1964 would make the authority the largest producer of electricity in the country and its steam plant generating capacity far greater than its hydroelectric capacity.[24] But the TVA would turn out to be a special case.

III

The Department of the Interior also sought authorization to build steam plants. It claimed the right under the Flood Control Act of 1944, which obligated the government to give preference to public bodies and cooperatives. The department reasoned that steam power was commonly required to firm up the secondary power usually produced at government hydro plants, which were normally located in highly variable water supply sources. This electricity then could be made available to preference customers. Private power proponents maintained, however, that no energy other than "electric power and energy generated at reservoir projects" was mentioned in the Flood Control Act. Furthermore, they argued, this law, like the Tennessee Valley Authority Act, contemplated only projects intended primarily for flood control and naviga- tion.[25]

In 1951, the question of federally built steam plants in the Northwest became especially important when a severe water shortage occurred there and when defense needs created by the Korean war made it essential that aluminum companies, electro-process industries and the Hanford atomic energy plant be supplied with sufficient electric power. Senator Warren G. Magnuson of Washington urged the Department of the Interior early in the year to consider steam plants for the Northwest because the threatened power shortage was being used as an excuse to move defense industries out of the area.[26]

Magnuson was referring to a proposal by Defense Electric Power Administrator Clifford B. McManus that no new, large power-consuming industrial companies be located in the Pacific Northwest until they could be assured that their electric power needs would be met during low water periods. McManus, President of the Southern Company, one of the largest private utility systems in the country, had been appointed by Secretary Chapman to head the Defense Electric Power Administration in the atmosphere of cooperation between public and private power engendered by the Korean crisis. Set up in the Department of the Interior in January 1951, the DEPA represented the department's successful bid to be named under the 1950 Defense Production Act as the primary coordinator for electric power. The agency was responsible for allocating materials to the electric industry, dealing with shortages and helping locate defense plants where there was sufficient power. Although McManus had alienated some of his private power colleagues in early 1950 by stating that the government should build hydroelectric power projects if private power could not, most of them applauded the appointment.[27]

As the person responsible for the Defense Electric Power Administration, the secretary of interior was expected to be a "neutral, impartial advocate of the nation's best interests" in any controversy that might arise between public and private power. In this spirit, Chapman appointed twenty-one private power representatives to a thirty-member advisory council and pledged that he "would not use the defense powers entrusted . . . [him] as a means of advancing public power development at the expense of private power development."[28]

This truce in the public versus private power fight broke down with a disagreement over steam plants in the Northwest. Interior Assistant Secretaries Davidson and Warne thought it imperative that the government build these facilities. Davidson assured Senator Magnuson early in 1951 that he would foster a plan that included three steam plants, to bring a million kilowatts of new power to the area in the next two years. Warne opposed the McManus proposal to delay locating industrial companies in the Northwest (the plant then being considered was Alcoa's new aluminum plant). He advised Secretary Chapman, "We must . . . expand the power facilities of the Northwest as rapidly as possible."[29]

D. L. Marlett, acting deputy administrator for Electric Power and vice-chairman of the Advisory Council on Electric Power Defense Production, agreed. He warned Chapman that the policy of locating large power-using industries outside the Northwest in high cost power areas would realize objectives sought by many private power executives: (1) to keep available federal hydroelectric power for their own use and minimize use of more expensive steam plants and (2) to show that industrial demands on the federal system were insufficient to warrant additional federal hydro projects and steam plants.[30]

Chapman was persuaded. Overruling his private power advisors who maintained that the Northwest could not support expansion of the aluminum industry, he decided that Alcoa, as well as other defense plants, could "be economically located in the Pacific Northwest and supplied with power."[31]

The secretary had alienated the private power industry, which charged that he had gone back on his promise not to use the wartime situation to extend public power. But he had succeeded in tying to the defense emergency the need for additional electric power and specifically fuel-fired steam plants to help firm supply when water was low and to conserve coal and oil when water was high.

Despite active promotion by the secretary of the interior, administration efforts to get funds for steam electric facilities from the Eighty-Second Congress failed. Before the House Committee on Public Works and in a letter to the chairman of the Senate counterpart, Chapman urged their authorization, basing his argument both on defense purposes and on "serving general area loads." Although he admitted that his department had taken a calculated risk in designating the Pacific Northwest as a location for defense industries needing large amounts of power, the secretary argued that steam plants could substantially reduce the risk posed by a critical water year. He also said the department wanted to avoid the mistakes made during World War II when aluminum plants were built in areas of high cost power. If these plants had been located in a low-cost power area, argued Chapman, it would not have been necessary to close them down as uneconomical after the war; they could have continued to contribute to the wealth of the nation, and their products would have been available in 1951 for defense purposes.[32]

The Public Works Committee favorably reported a bill authorizing the steam plants on October 9, 1951, and its backers predicted early passage. However, support dwindled when the need for the steam plants rather quickly diminished. Heavy rains fell in the Northwest during the last week of September, allowing interrupted power to be restored by the Bonneville Power Administration to the region's aluminum industry and prompting the Office of Defense Mobilization to announce that it was no longer necessary to move the aluminum plants out of the area. In early November, Charles Wilson, former president of the General Electric Corporation and now head of the new Office of Defense Mobilization, reportedly withdrew his support for the steam plants.[33]

The perennial question of whether there really was a power shortage in the Pacific Northwest also contributed to the administration's failure in this effort. A minority report on the House bill raised the issue, implying that the Department of the Interior had artificially created a shortage as an excuse to extend federal public power. Even after the Korean War broke out, private power executives insisted they could meet all power demands and maintained that the emergency was being "used to promote government power plants with the same old propaganda about 'power shortages.'"[34]

Although Truman again recommended in January 1952 that Congress authorize the plants, nothing came of his administration's efforts to build steam plants in the Pacific Northwest.[35]

Nor was the right of the government to build steam generating plants definitively established during this period. James Black and other representatives of the Pacific Gas and Electric Company managed to convince Congress every year that the proposed Delta steam plant for the Central Valley was unconstitutional and/or unnecessary, and it took the more liberal, Democratic Eighty-First Congress to finally approve the long-proposed Tennessee Valley Authority steam plant at New Johnsonville. Although appropriation requests for steam plants justified on the grounds of national defense for the Tennessee Valley Authority met with little opposition from Congress during Truman's second term, not even a power shortage or a war time national emergency could convince the lawmakers that the government should build steam plants in the Northwest.

IV

Interior Department requests for appropriations for transmission lines also came under fire from private power industry representatives. They maintained that if their companies were able and allowed to build any lines that were needed, duplication of lines would be avoided, and the utilities would pass along to consumers the savings from buying government power. To continue to allow the government to build these lines, they insisted, would lead to the socialization of the electric power industry.

In any case, the government had no legal right to construct such facilities, according to private power advocates. In arguing their case, they, like their public power opponents, referred to Section 5 of the Flood Control Act of 1944:

> The Secretary of Interior is authorized, from funds to be appropriated by the Congress, to construct or acquire by purchase or other agreement only such transmission lines and related facilities as may be necessary in order to make the power and energy generated at said projects available in wholesale quantities for sale on fair and reasonable terms and conditions to facilities owned by the federal government, public bodies, cooperatives, and privately owned companies.[36]

Private power proponents emphasized the words "as may be necessary," arguing that Congress intended to circumscribe the powers of interior. It therefore followed that if a private company was able and willing to build a transmission line, it would be improper for the government to build it.[37]

The Department of the Interior followed the policy on transmission lines as laid down by Secretary Ickes in the 1946 memorandum: "Transmission outlets to existing and potential wholesale markets shall be adequate to deliver power to every preferred customer within the region upon fair and reasonable terms."[38] The department maintained that the 1944 Flood Control Act, as well as related acts going back to 1906, obligated it "to get low-cost energy" to wholesale customers "with preference to public bodies." Federal transmission lines were necessary because this responsibility included ensuring that "equality of access to the power" was maintained. Since the department concerned itself with wholesale use rather than general distribution, interior argued that its power distribution did not conflict with that by private utilities.[39]

As private power sympathizers became more and more successful in persuading Congress to cut appropriations for transmission lines, Congress, in turn, began to pressure the government to negotiate "wheeling" contracts with private utilities. Under these agreements, the companies would agree to "wheel" or transmit all of the federally generated electrical energy at the dam over their lines to customers of the government. Thus, the government, in effect, would rent the companies' transmission lines. Assistant Secretary Warne said these contracts were "like taking a taxi rather than driving your own car, and like the taxi you ride only when there's room."[40]

Wheeling agreements were not new. By 1950, the Bonneville Power Administration had executed fifty of them over its more than ten years of existence. The government negotiated these contracts in order to meet its responsibilities for distributing power as dictated by law, and to delay investing in transmission facilities until load conditions increased. The Bureau of Reclamation had been forced to negotiate a five-year contract with Pacific Gas and Electric Company in 1944 after the company successfully lobbied Congress to deny funds for transmission lines from the newly built Shasta Dam in California to its California markets. It was "sign," complained interior officials, or "waste the water." Since 1944, the government had been trying to get wheeling rights over PG&E's lines, but local elections, the California Public Service Commission and Congress had foiled their attempts.[41]

The Interior Department's guiding principles for contracting wheeling arrangements with private utilities were set down in the Ickes memorandum and in a July 14, 1950 memorandum signed by Secretary Chapman. The Ickes directive specified that such contracts contain a time limit and guarantee the rights of public agencies and cooperatives as preference customers. The Chapman memorandum added a number of standards, including stipulations that the agreements (1) guarantee preference customers the same degree of service, chance to develop and serve greater power loads and right to contract with the government as if the government had built its own facilities; (2) not result in monopolization of the power at the bus bar; and (3) ensure that the government have an "equal or more advantageous" way of getting power to its customers than if it had constructed its own lines.[42]

Although the government was willing to execute wheeling contracts if these safeguards were included, in most cases it preferred to build its own facilities. Department officials contended that wheeling agreements saved the government very little money, and in some cases were more expensive in the long run than building new transmission lines. They also found that the monetary advantage in postponing construction of the facilities was usually temporary. And even if a contract were in place, according to President Truman, the government still needed continuing authority to build transmission lines in the event that the agreement didn't "bring the results it was intended to achieve." As he explained in a letter to Senator Carl Hayden,

Wheeling agreements, in general, do not guarantee the delivery of power to preference customers—they simply make the surplus-carrying capacity of the private power company's lines available to the government. At any time the private company makes use of its lines for other purposes, preference customers may be dropped from service.[43]

Because of this perceived threat of being put at the mercy of unfriendly private power companies, most preference customers opposed wheeling agreements.

Private power companies preferred wheeling agreements to additional federally-built transmission lines, but they would enter into these contracts only under certain circumstances. They disagreed with the Interior Department on such matters as whether they had to "wheel to any and all customers of the government, including any future customers; the duration and responsibility of the agreement; the geographical scope of the agreement; the amount to be paid for wheeling and the obligation of the company to increase its transmission capacity if necessary."[44]

V

In the Central Valley of California, controversy centered on whether the Bureau of Reclamation would build transmission lines from its Shasta Dam in the North down the east and west sides of the Sacramento Valley or whether the Pacific Gas and Electric Company would be allowed to buy the power at the bus bar and build its own transmission lines. The private utility also opposed the government's proposal to build the Delta steam plant at Antioch, California, as well as switchyards and other related facilities intended to firm up and integrate federal hydroelectric power.

The Interior Department's plans to construct a tie-line between the Central Valley project and the Bonneville Power Administration system in the Pacific Northwest also sparked opposition from private power. Long distance inter-ties related to the issue of whether public or private power would effect integrated power systems and reap the potential economic benefits. Tying widely separated systems also could make it possible to move power from one area to another where there was a shortage, thus saving the destination area from having to build more generating systems. Private power feared that federally built and controlled inter-ties could result in a national power pool, increase the number of publicly owned and nonprofit cooperatives and eventually lead to a national takeover of the power industry.

The Central Valley project had long been a source of contention among federal, state and private power proponents, as well as between the Bureau of Reclamation and the Corps of Engineers. Conceived and initiated with the goal of carrying water from the Sacramento Valley in the North to the semi-arid San Joaquin area in the South, it was authorized in 1933 by the California Legislature and taken over by the federal government at the request of the state by 1937 and 1940 acts of Congress. Initially, Californians had been concerned about the conflict between the Corps of Engineers and the Reclamation Bureau. Jealous guardians of states' rights, especially water rights, a majority of Californians opposed setting up a valley authority to administer the project. Some wanted the bureau to run it; others wanted the State of California to take it over again.[45]

Aware of the conflict between the two agencies regarding the Central Valley, Truman in 1945 had asked the secretaries of the army and interior to submit reports. On August 29, 1949, the Department of the Interior transmitted to Congress its comprehensive plan for development of the resources of the valley. Along with it went an endorsement from the president authorizing the so-called Folsom formula, which assigned responsibility for multiple purpose dams to the Bureau of Reclamation and jurisdiction over works built exclusively for flood control to the engineers. With the passage of the Engle Bill authorizing the Folsom Dam in October 1949, this formula was applied for the first time.[46]

With this argument resolved, the controversy between the Bureau of Reclamation and the Pacific Gas and Electric Company over the government's right to build transmission lines and steam plants in the valley assumed major importance. The bureau and the Office of the Department of the Interior, as well as local public power sympathizers, including Governor Earl Warren, took the view that such facilities constituted an integral part of the project itself because they were necessary to ensure a secure power supply as well as to comply with the spirit and philosophy of the Central Valley Act. Without transmission lines, they insisted, the preference policy could not be followed since PG&E would be the government's sole customer.[47]

Pacific Gas and Electric representatives, on the other hand, maintained that no statute granted the government authority to build a steam plant and transmission lines as part of the project and that their company was willing to supply all the necessary standby power and transmission facilities.[48]

Since 1941, the bureau had been seeking funds from Congress to build transmission lines south from the great multipurpose Shasta Dam, one on the east side and two on the west side of the Sacramento Valley. The Pacific Gas and Electric Company had consistently opposed these efforts, claiming that its lines were adequate and that it expected a leveling off in demand for power. When Congress appropriated funds to build the east side line, but denied funds in 1947 for the others, the private utility began building two lines on the west side. [49]

The next year, when the Interior Department sought funds for its proposed west-side lines, the company argued that these would duplicate the lines it was building. Interior's request for the two lines as well as for the Delta steam plant met the axe of the particularly hostile Eightieth Congress House of Representatives. The Senate followed suit, but it was responsible for a $1.5 million appropriation for fiscal 1949 to begin construction on a line from Shasta Dam to the Shasta Pacific Gas and Electric substation. After signing the Interior Department Appropriations Act for 1949, President Truman charged that in certain of its provisions Congress had "made a broad attack on the national public power policy." Included in his examples was the failure to grant funds for the west-side lines.[50]

The Central Valley transmission lines, substations and Delta steam plant seemed to stand a much better chance of approval in 1949, particularly since they had figured prominently in Truman's election campaign in the West. Worried about the possibility of a more pro-public power Congress, PG&E President James Black asked for a private meeting with Truman to try to convince him that his company "was being unduly mistreated" by the extension of government power lines in the Central Valley. The president agreed to see Black, but he "was not impressed" with his argument. Equally unconvinced was Krug, who wrote Truman that adoption of Black's position would mean "the complete negation" of federal power policy as it related to the Central Valley.[51]

When the Bureau of Reclamation again asked Congress for funds to build these facilities, Black testified in opposition before the subcommittees on interior appropriations of both houses. The private utility president presented his usual arguments—that the lines were unnecessary since his company's five lines were adequate; that if the bureau built its lines, the company would be severely hurt economically; and that the Delta steam plant was not needed because his company could supply the bureau with standby power at a price no higher than it would cost the government to produce it. Furthermore, said Black, Pacific Gas and Electric was willing to enter into a wheeling agreement with the government. Heretofore, he said, the two sides simply had not been able to get together.[52]

Ben Creim, the bureau's regional power manager at Sacramento, and Commissioner Straus responded that more lines were needed because all five generators at Shasta Dam would be working in the coming year; that if Mr. Black still did not believe in the great growth potential of California, the government would be glad to buy his company's transmission lines; and that PG&E lacked the capability to supply standby steam power much less produce it as cheaply as the Central Valley project could. As to the likelihood of executing a wheeling contract, Creim expressed astonishment at Black's testimony: "I want to state to you firmly and with all the emphasis at my command that the Pacific Gas and Electric Company has refused to favorably consider contractual terms on each and every occasion when the subject of exchange service was presented to them."[53]

During the House hearings, the question came up as to whether the previous year's appropriation had been intended for beginning the west-side lines or only for tying the Shasta Dam to the Shasta substation. In his statement on the 1949 appropriations act, the president had referred to the Shasta Dam-San Francisco area line as "previously authorized." Now Creim testified that Congress had granted the money to begin construction on these lines with the "stipulation . . . that the first service should be to the Shasta Pacific Gas & Electric substation." However, Representative Ben F. Jensen of Iowa insisted that "by no stretch of the imagination could one read into the language of the bill" that the west-side lines had been approved. Jensen charged that funds had been granted for the Shasta-Pacific Gas and Electric substation line only because the bureau had taken the funds appropriated earlier, struck off for "Timbuctoo" and then run out of money.[54]

The House of Representatives approved the funds for the facilities, although it cut the total amount for power by a sizeable amount. The Senate Appropriations Committee was hostile this time, striking out all three items and directing federal agencies to negotiate wheeling contracts with private utilities. After considerable debate regarding the dominance of the power lobby versus the dangers of socialism, the Senate restored the transmission lines item, and it appeared in the final bill.[55]

The Conference Committee refused to include a directive that the Interior Department make every effort to negotiate wheeling agreements before beginning to build transmission lines, a move that the Senate committee had admitted would involve Congress in setting national power policy. But when they accepted the conference report, on October 6 and 7, the two houses indicated they would ask for progress reports on this matter from the department.[56]

Public power liberals saw in this appropriations bill a victory of sorts because the funds for the transmission lines had been reinserted. The Department of Interior, however, knew it would have to proceed carefully on such matters because the opposition to government built lines and steam plants remained strong. Secretary Krug and Assistant Secretary Chapman agreed that Straus would have to be kept in line because he had "such a strong will to do things whether they . . . [were] approved or not."[57]

Private power could only view approval of the transmission lines as a defeat. The Council of State Chambers of Commerce had stated just a week previously that if the transmission lines were approved, the day would be "hastened when the nationalization of electric power in the United States will loom as a *fait accompli*." Private power could take heart, however, in the close vote in the Senate (45-38), the refusal by Congress to grant funds for the Delta steam plant and indications that in the future Congress would place increasing pressure on interior to negotiate wheeling contracts.[58]

Encouraged by its success, interior, in the next session of Congress, asked for $2 million for the Delta steam plant and switchyard as well as over $13 million for transmission lines and related facilities. It omitted, however, a request for a project it had been planning for some time—the Bonneville-Central Valley inter-tie. Krug, Assistant Secretary Davidson and Bonneville Power Administrator Paul Raver decided that the time was not yet ripe to ask for funds to interconnect the two systems. "If Reclamation puts in their justification," observed Davidson, "all hell will break loose."[59]

This inter-tie had been the subject of departmental discussion and study since early 1945. In January 1949, the Bureau of Reclamation presented a preliminary report indicating that the interconnection would be economically feasible and beneficial to California, the Northwest and the national interest. It would make available to California, which had a scarcity of water, possibly 600 million kilowatts of hydroelectric power then being wasted in the Northwest in off-peak (low demand) periods and would allow transmission of steam power from California to the Northwest during lower water periods in the Columbia River system.[60]

In 1948, Congress had granted the Interior Department's request for $70,000 for examination of power facilities, including a possible interconnection between the Central Valley project and the Bonneville system. However, it included a proviso that none of the funds for these purposes could be used outside California. In 1949, the bureau again asked for an appropriation to finance a similar study. Congress complied but stipulated in the appropriations bill that no more than $100,000 could be spent for examination and surveys of power facilities.[61]

The next year, interior included an item in its 1951 Central Valley budget estimates for over $400,000 for "development of project plans." Richard S. Boke, Sacramento regional director of the Bureau of Reclamation, testified that while it would like funds for the tie line at a future date, the bureau was not seeking money for construction at the present time.[62]

At the very moment that the House subcommittee was conducting its hearings on the interior appropriations bill for fiscal 1951, Commissioner Straus, unknown to interior as well as to Congress, was already "getting out of line." Bureau of Reclamation engineers were surveying a possible inter-tie. When Chapman, the newly named head of interior, discovered what was happening, he ordered the recalcitrant Straus on February 28, 1950 to stop the survey. Straus insisted that he was proceeding under the appropriations act for 1950, which, he reminded Chapman, had provided $100,000 "for surveying power facilities," but he did stop the work in March.[63]

In August, Commissioner Straus asked for permission to resume survey activities, but his request was denied. By now Northwest residents were expressing extreme opposition to the line because they feared loss of what they considered "their power" to California. To begin such work before action on the appropriations bill was completed, reasoned department officials, would look suspicious as well as possibly jeopardize the request for a line in Oregon (from Maupin to Klamath Falls), which represented two-thirds of the inter-tie. Furthermore, with the Korean conflict under way, the Interior Department began to consider the possibility of arguing its case on the basis of defense with particular attention to aluminum production and the expected shortage of power in the Northwest.[64]

Meanwhile, the House barred the bureau from spending any appropriation funds "available to the Bureau for reconnaissance, preliminary survey, design, or any other work" on the proposed inter-tie, and refused to approve interior's request for $4.45 million to build three transmission lines, the Delta steam plant and related facilities.[65]

As one of several Interior Department officials who requested restoration of these items by the Senate, Straus told the Interior Subcommittee of the Appropriations Committee that he believed the House had cut the $4.45 million "on the advice of Mr. James Black," president of Pacific Gas and Electric. The commissioner charged that Black had led the House committee to believe that his company would enter into negotiations for wheeling contracts with the bureau that were "satisfactory to the reclamation law" when in truth PG&E had never revealed such an intent.[66]

However, on the question of which side had shown a willingness to negotiate in good faith, it was the private utility that scored with the Senate committee, largely because of an error in judgment by Interior Department and Bureau of Reclamation officials.

In the most recent series of exchanges going back to October 1949, a first draft of a contract had been sent to PG&E by the Interior Department on December 19. At a meeting held on February 1, 1950 between the bureau and company representatives, the private utility offered substitute articles that the bureau and the Secretary of the Interior found "totally unacceptable."[67]

At this point the meetings were suspended because some members of the joint negotiating group had to be in Washington for hearings on the interior appropriations bill. At these hearings, Chapman told the senators on April 4 that the PG&E proposal could not be accepted because it contained conditions that ran "counter to the public power policy of the government." The secretary asked that funds for the transmission lines be granted, arguing that the department needed a strong negotiating position to protect the preference and other features of public power policy. When urging that the Delta steam plant item be restored, Chapman reminded the committee that it had cut funds for this plant in the previous year on the assumption the utility would agree to a suitable wheeling contract. "We have tried to get that contract," he said, but "the government cannot wait any longer for the company to make up its mind whether it can accept this committee's instructions of last year."[68]

A few days later Harvey F. McPhail, Director of the Branch of Power Utilization for the Bureau of Reclamation, told the committee that the company did not want to make a wheeling agreement that was "within the law and federal policy." Among seven reasons he listed as to why the PG&E counter proposal was unacceptable to the bureau were the charges that the contract would extend the repayment period by more than thirty years, limit preference customers to such a small number that the bureau could not carry out the law, make PC&E a preference customer contrary to federal policies and law, and prevent the bureau from directly serving any customer.[69]

This testimony backfired on April 17 when Black informed the committee that he had first and only learned of McPhail's points in a press release of the previous day. The head of Pacific Gas and Electric's negotiating team, General Counsel Robert H. Gerdes, thereupon offered to submit financial differences between the two parties to the federal Power Commission or the California Public Utilities Commission for a final decision.[70]

The private utility had gained the advantage with the committee. Republican Senator William F. Knowland commented that if it were true that the government had not notified the company until the day before, and then through the press, he would be "a little shocked." Pressed by committee members, McPhail could only admit that the bureau had not transmitted the seven objections to the company in two months' time, explaining only that the department had been short staffed and busy making a "complete repayment and financial analysis of the Central Valley project" based on the company's counter proposals. Still, Chapman maintained that the company had refused to sign a contract. He told the Senate committee, "We know when we have been given the run-around."[71]

Gerdes then suggested to Senator Hayden on May 8 that a meeting between the private utility and the government be held before the Senate Appropriations Committee to resolve their differences. Chapman refused, saying that he did not believe "a single meeting could hope to resolve the differences of policy which have been the subject of unsuccessful negotiations for seven years" and that in any event, the Senate committee was an inappropriate place for negotiations.[72] Interior had failed to make its case with the Senate. Funds for the Central Valley transmission and steam facilities were omitted from the final appropriations bill for fiscal 1951.

The next year, the department repeated its requests for funds to build transmission lines in the Sacramento Valley and between the Central Valley lines at Elverta and the new dam and power plant being built on the American River at Folsom. Funds for lines intended to serve government installations in the area that had a direct connection with the defense effort also were requested. However, interior temporarily abandoned hopes of getting the Delta steam plant item approved.[73]

Chapman had, in fact, already retreated, as he had on other public power issues in the face of the country's involvement in the Korean War. On April 4, he shocked public power advocates outside the government with an announcement that, while the House was considering the appropriations bill, the department had signed a ten-year wheeling agreement with Pacific Gas and Electric. The *New York Times* described the contract as the culmination of "one of the nation's bitterest battles since the formative stages of TVA."[74]

Administration insiders were not surprised at the outcome since the secretary had been steadily losing ground in his struggle for transmission lines funding. Denial of requests for lines in the Southwest by the Eighty-first Congress had compelled Chapman to sign an agreement with two Oklahoma private power companies that liberals generally regarded as disadvantageous to public power. Bureau officials in California had sensed that this contract, announced in July 1950, would make it difficult for the secretary to refuse one in their area that was, as Boke put it, "equally onerous."[75] Furthermore, the Eighty-second Congress, in which the Democratic majority was sharply reduced, was expected to be even less cooperative than its predecessor.

While most public power liberals saw the agreement with Pacific Gas and Electric as a sellout, private power proponents hailed it as a victory. Under its terms, the bureau would deliver power to PG&E at Tracy, California. When the company had transmitting capacity available, it would carry the power to customers of the government for which the government would pay the utility at an agreed upon rate. But the Bureau of Reclamation said that it put the government at the mercy of the company which could "at any time, notify the Bureau" that it had no excess capacity, thereby rendering it "unable to wheel the public power to public preference customers."[76]

Meanwhile, interior proceeded with its tactic of tying some of its California requests to defense. It turned the inter-tie question over to the Defense Power Administration, which found the interconnection to be in the national interest. Secretary Chapman consequently approved the line on January 3, 1951.[77]

The Department of the Interior then asked Congress for $6 million to build a transmission line from Shasta Dam to Klamath Falls, Oregon, justifying it on national defense grounds. Chapman thereupon ordered the bureau to begin "immediate steps for construction" of the interconnection, which he said had "been certified in the interests of national defense."[78]

Hearings were held in March on the bureau's request for the tie line appropriation. Opposition came from both regions involved. Northwest opponents, fearing the loss of low cost power to California, accused the federal government of "empire building." In California, some objected that making the Central Valley project a state one would now be more difficult to achieve.[79] Arguing the department's case on an urgent defense basis, Assistant Secretary Warne contended that the line would allow the equivalent of continuous operation of one complete aluminum plant in the Northwest. He also assured congressmen that both areas would benefit economically from the inter-tie.[80]

However, in this effort, the Interior Department appeared again to be its own worst enemy. Newspapers were reporting that Chapman had ordered that investigative and planning work on the inter-tie be carried out during the current fiscal year.[81] Since the Appropriations Committee had stated categorically in the previous year that no funds should be used in fiscal 1951 for any work on the tie line, the secretary could expect trouble if the press stories were substantiated.

Representative Henry M. Jackson, chairman of the House committee in charge of investigating the interconnection item and normally a public power liberal, was livid. Jackson directed the committee's attention to a February 1, 1951, Wenatchee (Washington) *Daily World* report of Boke's announcement that he had received orders to proceed with design work. Adding that Straus had said as far back as the preceding fall that he intended to go ahead with plans for the inter-tie, despite the congressional directive, Jackson demanded of Warne, "Why does the Bureau persist in defying a directive of the Congress?" Forcing Warne to admit that his department had no authority to proceed with the inter-tie, Jackson in effect accused the bureau of subterfuge when it included an item called "Shasta boundary terminal facilities" in the previous year's justification without making a full disclosure as to its intended meaning.[82]

On the same day that Warne was under fire before the subcommittee, Chapman asked the bureau for an explanation. The bureau reported that it had spent $157,117 in fiscal 1951 on planning for the line and reminded the secretary that the appropriations bill contained an item for $400,413 "for development of project plans" in the Central Valley. The bureau construed this to mean that surveys of marketing areas and transmission lines in California could be carried out if they related to the over-all Central Valley project.[83]

In its report to the House, the Appropriations Committee concluded that "a violation of comity between the Interior Department and the Committee on Appropriations and the Congress has been committed by the Bureau of Reclamation." And it asked the secretary to investigate the situation and to report promptly to the committee. Chapman turned the matter over to the Division of Budget and Finance.[84]

Thus, the Department of the Interior, especially through its Bureau of Reclamation, again found itself in the bad graces of the House Appropriations Committee. Straus tried to shift the blame within the department from himself to Chapman, while the secretary adroitly avoided taking the responsibility.

After Chapman had put the investigation in motion, the commissioner asked the secretary for "positive direction." Obliquely reminding his superior that he had been following his orders on the tie line, Straus suggested that Chapman might want to countermand his January 17 instruction that Straus and the BPA "take immediate steps . . . to initiate construction of, and to complete as rapidly as possible" the interconnection. The secretary cleverly replied that the directive did not need countermanding since it did not actually authorize the bureau to "obligate any funds" for the tie line. "On the contrary," wrote Chapman, "I reaffirm the instructions and ask that you continue to support the department's request for funds to initiate construction of the necessary facilities at the earliest possible time."[85]

On June 12, 1951, the Division of Budget and Finance sent its report to the secretary. It revealed that field survey work on the California-Oregon line had recommenced on July 31, 1950 on orders of Regional Director Boke and stopped again on May 25, 1951, after having obligated a total of $252,000. Thus, work had continued despite Chapman's February 28, 1950 order to cease and despite the House committee's directive that no funds be spent for any work on the proposed interconnection in fiscal 1951.[86] Placing the blame squarely on the bureau, Chapman reported to the chairmen of the House and Senate Appropriations Committees on August 1, 1951 that the investigation revealed that the bureau had spent money to conduct field surveys of the inter-tie "contrary to the directions of the Secretary of the Interior."[87]

The House of Representatives had acted on the appropriations bill before the report was finished. While it allowed funds for three transmission lines in the Central Valley, it cut items for three other lines (in view of the wheeling agreement executed between the government and PG&E) and eliminated funds for the inter-tie as well as banned all preliminary work on it.

In another move that would seriously tilt the struggle in private power's favor, the House accepted an amendment to the bill by Republican Kenneth B. Keating of New York. This amendment specified that the Bureau of Reclamation could use none of the money appropriated by the bill for construction of transmission lines in areas where wheeling agreements that provided for private utility service to government preferred customers were in force. Keating argued that this amendment merely put into law what members of interior subcommittees in both houses had been advising for several years—that taxpayers' money not be wasted on building transmission lines in areas where private utility lines already were in operation. The Interior Department took the stand that without sufficient appropriations to build or acquire transmission lines, it could not carry out the objectives of the 1944 act and would be left without effective bargaining power in negotiating equitable wheeling contracts.[88]

In general, the House had savagely cut the entire public power program. Reducing Truman's request for the Interior Department by 11 per cent, it had exceeded its predecessor's hostility to public power. One-third of the Democrats voting had said "yea" to the Keating Amendment, but most surprising was the revolt by congressmen from the Tennessee Valley Authority area who lined up 9 to 17 against the government's request, with 10 not voting or absent. This action by the House toward the administration's public power program symbolized the breakup of the Democratic Party's congressional strength and reflected the increasing shift toward the right that had taken place in the 1950 elections. Congressmen with strong ties to labor voted against public power for the first time, and some congressmen voted against it because public power meant loss of city and state taxes.[89]

Truman reacted strongly to the bill as passed by the House in June. The President wrote Senator Hayden, chairman of the Appropriations Committee, urging that the Senate restore the transmission lines and the inter-tie items and eliminate the Keating Amendment. Not to do so would "restrict the operation of federal hydroelectric power projects for the national defense and in the public interest," he wrote. Failure to comply also would drastically alter the government's basic power policies by removing its authority to "ensure widespread benefits from federal power at low cost" since wheeling agreements generally "do not guarantee the delivery of power to preference customers." The inter-tie, he insisted, was "a good, fast way to increase the nation's power supply."[90]

The Senate did soften some of the House blows to public power. It weakened the Keating Amendment by allowing the Bureau of Reclamation to construct lines when funds had already been appropriated for them, or when the secretary of the interior had determined that a private company was "unable to unwilling" to provide adequate wheeling either to service federal preference customers or to integrate government hydro projects. However, it stood squarely behind the House action on the inter-tie and was even more ruthless in cutting requests for Central Valley transmission lines.[91]

As the bill emerged from conference, it contained the Senate's wording on the Keating Amendment but authorized only one transmission line—the one to connect the Folsom Dam power plant to the east side Shasta-Tracy line. The conference report revealed Congress's irritation with interior over its handling of the Central Valley-Bonneville interconnection issue. Observing that it had received reports that work had continued on the proposed inter-tie "despite the categoric denial of funds" by both houses of Congress in 1950 and 1951, the conferees asked the secretary of the interior "to submit immediately a full and complete report including disciplinary action taken by him in this case."[92] The final bill, signed into law on September 6, 1951, was a resounding defeat for public power in general and the Department of the Interior in particular.

Despite this defeat, the bureau wanted to ask for funds for the interconnection in the next session of Congress, but Bonneville Power Administrator Paul Raver advised caution. However, circumstances were soon to change Raver's attitude. At just this time, a severe water shortage occurred in the Northwest, forcing the BPA to withdraw power from aluminum and electro-process industries and causing defense mobilization chief Charles Wilson to direct all major aluminum producers to plan to move out if the situation did not improve immediately. It was against this background that Raver requested the bureau to issue a strong statement regarding the necessity of the inter-tie as a means of alleviating such a shortage in the future. But Straus evidently had not recovered from the criticism leveled against him during his last experience with this issue. He refused, replying that "the Department and Congress have made this line question one of personal handling by the secretary."[93]

In his budget message to Congress on January 1, 1952, President Truman included a request for transmission lines for the Bureau of Reclamation, as well as for the Bonneville, Southwestern and Southeastern Power Administrations, and the Tennessee Valley Authority. For fiscal 1953, the bureau asked for funds for transmission lines in the Central Valley and a switchyard at Tracy, as well as for beginning the Bonneville-Shasta tie line. The Congress, however, was no more amenable to these requests than it had been in the last session. It approved just one transmission line (Tracy-Contra Costa) and switchyard and kept the Keating Amendment in force.[94]

The Interior Department had decided not to press for the California-Oregon interconnection. Realizing how politically infeasible the project was despite the defense justification, the department decided to wait for the results of a study of the inter-tie by the Federal Power Commission as requested by the DEPA "to determine the contribution such an interconnection could make to the national defense." Chapman believed that a positive FPC report might favorably influence the House Committee on Appropriations, which had stated in its report for 1952 that it would not be convinced of the need for the project until a thorough study was made of the possible effects on the economies of both California and the Northwest. The conference report on the Interior Department Appropriations Bill for 1953 contained a similar statement regarding the need for a study before a decision on the tie line could be made.[95]

As the Truman Administration came to a close, not only was the tie-line question left in the air, but there was a possibility that the Federal Power Commission would recommend connection of the two systems through the Pacific Gas and Electric Company's hydroelectric site on the Pit River.[96] Some funds for transmission lines in the Central Valley had been granted, and some lines had been completed, but the reluctance of Congress to approve such requests led the Interior Department to compromise on the wheeling agreement with Pacific Gas and Electric, which liberals felt placed government preference customers at the mercy of the private utility.

Although the administration could claim few successes in its efforts to secure funds for steam plants in the Northwest and California, transmission lines in the Central Valley and the inter-tie, it could chalk up one definite victory. In 1949, it succeeded in securing from Congress an appropriation creating the Southeastern Power Administration. However, the fledgling agency, as well as the six-year old Southwestern Power Administration, were slated for more and even tougher battles with private power.

5

Compromises and Unholy Alliances: The Southwest

To many on the private power side, federal marketing agencies represented key steps in a "master plan" to eventually nationalize the electric power industry. The *Electrical World* warned of the dangers: "These agencies are real political and economic forces of no mean proportions because they control all the federal power generated in these large areas. And it looks as if they can be set up wherever an army hydroelectric plant is erected."[1]

By 1949, the Department of the Interior had created two power marketing administrations, the Bonneville Power Administration and the Southwestern Power Administration, and for several years it had been trying to secure funds from Congress to establish a third, in the Southeast.

The precedent for marketing administrations had been set by the Bonneville Project Act of 1937, which authorized the Corps of Engineers to build the Bonneville Dam project on the Columbia River. A 1940 amendment made permanent a provisional Bonneville Power Administration and placed it under the jurisdiction of the secretary of the interior who was empowered to appoint an administrator to dispose of the power generated at the plant. The administrator also was directed to build, operate and maintain "such electric transmission lines and substations and facilities he finds necessary, desirable or appropriate" to get the available electric power to "existing and potential markets."[2]

In 1940, the BPA was authorized to market power from the Bureau of Reclamation's Grand Coulee Dam, and an act of 1947 empowered it to market surplus electrical energy from all Corps of Engineers projects in the Pacific Northwest.[3]

Private power proponents saw the BPA as a menace partly because a section in the Bonneville Project Act requiring that a minimum of 50 per cent of power be reserved for preference customers up to January 1, 1942, had enabled a number of public utility districts to enter the power business in the

Northwest. The first administrator, James D. Ross, encouraged this practice so energetically that private power proponents said it was only through "foresight, planning and tenacious spirit" that private utility companies in the area were able to remain in business. When Ross died in 1939, Interior Secretary Harold Ickes chose Dr. Paul W. Raver to replace him. A civil engineer and university professor, Raver guided Bonneville during its formation years and remained at this post throughout the Truman period.[4]

The establishment of the second marketing agency—the Southwestern Power Administration—grew out of the Grand River Dam project, which the federal government took over from the state of Oklahoma in November 1941 to complete and operate for defense needs. Responsibility for the project was placed in the Public Works Administration, but in 1943, it was transferred to the Department of the Interior, which established the SWPA to carry out this function. The new agency also was authorized to market power from Corps of Engineers hydroelectric plants at the Norfork Dam on the White River in Arkansas and the Denison Dam project on the Red River separating Texas from Oklahoma.[5]

Douglas Wright, an engineer then serving as administrator of the Grand River Dam project in Oklahoma, was appointed as administrator. Long associated with public power, he had worked for the Public Works Administration in the thirties and later for the State of Nebraska on its power projects.

II

A departmental order of November 21, 1945 designated the Southwestern Power administrator as the marketing agent for surplus electric energy generated at Corps of Engineers projects in Arkansas, Louisiana, Missouri, Kansas, Oklahoma and Texas. The administrator was directed to carry out the marketing policy and exercise the powers granted the secretary of the interior as set forth in the Flood Control Act of 1944.[6]

The Bureau of Reclamation handled the marketing of power from its own as well as from all Corps of Engineers projects west of the Mississippi River except those in the marketing areas of the Bonneville and Southwestern Power Administrations. The Bureau hoped also to handle this function for those Corps of Engineers projects that had been authorized in the area east of the Mississippi and south of the Ohio River. However, senior officials in the Interior Department advised in 1947 that a Southeastern Power Administration be established for this purpose and that in the meantime the job be given to the Division of Power, a staff agency that aided in supervising departmental power activities.[7]

Secretary Krug agreed but made an exception of eight of the Corps of Engineers projects that were located in the Cumberland River Basin. Since these projects fell naturally into the Tennessee Valley Authority system, it was decided that the TVA would distribute their surplus power.[8]

The Interior Department then began seeking appropriations to set up a Southeastern Power Administration but achieved no success with the Eightieth Congress. With the situation more promising following the 1948 elections, the department asked the Eighty-first Congress for $85,000 to create the agency. Opponents reacted strongly. Democratic Senator Elmer Thomas of Oklahoma accused the Interior Department of attempting to carve out a "power empire" in the area, and Senator Kenneth McKellar of Tennessee introduced a bill on May 25, 1949 intended to give the Corps of Engineers, rather than interior, authority to market surplus power from army dams.[9]

Outside Congress, a private utility representative, A. C. Spurr, president of Monongahela Power Company in West Virginia, charged that a federal marketing agency in the Southeast, covering eleven states from Maryland to Florida, would constitute the tie-up link in a chain by which the government could choke off private power in a vast area from the Tennessee Valley Authority to the Southwestern Power Administration.[10]

Despite this strong opposition, the public power forces won. The McKellar bill failed to emerge from committee, and the final interior appropriations bill as enacted on October 12, provided $70,000 for setting up a marketing agency in the Southeast. The secretary of the interior established the Southeastern Power Administration on March 21, 1950, to carry out the functions assigned him by the Flood Control Act of 1944 with regard to the marketing of power from army projects "in the states of West Virginia, Virginia, North Carolina, South Carolina, Georgia, Florida, Alabama, Mississippi, Kentucky."[11]

In addition to the issues of federal transmission facilities and wheeling agreements, the public versus private power debate concerning activities of the Southwestern and the Southeastern Power Administrations included Rural Electrification Administration loans to federated cooperatives. These so-called "super-cooperatives," composed of distribution cooperatives that banded together to secure REA loans to build steam plants and transmission lines, were seen by private power as another government effort to put them out of business. And when these federated cooperatives announced plans to lease to the marketing agencies the facilities that the loans made possible, the threat, according to private power, was compounded.

III

The comprehensive plan for power distribution and sales from federal hydroelectric projects issued by the Southwestern Power Administration shortly after its creation in 1945 had included a proposal to build transmission lines and substations costing $125 million and a steam plant costing $77 million. In early 1946, the administration asked Congress for $23 million to begin effecting this plan, which had as its main purpose the interconnection of the various federal hydroelectric projects in the area. While a subcommittee of the House Appropriations Committee was holding hearings on these budget requests and on the very day and hour that the Southwestern Power Administration was scheduled to appear on behalf of them, eleven private utility companies released to the press an offer to buy all of the electric power generated at the Denison, Norfolk and Pensacola projects. The timing and publicizing of this proposal were obviously intended to influence Congress, as Secretary Krug and Administrator Douglas Wright charged. Congress drastically cut the request to $7.5 million for construction and refused the steam plant.[12]

The Interior Department, which viewed the offer as hostile, explored the possibility of striking back with an antitrust suit. On March 7, Acting Secretary Chapman asked the United States attorney general to determine whether the eleven private utilities had violated any antitrust laws by apparently combining for the purpose of gaining control of all electric power sources in the Central Southwest. By controlling all outlets from the dams, Chapman pointed out, the companies could control the market.[13]

The following day, Wright informed the utilities that their offer was unacceptable and at the same time sharply criticized their tactics. The timing of both the offer and its release, he wrote, make "it clear that your offer was designed . . . for its psychological effect in assisting in the tremendous campaign you are making to prevent any appropriations from being made for the construction of facilities to distribute power to anyone but yourselves." The attorney general later advised the secretary that only an attempt to monopolize was involved, and since interior had rejected the companies' offer, the case was weakened.[14] Consequently, Chapman dropped the idea of an antitrust suit.

In early 1947, SWPA, with the funds appropriated by Congress, let contracts for the building of a transmission line to connect the Denison and Norfolk projects. Realizing that it was not going to be allowed to buy power at the bus bar, Texas Power and Light Company in April negotiated a contract with the Interior Department providing for delivery to the company of 70,000,000 kilowatt hours of primary energy and an average of 63,500,000 kilowatt hours of secondary energy yearly. The utility agreed to allow the government to withdraw up to 20,000 kilowatts from its transmission lines for Rural Electrification cooperatives and federal government purchasers. The power agency would buy this energy at a slightly higher rate than it would charge for it. Service to other preferred customers would have to be made over the government's own lines. For firming up these loads, the company would charge the government its lowest prevailing rates.[15]

The other private power companies in the Southwest were horrified at the terms of the contract and vowed never to negotiate on such a basis. The president of Southwestern Gas and Electric Company told the Senate Appropriations Committee, "I would feel that I was almost criminally to blame should I make such a contract with Southwestern Power Administration."[16]

Taking the offensive, representatives of the private power companies, in testimony before Congress over the next two years, vigorously opposed Southwestern Power Administration requests not only for further transmission lines and related facilities but for operation and maintenance as well. Congress responded by appropriating no funds at all for construction in either year. In 1947, it approved only $125,000 for operation and maintenance, forcing SWPA to cut its staff in half. In 1948, when Congress granted the agency funds for only eight months of existence, it looked as though the companies had succeeded in their attempt to emasculate, if not destroy, their enemy.[17]

IV

The November elections saved the power agency. Most area congressional candidates who opposed the SWPA were defeated. Furthermore, pressure began to come from various quarters for the president to include in his next budget funds that would allow the marketing agency not only to remain in existence but also to build transmission lines. One group that agitated in behalf of the agency was the rural electric cooperatives, who feared that the private power companies would come between them and the federal government for whom they were preference customers. They demanded that interior ask Congress for funds to build transmission facilities to reach them. Clyde Ellis, executive secretary of the National Rural Electric Cooperative Association, wrote Oklahoma Representative A. S. Monroney that if SWPA were not granted a deficiency appropriation, it would go out of business in February 1949 and added that it had to be granted permanent status in law. "Rural people everywhere in the area," he wrote, "are feeling the pinch."[18]

Cooperatives that had built or wanted to build their own transmission and generating facilities approached Southwestern Power to examine the possibilities of integrating their plants and lines with the agency's in the event they could obtain loans for construction from the Rural Electrification Administration. Approving the idea, SWPA included items in its budget to build transmission lines to these "generating and transmission cooperatives" and to investigate the possibility of leasing their facilities and buying power from them.[19]

Political figures also pressured Truman to help the weakened agency. Governor Robert Kerr of Oklahoma, House Minority Leader Sam Rayburn of Texas and Representative Carl Albert of Oklahoma were among those who urged the president late in 1948 to do everything possible to secure funding for Southwestern transmission lines and operation and maintenance.[20]

The private companies in the area became more conciliatory. They renewed attempts, made sporadically since 1946, to negotiate a contract with the government. Calling it their best and last offer, the eleven companies submitted a proposal on December 30, 1948. The Department of the Interior, however, rejected the offer on January 25, 1949. Among its reasons were the proposal's failure to grant preference to public bodies and cooperatives, encourage the most widespread use at the lowest possible cost, and assure the government payment for electrical energy sufficient to meet expenses. Interior also said that, if accepted, the offer would restrain trade and encourage monopoly, and its benefits would go to the companies rather than to all the people of the area.[21]

Before the House subcommittee on interior appropriations, Secretary Krug, SWPA Administrator Wright and Democratic Representative A. S. Monroney offered convincing arguments for approval of $31 million for fiscal 1950 Southwestern construction and against execution of a contract on the basis of the companies' last offer. Krug said that "after about three years of negotiation, it has become crystal clear that we will never get a proposal from the power companies that will protect the preferred customers."[22] Wright relayed the demand from REA cooperatives in the area "that the rights extended to them under the law as preference customers be carried out." Monroney defined the issue as whether Congress was going to go back to the old "bus bar philosophy" or allow the government to make its power available at a reasonable cost to public agencies and cooperatives.[23]

The committee recommended and the House approved the entire amount requested for construction and allowed $4 million in cash and $5 million in contract authority. The eleven companies thereupon reversed themselves. During testimony before the Senate Appropriations Committee, they offered to sign a contract of the type agreed to by the Texas Power and Light Company. The president of Southwestern Gas and Electric Company admitted that the private utilities had decided to make the offer after the House approved the funds for SWPA.[24]

Although this was the first time the companies had made such an offer and although this type of contract was considered acceptable to the government, the National Rural Electric Cooperative Association was opposed. Charging that "these power companies are out to kill us," Executive Secretary Clyde Ellis warned that even a "Texas" contract would endanger the rest of the Southwest area because the other states had regulatory commissions usually dominated by private power interests that could alter the terms of the contract at any time.[25]

Interior and its supporters then tried to persuade senators to approve the request for Southwestern on the ground it would put the power agency in a good negotiating position with the companies. However, the Senate Appropriations Committee approved only three of the forty-four projects approved by the House. It then directed SWPA to try to negotiate agreements with the companies similar to the Texas Power and Light contract and report back by January 1, 1950.[26]

Public power could claim a victory when the appropriation request survived the Senate and when the Conference Committee refused to adopt the direction that the government report to the Appropriations Committee regarding progress on wheeling contracts.[27]

But the administration understood the strength of the opposition. Although the Senate had approved the appropriation, the fight on the floor had been bitter. After the bill was passed on October 7, 1949, Senator Hayden, chairman of the Interior Subcommittee of the Committee on Appropriations, told the upper house that the president had assured him that the administration would continue "to encourage cooperation between the government agencies and private utilities to obtain the greatest possible benefits from electric power obtained from both sources." Hayden in turn promised his colleagues that he would monitor the administration on this promise when the Interior Department asked for appropriations for transmission lines in the following year.[28]

As a practical politician and a president who understood the limits of his powers over Congress, Truman knew that the marketing agencies would have to negotiate wheeling agreements with private power in certain cases. But he and Interior Department officials were determined to fight any congressional policy-making that would require entering into contracts harmful to public power principles. Outlining his department's position to Senator Thomas of Oklahoma, Secretary Krug noted "major differences" between many of the private power companies and interior regarding the government's "basic policies" on disposing power from its projects: "These companies . . . have done everything possible to force the power agencies of the government to enter into agreements which would, in effect, nullify those policies."[29]

After passage of the appropriations bill for 1950, Southwestern Power proceeded along two fronts. First, it continued negotiations with the generating and transmission cooperatives, concluding contracts with five of them between November 23, 1949 and January 9, 1950.[30] Second, it resumed talks with the private companies. Beginning with the Oklahoma Gas and Electric Company and the Public Service Company of Oklahoma, Wright aimed to execute contracts that could be used as a model for other agreements in the Southwest. On December 22, 1949, he submitted a draft of a proposed wheeling contract with the two companies to the secretary of the interior for his approval.[31]

The other power agencies in the department and the Bureau of Reclamation advised the newly named secretary, Oscar Chapman, to reject the proposal because of a protective provision that would in effect have granted a subsidy to the companies in certain cases.[32]

Meanwhile, Wright was defending the proposed contract. Before a meeting of Missouri REA cooperatives in February 1950, he said that Congress had appropriated funds for transmission lines with the expectation that the Southwestern Power Association would make agreements wherever possible, and he assured the cooperatives that this contract was a good one. "We have won in the Southwest," Wright proclaimed. While he commented that he had always supported "both public and private power," the administrator also felt compelled to evoke the name of the "father of pubic power": "Sixteen years ago I sat on a sand hill in Nebraska with the greatest man who ever used the world 'power'—Senator George Norris—and I got religion."[33]

Urging that it be accepted, the private companies used the proposed contract to argue that Congress should cut SWPA's appropriation requests for fiscal 1951. A special target was the power agency's continuing fund, established by Congress in 1949. Because this money could be used for "the purchase of power and energy," private power companies feared it would facilitate contracts between Southwestern and the generating and transmission cooperatives.[34]

Speaking before the House subcommittee about his work on the draft, Wright boasted that the terms of the agreement were "about three times as good" as the Texas Power and Light Company contract. When asked what action Secretary Chapman might take, the administrator commented, "If he disapproves it the thing has to be ended as far as I am concerned if I continue to work for the Department." As expected, Clyde Ellis spoke against the proposed contracts, but he surprised everyone concerned when he revealed their terms to the subcommittee since the two sides had agreed to keep them secret until Chapman acted.[35]

The secretary's decision came on April 3. Chapman pleased Ellis and other liberals when he directed Wright to present to the utilities an amended proposal that would eliminate the offensive protective provision. Suggesting language that would accomplish this goal, he declared that the clause was contrary to the law and established power policy. Four days later, the companies rejected the revised draft. The secretary then asked the administrator to try to work out a straight interchange and wheeling agreement.[36]

The House approved the budget estimates for SWPA construction, but not until Speaker Rayburn in a rare floor speech assured his colleagues that the $6 million would be returned to the United States Treasury if the agency signed wheeling contracts with the two Oklahoma companies. Rayburn defended the proposed contracts and charged that a man who claimed to represent the cooperatives of the country (an obvious reference to Clyde Ellis) had been "stirring up trouble" between the power administration and the rural cooperatives.[37]

While the Interior Subcommittee of the Senate Appropriations Committee was considering these budget requests for the Southwestern Power Administration, contract negotiations between the government and the two private utilities were resumed. Although the House committee had declared that it wanted action on these contracts, Chapman refused to be rushed into signing. When Wright submitted another draft to him in June, Chapman informed the administrator that its terms were "far more objectionable" than the earlier proposal. Rebuking Wright for not having followed his instructions, the secretary said the draft agreement failed to meet his objections to the principle of subsidy in the first drafts and would "freeze the status of customers as of the date of the contract." At the same time, Chapman was careful to update Congress on the course of the negotiations.[38]

Expressing surprise and "deep and genuine regret" at Chapman's response, Wright asked permission to arrange further talks between the government and the companies. Chapman consented, turning the negotiations over to his administrative assistant secretary, Vernon D. Northrop.[39]

Details concerning these negotiations were kept secret, but on June 14, syndicated columnist Doris Fleeson broke the news that Chapman had rejected the Wright contracts. The *Public Utilities Fortnightly* pointed out that these contracts, which Chapman had refused to sign because of an "alleged 'service charge' by the company for carrying the power," were the same ones on which Wright said he would stand or fall and the same ones Speaker Rayburn had defended before the House in his successful plea for SWPA construction funds. Some observers charged that the secretary was unwilling to sign any contract, so it was impossible for a company to come up with terms to which he would agree.[40]

Secretary Chapman surprised these critics, as well as public power proponents, on July 13, when he announced the signing of contracts between the Southwestern Power Administration and the two companies (Public Service Company of Oklahoma and the Oklahoma Gas and Electric Company) and added that the proposed transmission lines would now be unnecessary. The companies agreed to give SWPA full use of their networks in delivering electricity to its customers in Oklahoma and Arkansas, and the power agency, in return, promised to provide government produced power to the private utilities. Chapman said he was satisfied that the final version eliminated "provisions that would restrict distribution of public power to preference customers or provide a subsidy to the utility companies."[41]

Southwestern members of Congress, the private power companies, and the SWPA all praised the agreement. Incumbent Senator Elmer Thomas of Oklahoma said it would "save the taxpayers multiplied millions" because transmission lines would not be duplicated, and Representative Monroney, who was challenging Thomas for the Democratic nomination, agreed with his opponent. He called it the "most favorable contract ever written between public power and private companies."[42] SWPA Administrator Wright concurred with Richard K. Lane, president of Public Service Company of Oklahoma, that the signing would be remembered as "the beginning of profitable cooperation between public power projects and private industry." Wright predicted savings for SWPA of $6 million during the current year and $850,000 per year thereafter.[43]

Many public power advocates, however, thought the new era of coopera-tion between public and private power had come at the expense of liberal principles. They saw these contracts as at best a compromise. Clyde Ellis argued that government-owned transmission lines were much to be preferred over any wheeling contract, which in any case would not be permanent. He pointed out that the contracts with the two Oklahoma companies specified twenty years, but, at the end of that period, the companies could terminate their contracts and leave the cooperatives to die.[44]

Secretary Chapman was aware of the possible harmful effect of the contracts on public power principles and policies. As he remarked to Representative Clarence Cannon of Missouri, "Experience alone will tell how well this type of contract can serve" the public interest.[45]

Shortly before these contracts were signed and on the assurance from Chapman that they would be concluded, the Senate cut $6 million off the more than $16 million the House approved for Southwestern Power Administration construction and acquisition of transmission facilities, and the Conference Committee sustained the cut.

Private power viewed these developments as signs that its position *vis-à-vis* public power was improving. The *Electrical World* noted that although the amount was not large, the kind of saving that came from cooperating with private power was something congressmen and their constituents could understand. And it predicted that Congress would encourage the government to make more such agreements since these contracts were concluded only after it had directed the SWPA to negotiate.[46]

Chapman, of course, realized that this prediction was likely to come true. During the negotiations with the Oklahoma companies, he had struck a committee to formulate departmental policy on wheeling agreements. Chapman approved the policy on July 14, the day after the contracts were signed.[47]

V

Meanwhile, the leasing contracts being executed between the SWPA and generating and transmission cooperatives were becoming a controversial political issue. Although some opponents claimed that the Rural Electrification Adminis-tration loans that had engendered the contracts were a new development, the agency had made its first loan to a federated cooperative in 1941. By January 5, 1949, the REA had made 115 such loans in almost every area of the country. The agency justified these loans under Section 4 of the Rural Electrification Act, which authorized them for "financing the construction and operation of generating plants, electric transmission and distribution lines or systems." The REA's policy was to make these loans only where they were "required either to solve a problem of inadequate service or to give the members of the cooperatives electric service at a low cost."[48]

In March 1950, the REA granted three loans totaling over $30 million to "super-cooperatives" in Missouri, Arkansas and Oklahoma. These cooperatives planned to build steam and transmission facilities, sell power to the Southwestern Power Administration and lease most of the transmission lines to that power agency. Announcement of the loans brought charges of "unholy alliance," "iniquitous arrangement," "illegal contract," "duplication of existing facilities" and "an effort to circumvent Congress" from private utility executives testifying before the congressional appropriations committees considering Rural Electrification funds for fiscal 1951.[49]

SWPA Administrator Wright and REA Administrator Claude Wickard defended the loans before the committee, arguing that the Rural Electrification Administration had a continuing duty to see that its customers received adequate electric service at a reasonable rate.[50]

The controversy grew more intense as the Kansas City Power and Light Company and nine other private utilities in the Midwest sought an injunction against the REA, the SWPA and the secretaries of interior, agriculture, and the treasury to stop REA loans to five "super-cooperatives" in Missouri that planned to lease their facilities to the Southwestern Power Association. Calling the practice part of a plan to nationalize the electric power industry, Democratic Representative Boyd Tacket of Arkansas introduced a bill to require congressional approval of these "super-cooperative" loans. Other measures that would have had a similar effect also were introduced but none got out of committee.[51]

Although the Senate Appropriations Committee stopped short of recommending a ban on the use of the continuing fund for perpetuating this type of alliance, it did state in its report on the omnibus appropriations bill for 1951 that the SWPA had been using the fund to aid generating and transmission cooperatives "to an extent not contemplated" when it was established. The committee recommended that this money not be used unless "absolutely necessary to enable public bodies and cooperatives to secure sufficient power to supply customers."[52]

The following year (1951), the Truman Administration requested $4.1 million for construction for the Southwestern Power Administration. Including no new contract authority, this request was intended to cover only contracts then in progress; operation and maintenance estimates brought the total to $5.4 million. Controversy centered on proposed projects in Western Missouri, the use of the continuing fund and an effort by Congress to restrict the agency's power to build transmission lines where it had wheeling agreements with private utilities.[53]

The Western Missouri project, which called for building a transmission line, a switching station and substations to interconnect lines being built by cooperatives and under lease to the SWPA, was intended to provide additional transmission capacity to these cooperative lines in central and western Missouri so that the power agency could serve more municipalities. Congress had granted about half the estimated cost of nearly $5 million for fiscal 1951; now the marketing agency was asking for about $1.5 million more. Strenuous protests came from Kansas City Power and Light Company, which argued that the project would duplicate existing lines and that there was no power shortage in Missouri.[54]

While the House cut this item in the Interior Department Appropriations Bill, and the Senate sustained its action, the Conference Committee put an appropriation of $810,600 back into the bill. However, it stipulated in its report that the committee expected the secretary to make a "determined effort" to obtain a contract with the private utilities so that use of the funds would be unnecessary.[55]

When the Senate was considering the House passed Keating amendment, which applied only to the Bureau of Reclamation, another amendment was offered to apply its terms to the three power administrations so that they too would be unable to build transmission lines in areas where they had working agreements with private power companies. The proposal was defeated after it was pointed out that language already in the bill would accomplish the same purpose.[56]

Conferees agreed on a total appropriation of $4.6 million for SWPA. Funds for construction amounted to $3.375 million, but included in their report was a request that the agency quickly negotiate contracts with twelve private utility companies in the area.[57]

A restriction of Southwestern's use of its continuing fund to "emergency" expenses had been added to the bill in the Senate, but the Conference Committee softened the language so that the use of this fund for buying electric power and renting transmission lines would be limited to the amount set yearly by Congress.[58]

Behind this move was the desire of private power proponents to prevent the use of this money for leasing power facilities from the generating and transmission cooperatives. In August 1951, at the time of the final passage of the appropriations bill for 1952, the status of the alliance between the REA and the Southwestern Power Administration was uncertain. In December 1950, the Rural Electrification Administration had approved another controversial "super-cooperative" loan to an Arkansas federation. The suit filed in district court to try to stop three such loans already approved by the REA administrator to federated cooperatives in Missouri was still pending.[59]

Because of the restrictive language in the conference report on the appropriations bill pertaining to the continuing fund and the cut in the budget request for the Missouri project, the REA asked for a meeting with the Department of the Interior to determine whether the SWPA would be able to meet its contractual obligations to the generating and transmission cooperatives. The power agency representative said that the department's position had not changed—these facilities were necessary under the law even if wheeling agreements were signed with companies in the area.[60]

Still not satisfied, the secretary of agriculture asked Chapman for a current opinion from the Interior Department solicitor on whether "in the light of subsequent legislative developments," the SWPA could legally fulfill its obligations to the federated cooperatives. Solicitor Mastin G. White gave the opinion that the authority of the Southwestern Power Administration to purchase electric power and rent transmission facilities was lawful under Section 5 of the Flood Control Act of 1944, but the agency could exercise this right only to the extent that Congress granted money for this purpose.[61]

During this period President Truman spoke out against private power's treatment of rural electric cooperatives in the Southwest. In a speech delivered in Arkansas in 1951, he charged that private power interests were "trying to stop farmers . . . from getting the benefit of low cost hydroelectric power through electric cooperatives." These interests, he said, "have been bringing lawsuits, and running advertisements and appearing before Congress" so that farmers would have to pay more for their electricity.[62] And when president H. B. Munsell of the Kansas City Power and Light Company asked the president to temporarily delay the REA loan to a "super-cooperative" in Missouri, he received little encouragement. Truman's assistant replied that the cooperatives in the area had been trying for several years to get satisfactory service from private power companies and had failed; therefore, the "rural consumers in Northwest Missouri should not be denied the opportunity to obtain an adequate supply of low cost power."[63]

The Southwestern Power Administration had entered into contracts with a number of generating and transmission cooperatives, but whether this type of alliance would be allowed to continue was left in abeyance as the Truman Administration came to an end. The continuing fund request for fiscal 1953 of $1,425,000 was cut to a maximum of $1 million with the House Appropriations Committee stating that its actions were to be regarded as a deferral until the court case was decided. By January 20, 1953, the trial to determine if the REA and SWPA had violated the law in making the contracts with the Missouri cooperatives had been completed, but the district court judge had not yet handed down a decision. The case was certain to be appealed to the Supreme Court regardless of the outcome.[64]

VI

Nor was the other main issue concerning the Southwestern Power Administration settled during these Truman years. In 1952, the fight over wheeling agreements versus SWPA-built transmission lines was far from over. Government public power devotees were being pressured by Congress into cooperating with private power more than they had done in the past, but they continued to pursue their liberal goals.

The Interior Department asked for about the same amount for Southwestern construction for fiscal 1953 that it had requested for the previous year. Although the House slashed all of this $4.15 million, friends of public power prevailed in the Senate. The original figure was restored, bringing the total SWPA appropriation to $5.6 million. This victory was tempered by an expression of hope by House-Senate conferees that the negotiations for a wheeling contract with power companies in the Southwest could be concluded at an early date.[65]

Wright, who continued to tout cooperation with private power as a "better and cheaper way to get electric power" to all Southwesterners, had been working energetically to reach an agreement with private utilities in the area. In a speech delivered in Missouri in February, he discussed contracts with twelve companies that he said had been tentatively agreed upon and said that Chapman was studying them.[66]

Before the Senate subcommittee, Wright described this proposal as basically identical to the Oklahoma contracts. He called it "the best contract that was ever negotiated" and claimed it would "settle the power question in the Southwest." However, the administrator's statement that he had submitted the draft on January 21 prompted Senator Guy Cordon to question why, if it was such a good contract, it had not been approved in three months' time.[67]

The senator was implying, of course, that Secretary Chapman was purposely delaying the execution of these contracts. Others, including the *Electrical World*, drew the same conclusion. When asked about it at a news conference, Chapman said that he was waiting until a "thorough review" of cost figures could be made and that he was trying to see if the views of various government agencies could be reconciled. In September Wright explained the continued delay by saying the department was "giving it tremendous study." Perhaps as a final gesture toward the protection of his government's public power policy, Chapman left these contracts on his desk, unsigned, when he left office.[68]

6

Advances, Retreats and Holding Actions: The Southeast

After the Interior Department set up an agency in 1950 to handle its power marketing responsibilities in the Southeast, the administration also became embroiled in controversies with private power companies over federal construction and leasing of transmission lines in that part of the country.

Interior needed the Southeastern Power Administration because a number of Corps of Engineers multipurpose projects that would include hydroelectric power generation were nearing completion. Two dams, Dale Hollow on the Obey River in Tennessee and Allatoona on the Etowah River in Georgia, were finished, seven more were under construction, and thirteen were authorized and in the planning stage.

Private power interests were wary of this new body, which would have an operating area second in size only to that of the Bureau of Reclamation.[1] They feared that SEPA would quarrel with private utilities as interior's other two power agencies had; try to build transmission systems; and become a point around which public power movements in the Southeast could rally. More importantly, because it would connect federal power producing projects from Kentucky to Florida, many private power companies saw the agency as the last link of a public power chain that threatened to strangle them.[2]

Interior anticipated that within a few years the SEPA would market about one-tenth of all the power produced in the Southeast. Although it could be expected to ask Congress for funds to build some transmission lines to interconnect nearby plants, prospects for a grid the size of that of the Bonneville or Southwestern Power Administrations were slight because large capacity private transmission facilities already existed in the area owing to its highly industrialized nature.

II

The Southeastern Power Administration inherited a contract that the Interior Department had negotiated with the Georgia Power Company in 1948, allowing the utility to buy all of the power output from the Allatoona project. Preference customers were assured their rights by a clause authorizing the government to draw up to 2.5 million kilowatts per week for them. Public power proponents feared that this contract would be regarded as a precedent for future SEPA policy; however, Administrator Ben Creim assured the American Public Power Association that preference customers would be allowed access to federal power at the bus bar.[3]

The first quarrel between private power and the new power agency grew out of a proposal from this same private utility that, if accepted, would have violated that pledge. On March 24, 1950, just three days after SEPA opened its doors, the Georgia Power Company, acting on behalf of a group of private companies operating in the area of the Clark Hill project on the Savannah River, suggested to Creim that the utilities buy federally generated power at the bus bar. Under the proposed contract, the companies would agree to sell power to preferred agencies at the government rate, plus a percentage to be agreed upon. Creim rejected the offer because it meant that the companies would keep all the government's preference customers; the plan would not permit the government to serve any of these customers by wheeling, and it would allow them to get power directly from the government only over transmission lines SEPA might build in the future. Creim made a counter-proposal, which the private utility appeared unwilling to discuss.[4]

Pursuant to a request by the Defense Department, the Southeastern Power Administration, on October 6, asked the Georgia Power Company if it would transmit power for a reasonable fee from the Allatoona project to military establishments in the company's service area. At first, the company avoided giving an unequivocal reply to this contract offer, as well as to an earlier, February request that it supply Allatoona power to the Atlanta Penitentiary. But its vice-president, Charles A. Collier, warned Creim that although his company was not looking for a fight with his agency, "if you want a fight, we will fight and it will be a beaut."[5] In a reply that presaged difficulty for the government in its Clark Hill negotiations, Georgia Power informed the SEPA on November 17 that it would not give up any of its present customers to the government nor transmit power for it to government preference customers.[6]

Collier proposed another wheeling contract for Clark Hill power in February 1951, but Creim and Assistant Secretary Warne called it merely another version of the initial offer. Warne kept negotiations open, however, and several months later, the company presented a revised draft. Under its terms,

Georgia Power would buy Clark Hill power and resell it directly to preference customers at its purchase cost, plus a surcharge.[7]

The Southwestern Power Administration, the Bureau of Reclamation, the Bonneville Power Administration and the Division of Water and Power all perceived dangers in the proposed contract. They pointed out that it contradicted the established power policy of the government, conflicted with the 1944 Flood Control Act and threatened to jeopardize both the federal transmission program and any wheeling contracts under negotiation. Commissioner Straus found the proposed contract particularly odious and dangerously precedent setting. He told Chapman that even those who oppose federally built transmission lines had never gone so far as to propose that "the secretary sell power on a monopoly basis" to companies that agree to resell the power according to federal power policies set forth in acts of Congress.[8]

Secretary Chapman refused to accept this offer because he was convinced that signing such a contract would spell the end of the present government power policy. In response to a similar proposal in late 1952, he forcefully stated his objections to the president of the Southern Company (parent of Georgia Power Company): "It cannot be too strongly emphasized that the Secretary of the Interior, not the Georgia Power Company, is charged with the responsibility of giving preference in the sale of power to public bodies and cooperatives. He cannot delegate this function to a private power company."[9]

Georgia Power Company countered that no laws obligated the Interior Department "to enter upon a program of generating and supplying the present and future power needs of any class or classes of utility customers," and if it assumed it had such an obligation, the department must be "embarked on a policy of nationalization of that part of the electric power industry."[10]

Chapman, however, remained committed to preserving the preference clause. Shortly before leaving office, the secretary announced that he had rejected this latest Georgia Power Company proposal on the ground that preference customers must be the government's customers.[11]

III

Another major controversy in the Southeast concerned disposal of federally generated power at the Buggs Island Dam near the Virginia-North Carolina border. In this case, the Department of the Interior sought to build transmission lines and was met head-on by the Virginia Electric and Power Company.

The quarrel with this company began in December 1950 when interior asked Congress for $1,850,000 to build a line for carrying electric power from the Buggs Island project to Langley Field in Virginia, an installation that housed laboratories of the National Advisory Committee for Aeronautics. Intended for inclusion in the Second Supplemental Appropriations Bill for fiscal 1951, this item engendered heated debate on the floor of the Senate, on January 2, 1951, after conferees of the two houses failed to agree on the transmission line.[12]

Among those who spoke against going along with the House, which had approved the funds for the line, were Democrat Willis Robertson of Virginia and Republican Guy Cordon of Oregon. Robertson claimed the line would parallel the private company's facility, while Cordon argued that Virginia Electric and Power was "ready, able and willing to furnish the necessary power at a rate less than the government's rate." Defenders of the public power position included Senators Kenneth McKellar and Carl Hayden. McKellar said the company would have to build two new lines to carry the required power, and that denial of the line would give the utility the upper hand. Hayden argued that approval could provide a strong bargaining position for obtaining a satisfactory wheeling plan. With the debate taking place on the final day of the session, some members of the Conference Committee warned that the entire bill, which included defense appropriations, would die if the Senate failed to give its approval.[13]

On a motion by Senator Hayden to approve the House version, public power emerged the winner by a close vote of 43-41. But the victory was not as complete as it seemed. After the bill was passed, Hayden informed the Interior Department that he had obtained Senate authorization of the appropriation only on the assurance that the department would not build the line until after it had made a genuine but unsuccessful effort to execute a wheeling contract.[14]

Agreeing that Hayden's pledge was undoubtedly responsible for the narrow victory, Secretary Chapman informed the senator that his department would abide by it. He instructed Creim to commence negotiations immediately and ordered Assistant Secretary Warne to follow Creim's progress, so that in a "reasonable number of weeks we may have either a contract with the power company or a determination that no satisfactory contract can be had."[15]

The congressional appropriation apparently had the effect on the company that Hayden had anticipated, for it submitted a proposal to Southeastern that to Warne looked "like a fairly satisfactory contract." Despite this promising beginning, however, the negotiations became bogged down over three major points. Interior insisted that the company agree to wheel power on a system-wide basis to the government's preference customers, sell power at the ends of its transmission lines rather than at the bus bar and pay a flat, one mill rate, area wide. On March 20, Creim reported that if these problems could not be solved by the end of the month, survey crews would begin work on the transmission line. Another informal offer came from the power company, but Creim found the wheeling charge unacceptable.[16]

Agreement could not be reached. On April 6, 1951, Secretary Chapman informed Congress that all possibilities had been exhausted; therefore, work on the transmission line was commencing.[17]

In the meantime, interior had boldly asked for $4 million for fiscal 1952 SEPA construction, which included transmission facilities for disposal of power from the Buggs Island and Clark Hill projects. Interior based its request for the transmission lines on the need of South Carolina municipalities and REA cooperatives for additional power. Representatives of Virginia Electric and Power Company and Carolina Power and Light Company testified that their rates to cooperatives could not be beaten by Southeastern and that the cooperatives were satisfied with services from private power.[18]

With many of its members particularly irritated that interior had not concluded a wheeling agreement with Virginia Electric and Power Company, the House accepted an amendment by Democrat Vaughan Gary of Virginia that virtually eliminated all Southeastern construction. The Senate was a little kinder, but the final Interior Appropriations Bill allowed only $518,500 for SEPA and even rescinded the unobligated portion of the funds for the Buggs Island line that had been appropriated in the 1951 Second Supplemental Bill.[19]

The Keating Amendment was included in this act, but it applied at the moment only to Bureau of Reclamation requests for transmission lines. With funds for the Buggs Island line denied and this amendment presaging the wave of the future, interior was obliged to resume negotiations with the Virginia Electric and Power Company.

By November 1951, substantial agreement had been reached on all major points. The private utility agreed to the system-wide wheeling principle; SEPA agreed to let the company wheel from the Buggs Island project; and a compromise on the wheeling charge for an average of 1.375 mills was worked out.[20]

When he appeared before the House subcommittee in early 1952, Chapman surprisingly called these results "one of the Southeastern's major accomplishments" of the year. Asked by the Senate subcommittee why his company had been able to come to terms with the government when other utilities in the area had not, VEPCO Vice President T. Justin Moore admitted that congressional pressure had played an important role: "We really became convinced . . . that you gentlemen were probably going to make appropriations if we did not in some way get together."[21]

Because of the imminent signing of a contract, Congress also denied in the appropriations act for 1952 SEPA requested funds for a transmission line from Buggs Island Dam to Kinston, North Carolina. This line would have served municipalities and REA cooperatives in the area. Warne felt that too many public power advocates were giving up the battle for transmission lines. He wrote Clyde Ellis, "Only one voice from the area was heard by the committee in behalf of this line and that was an REA voice."[22]

Congress did, however, authorize, in the same bill, an appropriation of about $320,000 for commencing work on a transmission line to run from the Clark Hill Dam to Greenwood, South Carolina, despite a plea from South

Carolina Senator Clyde R. Hoey that the item be eliminated. This proposed line engendered another struggle between public and private power interests. In this case, two private utilities—South Carolina Electric and Gas Company and Duke Power Company—exerted pressure on Democrat Hoey to advance their interests. Hoey, in turn, kept a close eye on the Senate Appropriations Committee to see that it followed up on its assurances that it would supervise the Interior Department's efforts to execute wheeling agreements and if a reasonable offer were made and rejected, to forbid the use of funds already appropriated or ask for their cancellation.[23]

In January 1952, Chapman instructed the SEPA administrator to begin work immediately on the Clark Hill-Greenwood line so that a contract Southeastern had made to deliver power to the Greenwood county Electric Power Commission (a public body) could be fulfilled. Acting Administrator Charles Leavy reported that survey and design work was "going forward on the line," but that South Carolina Power and Light Company and Duke Power Company were trying "to create distrust on the part of the commission toward Southeastern."[24]

When they learned that this preliminary work was taking place, the private utilities became alarmed. The vice-president of the Duke Power Company, N. A. Cocke, wrote Senator Hoey that South Carolina Electric and Gas Company had offered to transmit power from Clark Hill to the Greenwood County Electric Power Commission and to provide the transmission facilities. He and the South Carolina Electric president then discovered that the Greenwood County Commission had offered to build the line and had even gotten approval from the Defense Electric Power Administration but that it had suddenly stopped its plans when interior told the commission that under no circumstances would electricity be sold at the project itself. Now, Cocke wrote, it appeared obvious that the department intended to build the line "irrespective of whether transmission facilities can be provided without expense to the government." And he reminded Hoey that this action was "directly in violation" of the understanding of the Senate "at the time funds were included for this project."[25]

Hoey immediately reported the information to Senator Hayden, and added, "I think your Committee should know that neither the Southeastern Power Administration nor the Interior Department has made any attempt to reach any agreement with reference to building these transmission lines." On January 30, Hayden asked the Interior Department to look into the matter.[26]

Replying six weeks later, Chapman explained to the senator that the Greenwood Electric Power Commission had negotiated a contract on April 27, 1951, which obligated the government to deliver power to the commission. Since no transmission facilities existed between the Clark Hill project and Greenwood, it was understood that interior would build a line. After funds were appropriated for their construction in the 1952 appropriations bill, SEPA tried to secure system-wide wheeling arrangements with Duke Power and South Carolina

Electric and Gas. These two companies offered to build the line and wheel power, Chapman said, but their proposed fee of one mill per kilowatt hour would far exceed the cost that the government would incur from building its own facilities. Furthermore, their offer would be inadequate for serving the growing needs of the Greenwood Commission, and the plan would fail to bring integration of Clark Hill with the Hartwell plants, necessary for defense, or with Duke Power Company. Therefore, after he learned in January 1952 that the commission had decided to build the line itself because of all the uncertainty, the secretary had decided that the interests "of the government, the preferred agencies and the entire Southeast," as well as the nation's defense, would best be served by Southeastern's beginning construction of the line immediately.[27]

Meanwhile, hearings were being held by the House on Southeastern's request for funds in fiscal 1953 to complete the Clark Hill-Greenwood line and build two additional transmission lines. The House allowed the full amount for the Clark Hill-Greenwood line but nothing for the other two.[28]

SEPA Acting Administrator Charles W. Leavy told the Senate subcommittee considering the requests that every line the department had asked for was in an area where it had been "unable to secure a proper system-wide wheeling and firming agreement."[29]

Denying the assertion, S. C. McMeekin, president of South Carolina Electric and Gas Company, charged that Southeastern had disregarded the fair offers of the two companies involved as well as the mandate of Congress. He argued that there never had been, nor would there be in the foreseeable future, a power shortage in the area and that the money appropriated in the previous year for the Clark Hill-Greenwood line would not be wasted if the appropriation were not granted because only a survey had been made.[30]

Although it retained the House-approved amount of $959,000 for the Clark Hill-Greenwood line and funds to plan a similar one in Georgia, the Senate committee added a clause that would increase pressure on SEPA to negotiate wheeling contracts with private companies in the area. It specified that none of the funds could be used for building transmission lines until a contract of basically the same type that had been made elsewhere had been executed with the affected power companies in the area, or until those companies had refused to enter into such contracts, and the secretary of the interior had so informed Congress.[31]

In consequence of this directive, Administrator Leavy suspended all work on the Clark Hill-Greenwood line, and, on July 8, 1952, the day before President Truman signed the appropriations bill into law, asked the two power companies if they were willing to sign contracts to deliver power for the government to its preferred customers. Leavy indicated the system-wide wheeling principles he wanted included and set a date by which he would like a reply. The private utilities sought to restrict the negotiations to the transmission of power to Greenwood, but, on July 22, following an exchange of several telegrams with the administrator, the South Carolina Electric and Gas Company agreed to commit itself to system-wide wheeling.[32]

By this time, the Department of the Interior appears to have determined that of the two private utilities, only the Duke Power Company would be affected in its operations by the transmission line, but it failed to inform the South Carolina Electric and Gas Company of its decision. The line would cross territory served by South Carolina Electric, but it would enter and end in territory partially served by Duke Power. It is unclear whether interior made this determination only after South Carolina Electric agreed to the department's system-wide wheeling condition. However, if this decision was reached shortly after the 1953 appropriations bill was passed, as Chapman was to make his case later, the logical course would have been for the Interior Department to simply inform the company of this decision in early July instead of asking if it would agree to wheel power on the department's terms.

In any case, Southeastern and the Interior Department seemed concerned only with the Duke Power Company. After SEPA made three inquiries about a contract and received one reply on August 26 from the company requesting more detailed information before it could give an answer, Leavy recommended that Chapman inform Congress that Duke Power had refused to wheel power system-wide for the account of the government.[33]

Chapman so informed Congress on September 15, in letters to the president of the Senate, Vice-President Alben W. Barkley, and the speaker of the House, Sam Rayburn. It was also in this correspondence that he first reported his determination that the transmission line would not affect operations of the South Carolina Electric Gas Company since the government's contract with the Greenwood Commission did "not provide for delivery of any power into the Company's territory."[34]

On the same date, survey work on the transmission line was resumed. Hearing of this development and unaware of interior's line of argument regarding his company's "unaffected" status, the president of South Carolina Electric and Gas Company feared that Chapman was about to inform Congress that his company had "refused to execute" a contract of the type referred to in the appropriations bill. McMeekin, therefore, wired Chapman a reiteration of his previous offer. Three weeks earlier, when he learned that SEPA was planning to invite bids for constructing the line, he had asked the secretary to inform him "when and to whom" Chapman had reported or would report that his company had "refused to execute a contract" in conformance with the congressional directive. McMeekin also complained to Senator Hayden that he had had no chance to talk with Chapman about his contract offer.[35]

The secretary finally replied to McMeekin on October 10. Verifying that the government was proceeding with plans to build the line, Chapman said that he had not and would "not report to anyone" that South Carolina Electric and Gas had refused to negotiate a wheeling agreement since the company would not be affected. Learning for the first time of this status determination, McMeekin was shocked. He asked the Interior Department to delay action on the line and grant him an opportunity to discuss his wheeling proposal. Acting Secretary Vernon Northrop merely agreed to discuss the Interior Department's action with the private utility president.[36]

Hayden, who had written the proviso in the committee report to the Senate, warned Chapman that both he and the secretary would be "accused of bad faith" if SEPA were to go ahead with the line: "I therefore urge you to stop all proceedings until you can meet with him [McMeekin]."[37]

McMeekin supporter Senator Cordon then asked the General Accounting Office to render an opinion as to whether, under the facts presented in Chapman's September 15 letter to the president of the Senate, the transmission line could be financed from the amount specified for that purpose in the appropriations act.[38]

When he heard that the bids for a construction contract were to be opened on the following day, Senator Hayden pleaded with Chapman on October 31 to hold off "until both of the South Carolina power companies have been given another opportunity to submit wheeling agreements." Undeterred, the department awarded the construction contract. Chapman informed Hayden, explaining that since the affected company (Duke Power) had failed after three requests to indicate a willingness to execute a contract for system-wide wheeling of federal power, he had had no other choice.[39]

On November 18, the two private power companies struck back by securing from District Court in Georgia a temporary order to stop construction of the transmission line. The court restrained the contractor from allowing the line to go any farther than one mile from the terminus at Greenwood and required the defendants to show cause by January 15, 1953 why they should not be so enjoined. Leavy had hoped for this development since it enabled construction of the line to continue, so the work could be substantially completed before the date of the scheduled hearing.[40]

On January 7, 1953, Comptroller General Lindsay Warren informed the secretary that the record of negotiations with the South Carolina Electric and Gas Company prior to September 15 did not support the conclusion that it was not an affected company. Furthermore, the department had not exhausted "every possible effort" to reach an agreement. He therefore stipulated that "any payment from funds referred to in the proviso" of the 1953 Interior Department Appropriations Act for building the transmission line would be disallowed.[41]

Private power hailed this opinion as a victory. The *Electrical World* declared, "Since Warren is Congress' watchdog over the federal treasury, his opinion is tantamount to a veto of the SEPA proposal."[42]

Chapman protested the comptroller general's definition of "affected" and considered asking the attorney general for an opinion on the validity of the finding. However, in the meantime the case was removed to federal district court, and for this reason, interior's solicitor advised the secretary that such a request would be useless because of a possible conflict of interest. There the matter rested when the Truman Administration relinquished power on January 20, 1953.[43]

The administration could claim little success in its efforts to win congressional approval for Southeastern Power Administration transmission lines. Funds for the Buggs Island line were authorized but later rescinded, and construction of the Clark Hill-Greenwood line was stopped by court proceedings. Significant in both cases was congressional insistence that monies for these projects could be used only if interior failed to negotiate wheeling contracts. In 1952, Congress began the practice of including this stipulation in Interior Department appropriations bills. At first contained only in committee reports, the proviso was based on the Keating Amendment of the previous year, which restricted the Bureau of Reclamation in a similar way. Interior's failures in this episode of the power fight contributed significantly to a strengthening of the private power position.

IV

Like its counterpart in the Southwest, the fledgling Southeastern Power Administration encountered opposition from private power not only when it sought to build transmission lines but also when it began to lease transmission facilities that were built by federated cooperatives with loans from the Rural Electrification Administration. Private power proponents had before them the example of the alliances already formed between the "super-cooperatives" and the Southwestern Power Administration and had seen the Senate Appropriations Committee criticize the agency's use of its continuing fund to strengthen this relationship. Private power companies viewed such contracts as an attempt to crowd them out and thus socialize the electric power industry. So, when Southeastern requested $200,000 in 1951 to establish a continuing fund in the federal treasury from power sale proceeds, which could be used to rent power facilities or buy power and energy, private power representatives vigorously worked to prevent it.[44]

Executives of the major private power companies in the Southeast argued convincingly before Congress against the fund. Arguing that it was unnecessary, T. Justin Moore of the Virginia Electric and Power Company reminded the Interior Subcommittee of the House Committee on Appropriations of the "acute controversy on the issue of abuses of the fund in the Southwest." L. V. Sutton, president of the Carolina Power and Light Company, charged that when Congress denied funds for the SWPA to build its own transmission and generating facilities, the agency had used the continuing fund to lease such facilities from "super-cooperatives" promoted by the REA for this purpose. Sutton warned that this same circumvention of Congress would occur in the Southeast if the appropriation were granted.[45]

Congress obliged these private power proponents by not only cutting the amount requested to $50,000 but also specifying that the money could be used only for emergency expenses. The following year, a realistic Interior Department asked for no additional monies for the continuing fund.[46]

In 1951, private power companies in the Southeast also were concerned about any strengthening of generating and transmission cooperatives because they had seen the private power companies in South Carolina lose in a fight with a state agency, the REA and a "super-cooperative" over the building of transmission lines and selling of electric power. In this instance, the Interior Department was not involved. Principals in the case were the Santee Cooper project, which consisted of the hydroelectric generating facilities owned and operated by the South Carolina Public Service Authority (a state agency); the Central Electric Power Cooperative of Columbia, made up of fourteen distribution cooperatives in South Carolina; the Rural Electrification Administration; and private power companies in the state, particularly the South Carolina Electric and Gas Company.

The REA's announcement, on January 7, 1949, that it would loan nearly $7.6 million to the Central Electric Power Cooperative for a 834-mile transmission system to carry low cost hydroelectric power from Santee Cooper to load centers of these fourteen distribution cooperatives caused a furor among private power companies in South Carolina. The new system was intended to effect substantial savings for the cooperatives as well as provide "better service and better assurance of enough power to supply their future needs." Power would be delivered to the load centers of the cooperatives at a rate of 6 mills per kilowatt hour as compared with the approximately 7.5 mills then being paid.[47]

In retaliation, South Carolina Electric President McMeekin took his case to the public. In full-page ads in New York, Washington, D.C. and South Carolina papers, he vowed he was fighting the loan to keep his company "from being threatened by an REA loan for transmission lines" that would duplicate his company's lines, and to "prevent the wasteful misuse" of taxpayers' money. One ad claimed that under the new arrangement the cooperatives would pay 10 per cent more for their electricity than the current rate of 5.5 mills per KWH.[48]

REA Administrator Claude Wickard and the cooperatives also used the media to argue their side of the controversy. Calling McMeekin's charge that the loan would kill his company "palpably absurd," Wickard told the press that according to a statement of the company itself before the Securities and Exchange Commission, South Carolina Electric and Gas Company's power sales to the cooperatives formed less than one per cent of its total revenue. He branded a 5.5 mill rate offer, which he had received only on the day after McMeekin's ad appeared in the paper, a "desperate effort" to block the loan.

Even if it were accepted, Wickard claimed it would affect only half of the fourteen cooperatives involved.[49]

His agency's annual report for fiscal 1950 characterized the attacks on such REA loans as part of a "nation-wide propaganda program" by the utility industry to take from cooperatives and public bodies their lawful status as preference customers of the government and to create a monopoly of federally produced power for private companies.[50]

The Central Electric Power Cooperative placed a full page advertisement in a Columbia, South Carolina newspaper, titling it "Thanks Mr. McMeekin, But We Don't Trust You. Why?" It contended that the 5.5 mill rate would be only a temporary measure designed to keep the cooperatives from getting a transmission system to the public power projects and that without these projects, South Carolina Electric and Gas Company would still be charging cooperatives 2 cents per kilowatt hour.[51]

Despite these rebuttals, McMeekin found support for his position. Most of the newspapers in the state supported it, as did a majority of representatives in the South Carolina House of Representatives. Several American Federation of Labor and Congress of Industrial Organization locals also joined the chorus opposing the loan and construction of the transmission lines, a move that seemed to be part of the general trend in which segments of organized labor were beginning to oppose public power.[52]

However, few office seekers for federal or state positions in South Carolina appeared willing to come out against the loan for fear it would hurt them in the November elections. (An exception was former Secretary of State James F. Byrnes, who, campaigning for governor, sharply criticized the "socialistic nature of REA's policies.")[53]

The action of the South Carolina House of Representatives had little effect. The REA and the cooperatives brushed off the resolution, the former saying that the planning of the lines had gone too far to stop and the latter that it would not defer building "to please the whim of a few politicians."[54] Hence construction of the lines went forward.

V

This loan to a "super-cooperative" in the Southeast, as well as loans then being made to generating and transmission cooperatives in the Southwest, created pressure from private power proponents in Congress to investigate not just the practice but also the Rural Electrification Administration itself.

Despite this pressure, Congress granted the agency's request for direct electrification loan authorization of $350 million, along with another $150 million available if needed, for both fiscal years 1950 and 1951.[55] However, in September 1950, the House decided to investigate the REA, and assigned the task to the government Operations Subcommittee of the Committee on Expenditures in the Executive Departments. The subcommittee found little to criticize about the agency, with the exception of making loans to "super-cooperatives," which it decided needed further study. After holding hearings, the House Agriculture Committee announced plans in May 1951 to make a complete investigation of the generating and transmission loans.[56]

Early the same year, the Executive Office of the President cut the Rural Electrification Administration's loan-fund request from the amount asked for and received over the past two years to a flat $100 million. President Truman said in his annual budget message that he was proceeding more slowly with the program because of the "shortages of metals, particularly aluminum and copper." The *Electrical World* interpreted the president's further comment that the reduction would require some curtailment of loans for new facilities as an "implied warning against loans for generating and transmission."[57]

A more realistic explanation for the cut, however, was that requirements for the Korean War were causing problems in allocation of materials. In early 1951 the Defense Electric Power Administration, which had been set up in the Department of the Interior, and the Rural Electrification Administration were quarreling over which agency should have responsibility for allocating such materials as copper and aluminum needed in the rural electrification program. DEPA administrator Clifford B. McManus, who was a former president of a private utility holding company, wanted the cooperatives to place their requests for materials with his agency, and he would process them in order of emergency. The Department of Agriculture, on the other hand, wanted McManus to make a lump allocation of these materials to the Rural Electrification Administration, which, in turn, would distribute the materials to the cooperatives as it saw fit.[58]

Wickard insisted that the procedure McManus advocated would slow up REA construction too much at a time when the war effort required maximum food production. Private power companies countered that their building plans also were being delayed.[59]

When McManus announced that he would pass on all REA "super-cooperative" loans amounting to more than $50,000 and stop any projects that would duplicate private power company facilities, public power advocates saw the move as an effort to circumvent Congress. Since private power had failed to stop REA appropriations for some generating and transmission loans, McManus instead could "blockade material" and prevent cooperatives from getting low cost electric power in that way.[60]

The rural cooperatives became impatient when the Department of Agriculture made little headway with efforts to change the allocation system. Clyde Ellis, executive secretary of the National Rural Electric Cooperative

Association, told Chapman that he had received "numerous complaints" from cooperatives about McManus, who was "listening too much to private power interests"; and he urged the secretary to make a decision immediately. NRECA President Clark T. McWhorter implored Truman to act on behalf of the REA. Complaining that the DEPA was "stacked with power company people," the member cooperatives charged that McManus's advisor, J. E. Moore of Electric Bond and Share, had participated in killing several generating and transmission cooperatives during World War II.[61]

Wickard's refusal to consider no other proposal than that advanced by the cooperatives, along with pressure from the cooperatives themselves and backing from Secretary of Agriculture Brannan, induced Chapman to fire Moore and to sign a memorandum of agreement with the secretary of agriculture. The accord stated that because rural electrification was "essential for defense and essential civilian needs," rural electrification cooperatives would be allowed to pool their share of construction materials through the REA. Under the agreement, the Defense Electric Power Administration would delegate authority to the Rural Electrification Administration to supervise the controls program for its borrowers.[62] This important victory enabled the REA to carry its program forward during the Korean conflict.

In the last two years of the Truman Administration, the REA continued to withstand attacks from private power sympathizers with a fair degree of success. The House Agriculture Committee investigating its practice of generating and transmission loans decided in 1951 to withhold further action until settlement in the federal district court of the suit brought by the midwest private utilities to enjoin the REA from making such loans to five cooperatives. Furthermore, bills that would have required congressional approval of each such loan did not reach the floor of either house. Although the government's requests for REA loan authorizations for fiscal years 1952 and 1953 were smaller than they had been in the two previous years because of defense needs in other areas, Congress did allow nearly the full amounts requested.[63]

Rural Electrification Administration loans for fiscal years 1951 and 1952 declined sharply, but this development was to be expected as backbone central station facilities in more and more rural sections were completed. Although the record amount of $136 million loaned for generating and transmission facilities during fiscal 1950 went down to about $51 million in fiscal 1951, the amount increased again, to about $61 million, for the following year.[64]

The REA continued to bring electricity to more and more of the nation's farms. By June 30, 1952, 88 percent of them were receiving electric service, as compared with about 50 percent when Truman became president and nearly 70 percent at the beginning of his second term.[65]

Throughout the struggle with private power over the REA's activities, President Truman consistently supported the agency and its purposes. For example, in reply to complaint from a personal acquaintance that the Missouri

Public Service Company, of which he was a director and an investor, was threatened by REA loans to cooperatives in the southwest, Truman wrote:

> Naturally I understand the viewpoint of the private power boys and to be frank with you I am not in accord with their viewpoint. I am sure that the program which the Rural Electrification Organization is trying to inaugurate in Missouri will help rather than hurt them.[66]

In a message sent to the Annual Meeting of the National Rural Electrification Cooperative Association in March 1952, the president summed up the public power view of his administration's struggle with private power that had culminated in the attack on the REA. He recounted the first round when private power interests had fought the yardstick and the valley authority concepts of public power policy; unsuccessful, they had then attacked the preference clause of this policy. Next, arguing that they were struggling to survive, some private utility representatives and sympathizers tried to destroy one government power agency and prevent the establishment of another. They challenged the right of government to build transmission lines and steam generators and attempted to execute contracts with interior on their own terms. Then they tried to stop the REA's practice of making loans to cooperatives for building steam and transmission facilities.[67]

In this speech, Truman defended the "long-established right" of each community to decide whether to supply its own electric services through a cooperative or municipality or to allow a private agency to do so under public regulation.[68]

7

Prizes to Be Won:
The Remaining Choice Power Sites

Four major power sites still undeveloped or only partially developed in 1949 were important prizes to be won in the battle between private and public power. Viewing these locations as integral parts of federal comprehensive river basin development plans or, in one case primarily as a potential source of large amounts of hydroelectric power, the administration sought authority to build power plants on them and distribute the electrical energy in a manner consistent with federal power policy.

Private power interests opposed these efforts. They sought the right to develop the sites themselves and to direct the sale and distribution of the hydroelectric power on their own terms.

The sites in contention were Kings River in the Central Valley of California, Roanoke Rapids on the Roanoke River in Virginia and North Carolina, Hells Canyon on the Snake River between Oregon and Idaho, and Niagara Falls on the Niagara River in New York.

II

The Kings River project had earlier been a source of conflict between the Army Corps of Engineers and the Bureau of Reclamation. In 1937 both agencies were asked by a local water users' association to investigate the Kings River area, apparently to determine which one would come up with a plan most beneficial to its members. Despite President Roosevelt's attempts in 1939-40 to avert the publication of two separate reports, each agency sent its own study to Congress. These plans exemplified the contrasting philosophies of the bureau and the corps. While the former agency viewed the Kings River development as part of a comprehensive plan for the whole Central Valley, the latter looked at the area almost entirely in terms of local flood control. The bureau's proposal included electric power development with government-built transmission lines connecting with other portions of the Central Valley project. The engineers' plan, by contrast, envisaged no federal hydroelectric construction, expecting it to be provided later by private enterprise.[1]

President Roosevelt decided in 1940, on the basis of the dominant interest theory, that since the project was concerned mainly with irrigation, the Bureau of Reclamation should build and operate it. The corps, however, because of its close relationship with Congress, felt no need to alter its position. Confusion multiplied when the secretary of the interior authorized the bureau to build the project under reclamation law, and Congress gave the corps the right to construct it under the Flood Control Act of 1944. The president's budget for fiscal 1945 called for a grant for the bureau to commence work, but Congress denied the request and instead included an appropriation for development of the Kings River area in the War Department Civil Functions Bill.[2]

Truman inherited this conflict when he became president. He asked the secretary of war to allow the Interior Department to participate in the project and then impounded the appropriated funds until the two agencies could agree on allocation of costs and negotiation of irrigation repayment arrangements. Reclamation and the engineers came to terms on February 17, 1947, and construction began soon thereafter.[3]

In 1949 President Truman directed that the "Folsom formula," which required all multiple purpose projects to be placed under the responsibility of the Bureau of Reclamation and all exclusively flood control enterprises under the jurisdiction of the Corps of Engineers, be applied to all Central Valley projects. To implement this policy, he asked that all multiple purpose enterprises under construction in the valley by the corps be transferred to the bureau.[4]

The Pacific Gas and Electric Company had earlier applied to the Federal Power Commission for a license to build and operate three hydroelectric projects on the North Fork of the Kings River, Kings River and Helms Creek. In a second application, the private utility requested permission to enlarge the Balch Powerhouse, which it had built on the North Fork of the Kings River in 1922. In February 1945, the Fresno Irrigation District also had filed an application with the commission for a preliminary permit to build a hydroelectric project on the Kings River. On April 6, 1948, the FPC ordered the consolidation of all of these requests.[5]

The stage was now set for a new round in the fight between public and private power. Invited by Federal Power Commission Chairman Nelson L. Smith to comment on the private utility's application, Secretary Krug replied that the plans of Pacific Gas and Electric were "in direct conflict with long-standing plans of the department of the interior."[6]

The secretary listed a number of reasons for his opposition. First, the Kings River area had been part of the Bureau of Reclamation's plan for comprehensive development of the Central Valley Basin since 1901. Second, the sites that PG&E was asking to develop were essentially the same as those in the bureau's 1940 plan. Third, the Pine Flat Dam, being built by the Corps of Engineers, was essential for economical construction of power plants on the North Fork of the Kings River because its reservoir would regulate the flow of water from the entire stream to meet downstream irrigation demands.[7]

At FPC hearings on the license application, which opened on May 17, 1948 in Fresno, the commission's staff counsel opposed the secretary's position. The attorney argued that the chief of engineers did not object to the license being issued to Pacific Gas and Electric Company if it would reimburse the government for reservation of power storage in Pine Flat. Second, the private utility had offered to supply energy at cost for irrigation and pumping from Shasta and Keswick. Third, the company's proposal to develop the North Fork of the Kings River fitted into the comprehensive plan for developing the area if the company and local groups could agree on joint use of the water for power and irrigation.[8]

At these proceedings the commission had before it applications by both a municipality (the Fresno Irrigation District) and a private company (Pacific Gas and Electric Company) for a preliminary permit and a license respectively for substantially identical projects. The Federal Power Act required the commission to grant preference to a municipality or state in such a case, but the counsel pointed out that the public body had failed to satisfy the commission that it could present a well-formulated plan.[9]

The Bureau of Reclamation countered that the Pacific Gas and Electric Company had made no firm offer to supply Shasta and Keswick energy at cost as the commission staff counsel had claimed. Furthermore, the private utility proposal "by no means fitted into" a comprehensive plan for water resources development in the Kings River area.[10]

These arguments pointed up the differing ways that interior and the commission conceived of the powers of the Federal Power Commission. The FPC believed that the Federal Power Act granted it "complete and final supervision over all non-federal development of water power resources subject to the jurisdiction of Congress." The Bureau of Reclamation, on the other hand, held that if the FPC did not agree that the United States should develop the Kings River resources, it should wait until Congress approved or disapproved the bureau's plans before acting on the application.[11]

While these hearings were taking place, the secretary of the interior presented to the president, on July 29, 1948, the bureau's proposal for the development of the entire Central Valley. This plan, which was made a part of the record of the Fresno proceedings, convinced the presiding examiner, Maximilian G. Baron, to find in the government's favor. On December 1, Baron recommended to the commission that "the development of the water resources of the Kings River Basin . . . be undertaken by the United States itself."[12]

Interior was not surprised when lawyers for Pacific Gas and Electric Company and the Fresno Irrigation District filed exceptions to the examiner's recommendation, but when the Federal Power Commission's staff counsel followed suit, Krug became furious. He complained to Chairman Smith in June 1949 that the commission's legal staff was showing "a hostile attitude toward the development of public power." Furthermore, in attacking the economic feasibility of the bureau's plan, the counsel was employing "the conventional line of the privately owned utilities" and completely ignoring the fact that the general public would gain "substantial benefits" by the bureau's proposed rates.[13]

Contributing to this divergence of views between the Department of the Interior and the president on the one hand and the Federal Power Commission on the other was the difficulty Truman was experiencing in realizing his aim to make the commission, through his appointments, a strong protector of the interests of the people.[14]

Since the resignation of Richard Sachse on June 22, 1947, there had been a split among the four remaining members of the commission, with Chairman Smith and Commissioner Harrington Wimberly leaning toward the private power point of view and Commissioners Claude Draper and Leland Olds generally upholding the public power position. Truman had hoped to bring about a public power majority with his interim appointment of Thomas C. Buchanan in April 1948, but Buchanan's confirmation was held up in the Senate and had not yet been confirmed when Krug made his objections to Smith.[15]

When the term of Commissioner Leland Olds expired at about this time, the president renominated the ardent New Dealer for a third term, sparking a lively debate in the Senate between public and private power proponents. Olds had incurred the wrath of natural gas producers, who included Senator Robert Kerr of Oklahoma, for taking the position that the FPC, under a recent Supreme Court ruling, had the right to regulate the production as well as the distribution of natural gas. Private power sympathizers lined up with the natural gas interests in opposition to Olds.[16]

When Olds's foes at the Senate confirmation hearings used the nominee's writings from the 1920s, which criticized capitalism, to brand him as a "radical" and a "pink," Truman defended his appointee's loyalty and claimed that powerful corporations were trying to prevent the nomination. However, the Interstate and Foreign Commerce Committee voted against confirmation. Although the president asked William M. Boyle, Jr., Democratic National Committee chairman, to apply party discipline, the full Senate delivered a resounding defeat to the administration by rejecting Olds 53 to 15. Truman then appointed an old Senate chum, Monrad C. Wallgren of Washington, to fill the vacancy. Wallgren, who was confirmed quickly on October 19, 1949, also was expected to vote in the interests of a strong public power program.[17]

Wallgren had been on the job only about three weeks when the Kings River vote came before the FPC in early November. Interior Department officials were astonished when Wallgren joined his colleagues in a unanimous decision to grant a fifty-year license to the Pacific Gas and Electric Company to build and operate water power projects on the Kings River, the North Fork of the Kings River and Helms Creek. A preliminary permit was granted to the Fresno Irrigation District to investigate the proposed development of a power plant at Pine Flat Dam.[18]

Liberals outside the government also were shocked by the new commissioner's vote. *The Nation* said that Wallgren's first decision showed that he had "made a poor start" as a federal power commissioner, and columnist Doris Fleeson dubbed the new appointee "Wrong Way Wallgren."[19]

By deciding to allow private development of Kings River, the FPC had rejected the recommendations of not only another government agency but also its own field examiner.

In its supporting arguments, the commission had included a statement Truman made to the secretary of the interior on August 5, when he returned the bureau's Central Valley comprehensive plan. The president wrote that the plans did not contain "sufficient information with respect to engineering and economic feasibility to justify their approval as a comprehensive valley plan." With the use of this comment, according to the opinion, the secretary withdrew the Kings River power projects from the list of projects for which he was asking authorization from Congress. Therefore, the commission was being asked to save the site for the government on the chance it "should sometime in the future come up with a more economic plan."[20]

Chapman immediately filed an application for a rehearing and intervention, arguing that the commission had erred in its interpretation of Truman's letter. He insisted that the president had not intended to veto federal development of the Kings River; rather, he had decided that the Pine Flat hydroelectric plant should be built and run by the Bureau of Reclamation and that other proposed works on the Kings River should be used as an inventory to be authorized according to the Folsom formula when found feasible. Furthermore, the secretary himself had not given up the North Fork projects but would be submitting a detailed report on them in the near future. In January 1950, Chapman was granted the intervention, which allowed review before a court of appeals.[21]

Another round of the fighting over Kings River began in mid-March. On the 17th, Budget Director Frank Pace, Jr. informed Secretary Chapman that he had approved interior's Kings River plan for submission to Congress: "The president has authorized me to reiterate that it has been and remains his view that the Federal Government must continue to undertake and accomplish development of the water resources of the Central Valley Basin, including those of the Kings River."[22]

The White House sent the plan to Congress on March 20. On the same day, all parties involved in the FPC proceedings submitted briefs, but they agreed that no one would present new evidence. About the same time, Representative Cecil White, Democrat of California, introduced a bill to authorize interior's plan.[23]

On April 13, Chapman made an unprecedented personal appearance before the Federal Power Commission to present his department's case. He was doing so, he explained, because the final decision would "have a vital effect on continuing or reversing a national power policy to which this government is committed." To correct what he perceived as the FPC's earlier misinterpretation of the president's views and despite his agreement that no new evidence would be presented, Chapman asked that Truman's position as set forth in the budget director's March 17 letter be put into the record.[24]

With his appearance, Chapman sent a signal that the administration planned to put up a vigorous fight. Some observers saw further evidence of this determination when Truman, on May 24, appointed Wallgren chairman of the Federal Power Commission. Under one of the approved reorganization plans Truman had sent to Congress, the president could now fill this post, and, instead of having just procedural authority, the chairman could choose and direct the staff. Private power exponents viewed the new regulations as "a challenge to FPC's traditional independence" and the president's choice of a personal friend to head the commission as an effort to strongly bind that body to the executive branch.[25]

At the same time, Nelson Smith's term on the commission was about to expire. Here was a chance for Truman to replace a man favored by natural gas and electric power interests with a Republican (as required by law to keep the party balance on the commission) more sympathetic to the public power view.[26]

Truman, however, failed to seize the opportunity. Two days after naming Wallgren as chairman, he nominated Smith for another six-year term. Truman may have chosen this course to balance off conservatives' criticism of his Wallgren appointment. In addition, it was possible that Speaker Rayburn pressured Truman to renominate Smith. Rayburn reportedly argued that if Smith were passed by, representatives of oil interests in Congress could jeopardize the president's program in the House.[27]

Interior's prospects for gaining the right to develop the Kings River appeared dismal in the summer and fall of 1950, when White's bill seemed sure to die in the House Public Lands Committee. Private power proponents viewed the bill both as an attempt by the department to pressure the FPC to find in its favor at the rehearing, as well as a move to help White in the November Congressional race in California.[28]

When the elections were over, the Department of the Interior had lost not only White from its small band of faithful congressional supporters of its Central Valley policy but also Helen Gahagan Douglas. White had made development of Kings River by the Bureau of Reclamation a main campaign issue, and in her attempt to move to the Senate from the House, Douglas, who lost to Richard Nixon, also had supported the White proposal and had herself introduced a similar bill.[29]

Some hope for interior came in December with the report of the President's Water Resources Policy Commission, which appeared to support the department's position both on the particular Kings River case and on the general question of whether the FPC should grant licenses to private power companies to develop sites that would otherwise be included as part of a federal comprehensive river basin development plan. The commission recommended that the FPC not license any private power projects that would "interfere with the carrying out of comprehensive river basin development, including marketing of the electric power produced incidentally to such programs." The report further advised that "no new licenses should be issued unless approved by the responsible river basin commission."[30]

The FPC hardly needed the general counsel for the Pacific Gas and Electric Company to persuade it to ignore these findings since, if followed, they would have lessened the authority of the power commission. But the attorney did so argue, maintaining that the PWRPC had authority only to recommend to the president, and, since no river basin commission had been established, the PWRPC advice could only refer to future legislative action.[31]

Approximately one year later, on December 21, 1951, the Federal Power Commission reaffirmed its 1949 decision to grant a license to the Pacific Gas and Electric Company for hydroelectric development in the Kings River Basin. Included were authority for the company to enlarge its Balch plant and a preliminary permit for the Fresno Irrigation District to investigate the possibility of developing a power plant at Pine Flat Dam. The commission also reduced the term of the license from fifty to thirty years.[32]

Despite what appeared to be a clear victory for private power, Chapman was not prepared to concede defeat. In early 1952, he decided to seek a judicial review of both the 1949 and 1951 opinions, and he requested Philip B. Perlman, solicitor general of the United States, to represent him in court.[33]

At this crucial stage, Thomas C. Buchanan, who finally had been confirmed as a commissioner in June 1949, became chairman of the FPC. The post had been vacant since Wallgren's resignation, for personal reasons, effective October 1, 1951. Still bristling over the Senate's rejection of Olds, Truman had told his friend Jonathan Daniels in November that he would take his time in choosing a new nominee since experience had shown that some "supporting and liberal Democrats" turned out to be opponents of "public policy when it comes to gas, oil and electricity."[34]

A Democrat, Buchanan had often taken the liberal side as a Pennsylvania Public Utility commissioner, but he proved to be little inclined toward upholding the public power viewpoint in this instance. He asked Perlman to refuse Chapman's request, arguing that the prestige of the Justice Department "should not be placed behind the position of the secretary as against this agency."[35]

Perlman, however, agreed that his department should present the case on behalf of the secretary of the interior, explaining to Buchanan that although he regretted that the case found them on opposing sides, he felt it "important that the questions of statutory interpretation be resolved." On February 9, 1952, the solicitor general filed the petition in the Ninth Circuit Court of Appeals in San Francisco, asking that the FPC opinions and orders be reviewed and set aside.[36]

In a second move, Chapman, on June 25, sent a new plan for the development of the Kings River to the president. Recalling that the November 10, 1949 FPC opinion had been "critical of the financial and engineering adequacy of the Interior plan," he said the new report was intended to correct any shortcomings the original plan might have had in that respect.[37]

Chapman was determined to keep the Kings River site out of the grasp of the "second largest private utility in the United States." At stake in this fight, he believed, was nothing less than "the administration's public power policy and program for the conservation and development of our publicly-owned natural resources." Frustrated because his department faced opposition not only from a powerful private utility, but also from another government agency, Chapman urged the president to see that unanimity prevailed in the executive branch. Agreement was essential, he said, to defeat PG&E, "one of the most articulate, clever and effective in the dissemination of the industry's propaganda against public power."[38]

That the secretary was asking Truman to bring the Federal Power Commission into line was obvious, but it was an unrealistic request. Although both the executive and Congress claimed the independent regulatory commissions as arms of their respective branches of government, neither was exactly correct. The president could pressure the FPC through budget control and the power of appointment, but Congress restricted his power to dismiss commissioners and set their terms, and in other ways protected them from his authority. Moreover, it was unlikely that Truman would intervene since he had a record of steadfastly refusing to pressure any of the commissions. On one occasion, he had, in fact, encouraged Federal Power commissioners to come to their own decisions.[39]

Nor could Chapman hold out much hope for a judicial reversal of the FPC opinions. His adversary, on the other hand, appeared confident of an outcome favorable to private power. James Black, president of Pacific Gas and Electric Company, told members of the National Federation of Financial Analysts in

May that the threat of federal power to private utilities in California had been exaggerated.[40]

When the Truman Administration left office in January 1953, the courts still had not acted on the petition for review of the commission's opinions on the Kings River case.[41]

III

The Roanoke Rapids power site on the Roanoke River in Virginia and North Carolina engendered a struggle between the Interior Department and a private utility company that in many ways resembled the Kings River case. The Virginia Electric and Power Company sparked the conflict on October 6, 1948, when it filed an application with the Federal Power Commission for a license to build a $27 million, 91,000 kilowatt hydroelectric plant on the Roanoke River. On April 4, 1949, Secretary of the Interior Krug filed a petition to intervene in the proceedings. Throughout the spring and summer, the license applicant vigorously opposed intervention by the Interior Department.[42]

The position the Department of the Interior took on this matter, as worked out by Counsel for the Secretary Gregory Hankin and Assistant Secretary C. Girard Davidson, was that by approving Section 10 of the Flood Control Act of 1944, Congress had "adopted and authorized," among a number of other public works, a general plan for the comprehensive development of the Roanoke River Basin to be carried out by the secretary of war. In so doing, it had reserved all of the eleven projects that comprised the plan, including Roanoke Rapids, for federal development. Since the law could be amended only by Congress, interior argued, the FPC had no power to dispose of the site in any other way, even if the government should delay the development of this site while awaiting congressional authorization or appropriations.[43]

Krug, however, had reasons to back off at this point. First, he learned from the department solicitor, Mastin White, that the army was unwilling to get involved in a fight with the FPC to gain jurisdiction over Roanoke Rapids. Second, White told the secretary privately that he believed Congress had authorized only a general plan, not Roanoke Rapids specifically, and that interior had no "legal basis for going to court on it."[44]

Despite the solicitor's advice, Krug continued his efforts. His request for intervention was finally granted, and on August 31, he filed a brief with the commission, spelling out the department's position on jurisdiction. In an additional point, the brief argued that the FPC had divested itself of power to approve the application by the Virginia Electric and Power Company when it concurred in the engineers' comprehensive plan prior to its submission to Congress.[45]

The department contended that private development of Roanoke Rapids would, for a number of reasons, adversely affect the entire basin development. First, since its great value was attributable to a large reservoir then being built by the government at Buggs Island, removing Roanoke Rapids from the federal plan would greatly reduce the feasibility ratio of the whole project by reducing net power benefits. Therefore, a private power company should not be allowed to "skim the cream" off the government's expenditures by reaping the benefits from Buggs Island. Second, the reservoir of the private company's Roanoke Rapids plan would back up against a planned unit in the government's comprehensive plan at Gaston, thus reducing its capabilities and adding to its costs. Third, if the Roanoke Rapids project were built and operated by a private utility, the secretary of the interior would have less, and more expensive, power to dispose of to preference customers.[46]

The Virginia Electric and Power Company argued that there was no merit in any of these arguments and insisted that its proposed project was economically sound and structurally feasible. In action reminiscent of the Kings River case, the FPC legal staff also presented arguments in opposition to the administration. The staff counsel maintained that the United States should not build and operate a hydroelectric plant at Roanoke Rapids because the Buggs Island, Gaston and Roanoke Rapids installations all would be peak load plants that could not be operated efficiently unless they depended on loads of the large utility company systems.[47]

On March 17, 1950, the Federal Power Commission's chief examiner, Frank A. Hampton, recommended that the license be granted to the Virginia Electric and Power Company. Using the Kings River opinion of November 1949 to back up his recommendation, Hampton cited two important conclusions he had reached: (1) Congressional "approval" of a comprehensive river basin plan does not constitute "authorization"; Congress could have specifically set aside the Roanoke site for federal development if it had so desired; and (2) there was little likelihood that the government would develop the site in the foreseeable future; therefore, early development by private enterprise would be in the public interest.[48]

The *Nation* commented that the decision, if upheld by the FPC, would "allow private interests to encroach upon river basins set aside by the government for flood control and public power projects."[49]

On the private power side, the *Electrical World* warned that if its interpretation of congressional "approval" of federal development plans were accepted, the Department of the Interior could protest most future private utility applications to the FPC for developing power sites.[50]

The secretary of the interior was granted a rehearing and allowed to present more testimony in June and July, but on November 15, Hampton reaffirmed his initial recommendation that Virginia Electric and Power Company be granted the license. Taking note of the Korean emergency which had arisen since his first decision, he said the need for more power for national security only strengthened his original opinion.[51]

On December 22, Chapman filed an exception to Hampton's ruling and asked that the FPC dismiss or deny the private utility's petition. As he had very recently done at the Kings River rehearing, the secretary referred to the section of the report by the President's Water Resources Policy Commission stating that the issuance of such licenses would have tremendous effects on government power policy partly because these sites would then be used for private gain rather than for increasing the use of electricity and lowering rates.[52]

Despite interior's efforts, the Federal Power Commission, in a unanimous decision, approved the examiner's report and, on January 24, 1951, issued a license to the Virginia Electric and Power Company to develop the Roanoke Rapids site.[53]

Private power hailed the victory as the sharpest curtailment ever placed on federal power plans. Ironically, a federal agency had contributed greatly to private power's success. Colonel H. S. Bennion, vice-president and managing director of Edison Electric Institute, termed it the first instance of one government agency setting back another so decisively. Especially pleased by the commission's private power bent were the Pacific Gas and Electric Company, for the effect it might have on the Kings River case, and the Idaho Power Company, which had recently requested a license to build hydroelectric plants on the Snake River, including one at Hells Canyon.[54]

Chapman continued to fight the ruling. First, he and the Virginia Rural Electric Association Cooperative, which had objected to the license on the ground that power would cost more from a private utility, tried to obtain a rehearing. After the FPC denied the requests on February 27, the secretary applied for a review of the FPC order in the United States Court of Appeals.[55]

The Interior Department and the Federal Power Commission appeared hopelessly deadlocked. Private power sympathizers, including at least some of the commissioners, saw this contest as an effort by interior to gain "top control of hydroelectric license authority in the United States." But to Chapman the basic issue was "whether after a policy has been decided on, an agency of the government may overturn that policy."[56]

Chapman and the department attorneys, however, neither relished the prospect of litigation between the two government agencies nor expected Truman to exert pressure on the commissioners, so they decided in mid-January to take a more conciliatory approach. Gregory Hankin, whom, ironically, Krug had recognized as extremely hostile to the commission, tried to persuade FPC lawyers to agree to limit presentation before the court to substantive questions of law. This course, he said, would "lend dignity to the government's appearance before the court with two federal agencies contesting." The Power

Commission attorneys rebuffed the attempt, replying that they would use all means at their disposal to win.[57]

Not only would the Interior Department have to face determined opposition from the FPC in this struggle, but it could count on no support from the government agency most directly involved in the outcome. Although it was designated to develop the Roanoke River Basin under the comprehensive plan approved by Congress, the Army Corps of Engineers never expressed a willingness to help interior. Chapman complained to Truman later that the engineers' attitude had been a "major problem" in his effort to "preserve the site at Roanoke Rapids for federal development."[58]

On September 5, 1951, the Roanoke Rapids case was argued in Baltimore before the Fourth United States Circuit Court of Appeals, with three judges presiding. Hankin found himself pitted against eight lawyers representing Virginia Electric and Power Company and two other power companies with a collateral interest in the case, plus two lawyers defending the Federal Power Commission's decision. His only support came from the Virginia Rural Electric Association Cooperative, which merely presented a short statement agreeing with Hankin's brief.[59]

The attorney for interior reiterated his department's position: Congress had withdrawn the site from private development by passing the 1944 Flood Control Act; the Interior Department had an interest in the case because it would market the power from the plant when built by the Corps of Engineers; and the FPC had abused its discretion in approving the license application. Hankin warned that allowing the Virginia Electric and Power Company to build the dam would mean that a private utility could interrupt any government river basin development plan simply by securing a license from the Federal Power Commission.[60]

The judges, however, on October 1, unanimously rejected all of interior's arguments. They held that (1) the secretary of the interior was not a party "aggrieved" by the commission's orders; (2) Congress had not reserved the water resources of the Roanoke River Basin for development by the United States; (3) the FPC had not precluded itself from granting the application by its prior approval of the Roanoke River Basin development plan as a federal undertaking; and (4) the commission had not exceeded its authority when it issued the license.[61]

Still Chapman persisted. After the court denied his request for a rehearing, Chapman recommended to the solicitor general that the case be appealed to the Supreme Court, and he asked the Department of Justice to handle the appeal. After some delay and finally, intervention by Truman, the Justice Department granted Chapman permission to proceed; however, it refused to carry on the litigation. Chapman was again left to fight alone.[62]

The administration's public power fortunes were at a low ebb at this time. In a letter to Jonathan Daniels, Truman referred to the Roanoke Rapids case as one of several losses to private utilities over the past three years. Characterizing them as a "pattern and a swing to the extreme right," he blamed gas and electric companies for blocking his Missouri-Mississippi flood control program, the Northwest-Central Valley power inter-tie and, through winning the court case, the Roanoke Rapids project. This suit, he said, "will completely upset our whole power policy unless we can prevent its being confirmed by the Supreme Court."[63]

Not until March 1952 did the secretary officially petition the Supreme Court to review the decision of the Court of Appeals. The *Electrical World* speculated that the Interior Department had been stalling in order to postpone a decision until after the November elections. This strategy, it said, would help the administration since a possible reversal of its public power policy would hurt public power supporters at the polls.[64]

The case was argued on October 22. Petitioners were the department of the interior and the Virginia Rural Electric Association Cooperative, *et al.*; respondents were the Federal Power Commission, Virginia Electric and Power Company, Carolina Power and Light Company and Appalachian Electric Power Company. Essentially the same arguments made by both sides before the Fourth Circuit Court of Appeals were again presented.[65]

A new element appeared in the Interior Department's effort to establish its interest in the case. Gregory Hankin referred to the secretary as a competitor of Virginia Electric and Power Company "in the disposition of power in the Buggs Island-Roanoke Rapids area to public bodies, cooperatives, and others," and compared his duties to those of a manager of a private utility company.[66] Private power exponents claimed this line of reasoning was proof that the government no longer defended its power operations, as it had in early court cases involving the TVA, as being incidental to navigation and flood control, which were authorized by the commerce clause of the Constitution. In those days, the utility companies had tried unsuccessfully to convince the courts that the government was their competitor.[67]

The Supreme Court's decision on the Roanoke Rapids case came shortly after the Truman Administration left office. On March 16, 1953, it affirmed the lower court's denial of the petition to set aside the Federal Power Commission's order and essentially agreed with the findings of both the Court of Appeals and the FPC.[68]

The result of the Roanoke Rapids case was clearly a loss for the secretary, Truman, and all public power exponents. For although they disagreed with the decision, they agreed with the court's estimation of the significance of the questions raised by the case. These questions, said the tribunal, involved "a conflict of view between two agencies of the government having duties in relation to the development of national water resources," and the decision of the court with regard to them could "affect a substantial number of potential sites for the development of hydroelectric power."[69] The resolution of these problems, in favor of private power and against the Department of the Interior, meant that public power devotees could expect in future years a reversal in federal public power policy as it had developed under Presidents Roosevelt and Truman.

IV

Hells Canyon, a deep gorge of the Snake River located on the Idaho-Oregon border, was another site that public and private power fought over during the Truman years.

Calling for a reservoir that would hold 4.4 million acre feet of water, a power plant with an ultimate installed capacity of nearly 900,000 kilowatts and transmission lines running to Pacific Northwest market areas, the government's Hells Canyon scheme included flood control, navigation and recreation benefits, as well as the use of surplus power revenues to aid irrigation in eastern Oregon and West Central Idaho. The project was a part of the Reclamation Bureau's 1947 plan for the comprehensive development of the Columbia River.[70]

This proposal presented, for the first time, the possibility of competition for what *The Nation* called the "Idaho Power Company's economic barony." In reaction, the private utility applied to the Federal Power Commission, on June 24, 1947, for a preliminary permit to develop its nearly abandoned plant at the Oxbow site. Located in what would be the future Hells Canyon reservoir, the project would make construction of the federal high dam impossible. Idaho Power's plant, with a run-of-the-river dam and an installed capacity of 140,000 kilowatts, would produce only a fraction of the potential output of the proposed Hells Canyon project. Facing opposition from the Department of the Interior, as well as from Democratic Senator Glen H. Taylor of Idaho, and realizing it would have to revise its plan to offer more kilowatts of power, the company asked the FPC on September 8 to suspend action on its license application.[71]

The 1948 Corps of Engineers' report on the comprehensive development of the Columbia River also included Hells Canyon Dam as part of its main control plan. The April 11, 1949 agreement between the Departments of the Army and Interior coordinated the two reports, but Truman, fearful that it would scuttle his own plan for a Columbia Valley Authority, delayed approving the joint report until February 2, 1950.

By this time, the president realized that his CVA proposal held little chance of being approved by Congress. Deciding that adoption of the agencies' comprehensive plan represented the next best solution, he had the two reports sent to Congress shortly thereafter. In approving two lists of projects to be built by the Corps of Engineers and the Bureau of Reclamation for development of the Columbia River Basin, the director of the Bureau of the Budget, acting for the president, cleared the Hells Canyon project to be built by the bureau.[72]

When it appeared unlikely that Congress would adopt this Newell-Weaver plan, the administration tried to get authorization for the bureau to build Hells Canyon Dam and other projects included in the pending Omnibus Rivers and Harbor and Flood Control Bill. The Senate, however, tabled, and thus killed, an amendment by Senator Joseph C. O'Mahoney of Wyoming that would have added the item.[73]

The administration then began drafting legislation to authorize Hells Canyon and other projects. On October 16, 1951, Democratic Representative John R. Murdock of Arizona introduced a bill to authorize the construction of the dam by the Bureau of Reclamation, but no action was taken on it in the first session of the Eighty-Second Congress.[74]

Meanwhile, the Idaho Power Company, in its December 15, 1950 application for a license, had presented its revised plan for Snake River power development to the Federal Power Commission. Providing for five low dams instead of one, the altered Oxbow project called for an installed capacity of 695,000 kilowatts, still below that of the single high dam proposed by the government. Its only purpose remained power production, and the dam farthest downstream was to be located essentially in the same place as the federally planned Hells Canyon Dam.[75]

The intensity of the controversy stirred up by this public versus private power issue equaled that of the Columbia Valley Authority debate. The two sides—those who favored the high, federal dam and those who wanted the low dams built by private enterprise—presented their respective cases in the states involved, in the Congress, before the FPC and before the courts.

The Idaho Power Company began an ambitious program to win over organizations in Idaho and Oregon. It opened a publicity campaign, sending representatives to speak at meetings of Chambers of Commerce, Kiwanis and other organizations and to present the private power position at hearings held by the Corps of Engineers. Idaho Power argued that it was ready and able to do the job, its project would pay $3 million in property taxes annually to Oregon and Idaho, and its low dams would provide better recreational facilities than would the high dam. Calling the federal high dam a back-door path to a socialistic Columbia Valley Authority, the company said the project would cheat Idaho businesses by draining off power to the Bonneville system and the West coast and deprive southern Idaho farmers of their irrigation rights.[76]

The Department of the Interior and its Bureau of Reclamation also mounted an effort to sell their plan to citizens of the states directly affected. In November 1950, Assistant Secretary Warne reported to Chapman that he had been "plugging it strongly" in eastern Oregon. Assistant Secretary Davidson held about fifty conferences with governors and groups in Idaho, Montana, Oregon and Washington in an effort to reach agreement on a "unified program for power development."[77]

Interior argued that the federal high dam would provide much more power to fill the needs of Pacific Northwest residents than would the private company's plan; additionally, it would provide recreation, flood control and navigation benefits that the five-dam scheme would not. Surplus power revenues would aid the development of irrigation, and under the department's proposed legislation, all present and future upstream water rights would be guaranteed.[78]

After December 1950, the department used the report of the President's Water Resources Policy Commission to bolster its position. The report stressed the need for comprehensive river basin planning and recommended that Hells Canyon Dam be finished as soon as it was practicable as part of the Columbia River Basin program.

Citizen groups in the area actively promoted interior's plan. The Hells Canyon Development Organization had been formed in Baker, Oregon in 1949 to counteract the efforts of the Baker Chamber of Commerce and the Idaho Power Company to sell the low dams idea to the people. By March 1952, this group claimed a paid membership of 400. In December 1951, citizens in Idaho and Oregon organized the Idaho-Oregon Hells Canyon Association, which soon boasted a membership of 8,000 people.[79]

The comments that the Interior Department received from state governments on the Bureau of Reclamation's 1947 report on development of Columbia River water resources had been either favorable or noncommittal. The governor of Washington, for example, wanted certain unspecified points cleared up before approving the plan, and the governor of Oregon wanted first to consider the army's report. The governors of Montana and Utah generally endorsed the entire plan, while Nevada and Wyoming state engineers approved of the portion that affected their states. The governor of Idaho refused to give his final opinion.[80]

Davidson informed Secretary Chapman in February 1951 that at the meetings he had held with Northwest governors and organizations during the previous fall, he had found "no known controversy, or only limited or surmountable controversy or objection to the Hells Canyon Project."[81] But Republican Governor Len Jordan of Idaho was already leaning more and more toward the private utility plan until he finally went all the way. In March 1951, Jordan argued publicly that development of Hells Canyon by private power would bring in about $3 million a year in tax revenues to the state. By 1952, he was traveling about the state making pro-Idaho Power speeches.[82]

In 1951 and 1952, the focus of the Hells Canyon controversy shifted from the states to Congress. With defense needs of primary importance in 1951 and a power shortage threatening in the Northwest, the president and the Interior Department began to justify the Hells Canyon Dam, along with other proposed hydroelectric projects in the area, in terms of national security. Truman included it in his annual budget message among new starts needed for the defense program.[83]

Before the Civil Functions Subcommittee of the House Appropriations Committee on May 10, Assistant Secretary Warne argued for the immediate start of the Hells Canyon project as a means of aiding the defense effort. But this argument failed to convince Congress.[84]

Truman again recommended that work be initiated on Hells Canyon in his 1952 annual budget message. A bill authorizing the project was introduced in the House in March, and hearings were held by the Subcommittee on Irrigation and Reclamation of the House Committee on Interior and Insular Affairs during March, April and June.[85]

"Raucous and rowdy" was how the *Electrical World* described the first seven meetings: "Not since the members of the House Public Works Committee went at each other's throats on the St. Lawrence Seaway bill last year have there been such spirited sessions."[86]

Leading off the list of witnesses was Secretary Chapman. He emphasized that the Hells Canyon Dam would supply a large amount of electric power, which was "urgently required for national security . . . and for the continued economic growth of the Pacific Northwest." He also argued that providing this power at low cost would "make possible expanded production of badly needed fertilizer through the development of the enormous phosphate deposits in Idaho" and that the project would "stimulate business, agriculture, and particularly the metallurgical and chemicals industries."[87]

During fierce and lengthy cross examination, Republican Congressmen John P. Saylor and Norris Poulson of California tried unsuccessfully to get the secretary to admit that the Hells Canyon project was intended strictly for power. Poulson scoffed at the proposed navigation, flood control and recreation benefits, pointing out that $37 million was to be spent for one foot of flood control, that there would be no place to go on the Snake River once navigation was made possible and that little recreation would be feasible since the water would be unstable during most of the year.[88]

The bill contained no mention of "irrigation" among its purposes, but Chapman insisted that it would allow the development of irrigation at a later time. Representative Hamer Budge of Idaho pointed out that this would be the first time that the Bureau of Reclamation had ever built a dam for which no irrigation was "mentioned in the purpose." Charging that the bill's main reason was electric power, Budge accused Chapman of trying to "bring this river under the commerce and navigation clause so the federal government would run it."[89]

Among those outside the government who urged passage of the bill were Northwest businessmen, newspaper publishers, the Idaho State Federation of Labor, the Oregon State Grange, local granges in Idaho and Oregon, the National Farmers Union, the Idaho State Legislature, the Idaho secretary of state, Senator Wayne Morse of Oregon, the Idaho National Rural Electric Cooperative Association, the Hells Canyon Development Association and the Idaho-Oregon Hells Canyon Association.[90]   In his testimony, Al Ullman, chairman of the Idaho-Oregon Hells Canyon Association, claimed that the people of Oregon and Idaho were "overwhelmingly in support of the Hells Canyon proposal."[91]

The senators also heard arguments from witnesses committed to scuttling the federal high dam scheme. These included Northwest irrigation districts, water user groups, cattlemen's associations and major newspapers. Among Idaho opponents voicing their opposition were the State Reclamation Association, Mining Association, Chamber of Commerce and Farm Bureau Federation, as well as Governor Len Jordan.[92] Jordan argued that interior's plan would violate state's rights because it would limit the amount of water Idaho residents could use, would mean loss of tax revenue to Idaho and the country, and would increase the federal debt.[93]

When the hearings recessed in early April, observers, including proponents of the plan, conceded that the bill had little chance of passage in the second session of the Eighty-Second Congress. When, only a week after the hearings resumed in mid-June, Poulson moved to recess the hearings indefinitely, not even Chairman John Murdock, who had introduced the bill, objected.[94]

The focus of the Hells Canyon struggle then moved to the Federal Power Commission, which scheduled the first hearings on the Idaho Power Company's applications for July 14, 1952. Granted permission to intervene, the Department of the Interior asked the FPC to reject the Idaho Power Company's request to build the Oxbow project on the ground it would prevent the future construction of the Hells Canyon Dam by the government.[95]

In November the Idaho Power Company filed with the FPC a supplementary application amending its 1950 one. Under its new plan, the private utility would build three dams, at the Brownlee, Oxbow and Hells Canyon sites, instead of the five proposed earlier. The other major change concerned the plans for the Brownlee site where the dam would be raised over 200 feet above the height specified in the original plan. Total kilowatt capacity now would be 783,000 as compared with 714,000 kilowatt capacity under the five-dam scheme. The FPC postponed the hearings until 1953. The reason it gave was to allow the private utility company time to prepare more engineering data for its new proposal, but public power proponents suspected its real reason was to wait until a new, more private power oriented administration took office.[96]

By failing to issue an opinion during 1951 and 1952, the Federal Power Commission jeopardized chances for congressional action on the bill authorizing the government's high dam at Hells Canyon. Bonneville Power Administrator Paul Raver observed to Chapman: "This failure permits the Congress to take the position that it will wait and see what the FPC's Oxbow finding is."[97]

Thus, in another instance, the question of whether the government or a private utility company would develop a hydroelectric site that the Department of the Interior regarded as a key element in the comprehensive development of a river basin was left in abeyance as the Truman Administration expired.[98]

V

Renewed interest in the proposed Niagara River power redevelopment project during Truman's second term revived the dispute between public and private power over which side would develop the additional power.

The Niagara project was related to the Great Lakes-St. Lawrence Seaway and power question in that Niagara redevelopment had been included in a 1941 executive agreement between Canada and the United States on the Great Lakes-St. Lawrence Basin. In the same watershed, the Niagara and St. Lawrence Rivers were among the major power resources in the nation. Both had been the focus of a public versus private power controversy in New York State and at the federal level for many years, and both had been partially developed by private power interests.[99] Policies adopted for the rapids of the St. Lawrence River could influence the Niagara controversy since some of the same principles were involved. However, basically, Niagara redevelopment constituted a separate and distinct problem.[100]

Truman's efforts to gain congressional approval of the 1941 agreement, which would have made possible ocean navigation to the Great Lakes as well as created 2.2 million horse-power of hydroelectric capacity to be divided between the two countries, have been adequately treated elsewhere.[101] They are considered here only to provide background to the struggle over Niagara redevelopment.

Truman continued Franklin Roosevelt's policy of tying the seaway and federal construction of power facilities together in one plan with the understanding that the United States power facilities, once built, would be turned over to the State of New York. The power part of the plan engendered opposition from the private power industry, while railroad and port interests fought the seaway plan.

Nearly every year since becoming president, Truman had asked Congress to approve the 1941 agreement on the St. Lawrence Seaway and power project, but Congress did not comply. Finally, in 1951, the Canadian prime minister announced, after meetings with Truman, that his government was prepared to build the seaway on its own. Truman then warned that if Congress again refused, he would support Canada's plan, along with United States participation in just the power project.[102]

When he asked Congress in 1952 for approval of the executive agreement, Truman said Canada's plan made action all the more urgent since United States partnership in the seaway project was vital to the nation's interests. But, as in 1948 and 1951, a bill to authorize United States participation was opposed by shipping and private power interests and killed in Congress. Truman then decided to allow the power project at the International Rapids to go forward through cooperation between New York and Canada, without federal participation. This separation of the power portion from the St. Lawrence Seaway and power project in effect nullified the 1941 agreement. In June, The United States and Canada applied to the International Joint Commission for authorization of the joint project to be carried out by bodies chosen by each government.[103]

The administration decided to delay choosing the agency (which everyone expected to be the New York Power Authority) to build the United States' share of the hydroelectric project until the International Joint Commission completed hearings in the fall of 1952. Then, the administration would make a last-ditch effort to get the seaway plan approved before adjournment of the Eighty-Second Congress.[104]

This attempt failed, but some success for the revised plan seemed likely in the future. The Joint Commission approved the application in October, and hearings by the Federal Power Commission got underway on the New York Power Authority's request for a license to build the United States' portion of the power project. As Truman prepared to leave office, it appeared virtually certain that the license would be granted since surprisingly little opposition had come to light. In his January 1953 budget message, President Truman expressed the hope that a new arrangement could be worked out on the seaway, and the Canadian Government announced that it would consider any new United States seaway proposal.[105]

Meanwhile, in 1949, interest in Niagara redevelopment increased. Temporary agreements to divert more water for badly needed power during World War II had proved that more water could be used for developing power without harming the scenic beauty of the falls. This fact, together with pressure from the Province of Ontario and the Niagara Falls Power Company to make these energy diversions permanent, prompted the Federal Power Commission to make an engineering study in 1949 on the possibilities of redeveloping the Niagara River.[106]

When the FPC's report was published in September, Leland Olds, who had negotiated and signed the 1941 agreement with Canada, pressed Truman to seize the "splendid opportunity" to urge that Niagara power be publicly redeveloped and in coordination with St. Lawrence power. Truman, however, had decided before the study was completed that he would proceed with negotiations with Canada for a new agreement on the Niagara.[107]

The two governments signed a treaty on February 27, 1950, providing for construction of works to conserve the beauty of Niagara Falls and allowing redevelopment of the falls and the river to permit more hydroelectric power production. As the FPC report had recommended, the United States' share of the power capacity would exceed 1.5 million kilowatts.[108]

Public power liberals saw this treaty as an opportunity for the president to make an important public power statement on both the Niagara and St. Lawrence questions. On its way to Truman's desk, the Olds memorandum had passed through the hands of presidential aide David E. Bell, who agreed with its ideas. Bell advised that the president now make a formal recommendation to the Senate, arguing that Truman always gained when he stated his views "forthrightly" and that to do so would help politically "vis-a-vis Governor Dewey," who could then only "oppose public development or me-too the president."[109]

In his message transmitting the Niagara Treaty, Truman followed Bell's advice: "I believe that the additional power facilities should be publicly constructed, in order that the benefits of the hydroelectric power produced there can be passed on to the people at the lowest possible cost to them." On August 9, 1950, the Senate Foreign Relations Committee approved the agreement, which included a reservation giving the United States the right to determine the method of development of Niagara water power.[110]

Three bills for Niagara redevelopment were subsequently introduced in Congress. One, sponsored by New York Democrats Senator Herbert Lehman and Representative Franklin D. Roosevelt, Jr. and supported by the Department of the Interior, provided for construction of the power works and installation of transmission facilities by the federal government. Under this proposal, operation would eventually be turned over to an agency of New York State under terms that would safeguard the federal preference principle. A second bill, introduced by Republicans Senator Irving M. Ives and Representative W. Sterling Cole of New York, allowed the New York Power Authority to build the project, provided for regulation only by the New York State Legislature and contained no assurance that the federal preference policy would be upheld. A third, sponsored by Republicans Senator Homer Capehart of Indiana and Representative William E. Miller of New York and supported by the National Association of Electric Companies and the New York State Chamber of Commerce, provided for turning the entire redevelopment of the Niagara over to five private companies. The companies would build the project and distribute the power with no concern for government preference customers, and rates would be subject only to state regulation.[111]

At hearings on these bills before subcommittees of the Senate Public Works Committee and the House Public Works Committee in August and September 1951, the president of Niagara Mohawk Power Company urged passage of the Capehart-Miller bill. Earle J. Machold argued that with private development, citizens from other parts of the country would not have to pay for building the project; approximately $23 million annually would be paid in local, state and federal taxes; and the power would be distributed so as to provide maximum benefits to as many consumers as possible.[112]

The chairman of the New York Power Authority, John E. Burton, testified that the Ives-Cole bill, which called for state development and control, was the way to get "the most power to the most people at the lowest cost" in the Northeast.[113]

Presenting interior's case for choosing the Lehman-Roosevelt approach, Assistant Secretary Warne said the Ives-Cole Bill "would amount to a surrender of elementary responsibilities of the government for this project" because it made no provisions for supplying preference customers with low cost power. The Capehart-Miller measure, which also lacked such safeguards, would turn over to private power companies a project second in capacity only to the Hoover and Grand Coulee Dams.[114]

The Eighty-second Congress took no action on any of these bills during its first session. With the opening of the second session, Truman asked Congress, in his 1952 annual budget message, to appropriate $1 million in planning funds for the "urgently needed redevelopment of Niagara power facilities made possible by the treaty with Canada," and recommended that Congress pass the necessary legislation to allow construction to begin.[115]

Perhaps anticipating a Republican victory in the 1952 presidential election, private power stepped up its attack on the Niagara project and on Truman Administration's public power policies generally. Focused in the East, the campaign relied largely on advertising in major magazines and newspapers, as well as on the radio. Its recurrent theme was the claim that public power posed a threat to the free enterprise system. An advertisement in an April issue of *Colliers* magazine proclaimed that "the baddies never ride white horses" and warned readers that "sure signs of socialism" could be found in phrases like "government can do it better and cheaper." And one that appeared in *Life* declared that the Niagara project represented a "long step toward socialized electricity" because only the issue of power production was involved.[116]

Private power proponents succeeded in rallying considerable support. Since the Niagara redevelopment project was a clear-cut public versus private power question, with no side issues such as flood control, navigation or irrigation, these advocates could effectively appeal to people outside the electric power industry who feared that their sectors of the economy might eventually become "socialized" as well. Medical societies in some New York counties and the American Medical Association itself jumped on the bandwagon. Other organizations that supported the Capehart-Miller bill included the New York City Federation of Women's Clubs, the Pomona Grange, the New York State Chamber of Commerce, and utility and electrical workers' unions of the American Federation of Labor and the Congress of Industrial Organizations in New York.[117]

The utility and electrical workers unions backed private development of Niagara, as unions were tending to do in other public power controversies in this period, largely because private power companies practiced collective bargaining. Spokesmen for the Congress of Industrial Organizations utility workers and the International Brotherhood of Electrical Workers (American Federation of Labor) told Interior Department officials that workers were often deprived of bargaining rights on public projects and invariably received lower wages and less favorable working conditions than on private power jobs.[118]

Attacked on all fronts, some 500 public power proponents met in Washington, D.C. in May to organize a permanent pressure group. At this charter meeting of the Electric Consumers Conference, representatives of labor, farm and consumer groups formed a committee, headed by Clyde Ellis of the National Rural Electric Cooperative Association, which was empowered to visit the president and maintain contact with Congress.[119]

The administration also was considering ways to seize the offensive. President Truman asked Secretary Chapman to look into the attacks, both from within and without the government, and on February 5, Chapman reported that private power had launched a campaign that was "clearly timed and directed to take over the control of federal power projects and our major undeveloped power resources as one of the big stakes in the 1952 elections."[120]

Liberal columnist Thomas L. Stokes took the administration's side of the story to the public in a February 25 article charging that the private utilities had recently "launched the most extensive and highly financed campaign since early New Deal days" in an effort to strangle the government's public power program. Stokes wrote that the attack was concentrated on the Niagara River Project but was being waged "along a wide front." Senator Murray, the long-time public power defender, entered the article in the *Congressional Record*.[121]

But such efforts could hardly counteract the extensive and costly media advertising campaign that the power companies were waging. Truman tried to seize the offensive by publicly decrying the practice. In a speech to the National Rural Electric Cooperative Association in March, he branded the propaganda campaign "one of the most cynical and dangerous developments in many years." Behind it, the president said, was a desire to restore the "unlimited right of private monopoly to exploit this Nation's water-power resources," and he cited as examples private power's attempts to block public power development at Niagara Falls and Hells Canyon.[122]

Speaking at the charter meeting of the Electric Consumers Conference, President Truman said that the aim of the campaign, in the words of the private utilities themselves, was to "influence the mass mind in this country by playing on peoples' emotions." Then, retaliating for their years of branding public power as socialism, he declared that the power companies had "taken a leaf right out of the books of Karl Marx and Adolf Hitler. They are following the Soviet and Fascist lines."[123]

By June the administration was giving serious consideration to launching an investigation of the private power industry by the Federal Trade Commission, similar to the one it had conducted between 1928 and 1935. Senator Warren G. Magnuson of Washington introduced a joint resolution authorizing such an inquiry on June 19. FTC Chairman James M. Mead assured the Committee on Interstate and Foreign Commerce that the FTC would be glad to make the investigation if Congress authorized it and appropriated sufficient funds. As the summer wore on and no action had been taken on the resolution, FTC Commissioner Stephen Spingarn suggested that the president direct the Federal Power Commission to make a preliminary investigation of purported antitrust violations by the private power industry, in the hope its findings would "provide the impetus for passage of the Magnuson Resolution."[124]

Complications arose, including the president's reluctance to provide any money from his emergency fund for the investigation, the FPC's lack of enthusiasm for participating and Spingarn's estimate that the preliminary probe would take about five months to complete. The White House began to think it would be best to defer the preliminary inquiry until after the elections, and nothing came of it or the joint resolution.[125]

Truman undoubtedly had expected his new appointee to the FPC to support the administration on this and other public power issues. To fill Wallgren's spot on the commission, the president in February finally had sent to Congress the name of Dale E. Doty, who had been with the Interior Department since 1939 and an assistant secretary since 1950. Doty, however, gave indications that he would be as disappointing as Buchanan (whom Truman nominated in May for a full, five-year term). Confirmed unanimously in May, Doty told the Senate Committee on Interstate and Foreign Commerce that although he had tried to support interior's public power program, he was "not one who thinks that the two cannot live together and that it has to be a dog and cat fight."[126]

Secretary Chapman, who viewed the Niagara and St. Lawrence development proposals as key issues on which the administration should make its last stand, urged the president in June to maintain the administration's "strong and consistent" record in handling further proceedings concerning these two plans:

> As you know, the opponents of public power, who already have gained substantial victories in the Roanoke Rapids case, Hells Canyon, Kings River and the Southeast transmission program, are eyeing avidly the outcome of the St. Lawrence so as to seize upon new devices for wrecking completely the Administration's program.[127]

In the fight over Niagara River redevelopment, the administration was battling not only private power proponents but also those who favored New York State development. Animosity between the Interior Department and the New York Power Authority increased during 1952 when the administration came to believe the authority was lining up on the side of private power. It was then that the New York public body published, in its annual report, a repudiation of its prior commitments to follow basic federal power policy in handling St. Lawrence-Niagara power. The authority now backed a plan for selling the power to private utilities at the bus bar and sending it over their lines without adequate preference safeguards for Rural Electrification Administration customers and public bodies. Calling the report a "political document," Chapman wrote the president, "It confirms my impression . . . that the Power Authority is a vigorous tool of the private utilities."[128]

When the secretary charged in a speech to the National Rural Electric Cooperative Association's annual convention in March that the authority aimed to "turn over Niagara and St. Lawrence power to private companies at the bus bar," the authority chairman countered that Chapman had "clearly spelled out" a fight and added that "no responsible state can bear his insult or avoid the challenge."[129]

Thus the three-sided argument continued, with the only chance for resolution lying with Congress. But 1952 was an election year, and no side to the controversy could be sure enough of victory to push for a decision. No hearings were held on any of the bills concerning Niagara redevelopment, and none emerged from committee during the second session of the Eighty-Second Congress. As it was with the Kings River, Roanoke Rapids and Hells Canyon sites, the question of whether public or private power would develop the Niagara River was left unanswered when the Truman Administration ended on January 20, 1953.

VI

No final determination was reached in any of the Truman Administration's attempts to save these four choice power sites for government development. In two of the cases, however, only court rulings could alter outcomes that were contrary to public power goals. The Federal Power Commission had made two decisions in opposition to the administration on the Kings River question, and the petition for their review was still pending before the Circuit Court of Appeals. In the case of Roanoke Rapids, both the FPC and the Circuit Court had ruled against federal development, and the final decision rested with the Supreme Court.

The controversies surrounding the other two sites continued unabated. Attempts by the administration to persuade Congress to authorize its Hells Canyon project had failed. Since its opinion on the Idaho Power Company's license application would bear on legislative decision making, the Federal Power Commission contributed to congressional inaction by postponing its hearings on the Idaho Power Company's license application until 1953. A deadlock in Congress among federal, state and private development exponents had prevented any resolution of the Niagara redevelopment issue.[130] In this situation, the FPC was powerless since, by a reservation to the 1950 treaty, Congress had to act before a license could be granted. With a Republican administration and Congress about to assume power, the prospects for outcomes to these cases favorable to public power liberalism appeared highly improbable.

8

War of Words:
Efforts to Enunciate a Power Policy

All of the significant aspects of the public versus private power struggle during Truman's second term—controversies over water resource organization, federal power marketing agencies, steam and transmission facilities, and remaining power sites—demonstrated the lack of a clearly enunciated federal power policy.

Private power exponents, especially those in Congress who served on committees that considered appropriation requests for expansion of public power, often deplored the absence of a broad policy statement that could guide decision making. For the most part, they preferred to have Congress, rather than the executive branch, set the policy because it would be more likely to create one that coincided with private power aims.

During a discussion about granting funds for the Bonneville Power Administration before the Interior Subcommittee of the Senate Appropriations Committee in 1949, Republican Senator Kenneth Wherry of Nebraska, who usually sympathized with private power interests, expressed his frustration: "In one place we furnish a substation; in another place we do not. In one place we build a transmission line and carry the juice hundreds of miles; in another place we make the purchaser take the juice at the bus bar. We have a conflict because we do not have a uniform policy."[1]

Democratic Senator Elmer Thomas of Oklahoma, a member of the subcommittee considering appropriations for the Department of the Army's civil functions, commented during an exchange about whether private power companies or the Interior Department should market power from Corps of Engineers projects in the Southeast, "I am going to insist that we have a public power policy developed and announced, so that everybody, private and public power advocates, can know exactly what they can expect."[2]

The Agriculture Subcommittee of the Senate Appropriations Committee in July 1950 lamented the fact that there was no established policy to help it decide whether the Southwestern Power Administration should use its continuing fund for leasing generating and transmission facilities from "super-cooperatives."[3]

During 1949 and 1950, the appropriations and conference committees experimented with directing the Southwestern and Southeastern Power Associations to try to negotiate wheeling agreements before using funds appropriated for transmission lines. After the Senate appropriations Committee gave SWPA such a directive in July 1949, Senator Thomas, who sided with private power on this issue, observed that because Congress had not developed a public power policy, the appropriations committee was forced to write it.[4]

Congressional private power supporters made several efforts to include in Department of the Interior appropriations bills a requirement that the Bureau of Reclamation attempt to negotiate wheeling contracts with private utilities before beginning construction of transmission lines. The majority in the Democratically controlled Eighty-first Congress, however, successfully opposed a move to set the practice in law, largely on the ground that Congress should not make power policy.

Private power proponents outside the government also became increasingly interested in the promulgation of a national power policy. In March 1950, discussion of the need for such a statement was placed on the program of the annual meeting of the United States Chamber of Commerce. Commenting that so important a policy point at issue in the Roanoke Rapids and Kings River cases should not be decided by a federal commission "which is necessarily a creature of the president in office," the *Wall Street Journal* urged the private power industry to ask Congress to declare a national power policy or risk facing "ultimate destruction."[5]

In 1951, Senator Guy Cordon, a member of the Interior Subcommittee of the Senate Committee on Appropriations, took up the cause. During discussion of a contract that Pacific Gas and Electric Company had offered the government, he declared that since private utilities in various sections of the country were attempting similar negotiations, Congress was "going to have to enunciate a power policy."[6]

This time, a more conservative Eighty-second Congress went along to the extent of passing the Keating Amendment, which, in effect, forbade the Bureau of Reclamation to build transmission lines where sufficient wheeling agreements were available. Interior appropriations bills in subsequent years contained the same stipulation, and similar language was later used to apply to the Southwestern and Southeastern Power Administrations. But Congress set no broad power policy.

Public power proponents from time to time also advocated a more clearly defined national power policy. They wanted the initiative to come not from Congress, however, but from the executive branch, which, under the Truman presidency, would be more likely to set down a policy in line with their beliefs.

The administration did make several attempts to come to grips with the problem during Truman's second term.

II

One possibility was to rejuvenate the old National Power Policy Committee that President Roosevelt had established in 1934. After Truman told the secretary of the interior in 1947 that he was interested in reactivating the body, Krug asked the former executive secretary of the committee, Joel D. Wolfsohn, to circulate a letter to other member agencies, asking their opinions. These agencies were the Reconstruction Finance Corporation, Securities and Exchange Commission, Tennessee Valley Authority, Federal Power Commission, Federal Works Agency, Rural Electrification Administration, War Department and Bonneville Power Administration. All except the War Department and the Bonneville Power Administration replied that they opposed regenerating the committee.[7]

The Interior Department was divided on the question of reactivation. Assistant Secretary Davidson favored it, while Arthur Goldschmidt, who represented the department on the committee, opposed it. Secretary Krug was unenthusiastic, but because he thought the president wanted the committee revitalized, he called a September meeting of representatives of the member agencies to give those who had voted "no" a chance to reconsider.[8]

Some of the agencies were skeptical about the possible strategy behind this move. Conjecture among REA officials ranged from the suggestion that interior was about to make a "frontal attack," to the possibility that the president had decided to use the National Power Policy Committee to analyze the vulnerability of Congress and form a campaign plank on the issue. When the representatives convened, Krug told the group that it should become a policy-making body and serve as an advisory committee for the president, and he indicated that Truman agreed.[9]

Many of the participants were anxious to examine Roosevelt's 1934 letter establishing the committee because they apparently had no inkling of the intended function of the body. The War Department and Bonneville Power Administration expressed a continuing interest in reactivating the committee, but no other agency followed suit. The REA representative opposed the idea on the grounds that any stirring in the area of power policy "would be seized upon by our enemies and interpreted . . . to suit their views." The REA took the position that no broad policy needed to be set down because the Flood Control Act of 1944, the Rural Electrification Act and other basic laws provided "the pattern for the present power policy." The FPC representative expressed willingness for the committee to continue if it did no more than "coordinate in a loose sort of way."[10]

This meeting underlined the strife, jealousies and suspicions that existed among the federal agencies concerned with power activities and foretold the difficulties that the administration would experience in efforts to spell out a power policy. Apparently feeling that the Bureau of the Budget often worked against their interests, all of the agencies wanted to exclude it from the committee except perhaps as an observer. As the REA staff member put it, "Everybody gave the Budget Bureau a good kick as they went by." The Departments of Agriculture and Interior teamed up against the Federal Power Commission and the Corps of Engineers as they had done in other such skirmishes. After the meeting, Interior Assistant Secretary Davidson told Carl Hamilton of the REA that he thought the committee could be reorganized so as to keep the FPC and the War Department in a minority position.[11]

On October 22, the secretary of the interior reported to the president that the agencies had indicated that the committee could serve a useful function, and plans went forward to reactivate it. Each of the nine agencies appointed a representative to serve on the committee; Krug was named chairman, and FPC Chairman Nelson L. Smith was picked to be vice-chairman, but the executive secretary position remained vacant.[12]

In October 1948, John P. Robertson, assistant to the director of interior's Division of Power, explained that the purpose of the National Power Policy Committee was to work out a national power policy that would serve the needs of both national defense and peace. As an advisory committee to the president, its duties were to study power problems common to the departments and agencies represented on the committee in order to coordinate the "development of a consistent Federal power policy." It planned for "closer cooperation" between public and private power so that electricity could be made "more broadly available at cheaper rates."[13]

However, these functions existed only on paper. The committee failed to meet at all between September 9, 1947 and late July 1950, when Joel D. Wolfsohn, who recently had been named an assistant secretary, suggested that Chapman consider activating the committee. At a time when Congress was debating the Hoover Commission reorganization proposals, Wolfsohn reasoned that since one agency might be designated as the leader in power matters, it could be wise to have a government-wide advisory organization on power policy.[14]

The committee, however, was allowed to die a natural death; for, by this time, the administration was exploring other avenues for enunciating a broad, national power policy. One of these was the President's Water Resources Policy Commission, established in January, which was studying major questions relating to water resources. Another was the current interior investigation into the possibility of revising the 1946 Ickes memorandum on which much of department power policy was based.

III

In July 1950, shortly before Wolfsohn inquired into the likelihood of pumping some life back into the National Power Policy Committee, Secretary Chapman asked the commissioner of the Bureau of Reclamation; the administrators of the Bonneville, Southwestern and Southeastern Power Administrations; the director of the Division of Power; Assistant Secretary William E. Warne and the department solicitor to submit a revised draft of the January 3, 1946, Ickes Memorandum on Power Policy to All Staffs of the Interior Department. Chapman said the memorandum should be reviewed and revised because of new legislation and increased Interior Department power activities since 1946. The secretary asked that special attention be given to "basic principles," some of which, such as those pertaining to wheeling contracts, had recently been subjects of controversy.[15]

The project failed to create enthusiasm among the agencies approached. At least some of the officials solicited could recall the difficulties that had arisen when the original memorandum was written. In 1945, then Secretary of the Interior Harold Ickes had considered two drafts, one sponsored by Bureau of Reclamation Commissioner Michael Straus and the other by Under-Secretary Abe Fortas. Fortas's statement contemplated an aggressive public power policy for the Interior Department. Its position that transmission lines to present and potential preferred customers be built, owned and operated by the government went beyond statutory authority and, if followed, would have ruled out the use of private utility transmission facilities and the wheeling contracts negotiated by the Department of the Interior with private companies later on. The draft also called for interior staff to give "active assistance" to the organization of public distribution agencies "in each project area." Straus had objected to these two aspects of the Fortas draft, and submitted his own statement, omitting these items.[16]

Asked by Ickes to compare the two drafts and make suggestions, Interior Department solicitor Warner Gardner advised a deviation from the Fortas principle on transmission lines. The solicitor's version allowed privately-owned transmission outlets to deliver power to government preferred customers within the project region if they offered terms that would "assure full accomplishment of the basic objectives of the congressional power policy."[17]

The Fortas principle on government aid for establishing public bodies remained substantially the same. Straus told Ickes that he approved of the draft memorandum with the exception of this portion, designated as II-a. Although the commissioner sympathized with this principle, he felt that since the law did not warrant so strong a statement, it would be open to criticism "by both sides."[18]

Warne, then assistant commissioner of the Bureau of Reclamation, approved of paragraph II-a, but agreed with Straus that declaring it would evoke criticism from both public power opponents and advocates. He recommended that the secretary abandon the idea of enunciating a statement of power policy because it was a subject that did "not lend itself to generalization."[19]

Ickes, however, approved the memorandum, effective January 3, 1946. It contained three parts: (1) a list of the five "primary objectives of the acts of Congress" that pertained to federal power policy, together with the titles of the laws that documented each aim; (2) a number of principles "designated to implement the Congressional policy" and (3) a summary explanation of the congressional acts that provided the basis for the power policy.[20]

The five objectives provided that federal dams should, where feasible, include hydroelectric power facilities; preference in sale of power should be granted to public agencies and cooperatives; disposal of electrical energy should be for the particular benefit of domestic and rural consumers; power should be sold at "the lowest possible rates consistent with sound business principles"; and power should be disposed of in a way that would encourage widespread use and prevent monopolization.[21]

It was against this background that Secretary Chapman, in July 1950, asked Assistant Secretary Warne to chair a committee to examine the 1946 memorandum and "revise it as necessary or desirable in the light of the many developments since its issuance." Composed of the commissioner of the Bureau of Reclamation; the administrators of the Bonneville, Southwestern and Southeastern Power Administrations; the director of the Division of Power; the Interior Department solicitor and Warne, this group was instructed to complete its task no later than September 1, 1950.[22]

At the same time, Chapman apparently decided that the need had become urgent for providing some written guidelines for his agency heads in their negotiations with private power companies for wheeling contracts. The Reclamation Bureau had recently been discussing wheeling contract proposals by the Pacific Gas and Electric Company that Chapman deemed unacceptable, and the newly formed Southeastern Power Administration had received an offer from a group of private companies to buy federally generated power at the bus bar. Furthermore, Chapman feared that Southwestern Power Administrator Douglas Wright was failing to adequately protect government power policy in negotiations with two Oklahoma power companies concerning a wheeling agreement. The secretary, therefore, created a committee, with Warne as chairman, to draft a statement covering the "requirements, terms and conditions" upon which wheeling agreements were to be negotiated.[23]

On the same day that he announced the signing of an agreement with the two Oklahoma companies on July 14, Chapman approved as departmental policy the principles that his committee had recommended. He sent these criteria to the administrators of the three power agencies, the acting director of the Division of Power and the commissioner of the Bureau of Reclamation, and directed them to ensure that any contracts they negotiated conform with these principles. In his guidelines, the secretary repeated the major basic objectives of the public power marketing program as set forth in the Ickes statement. To them he added some points intended to carry out basic objectives in the earlier statement: (1) "integrating Government-owned power facilities"; (2) "interconnecting such facilities with other power systems"; and (3) "constructing such transmission facilities as may be necessary, desirable, or appropriate to the foregoing purposes."[24]

To accomplish these aims, according to this directive, transmission lines that connect government projects with each other and with load centers generally should "be owned and controlled by the Government." In instances when this rule is not followed, the government must be able to operate with the same economy and available capacity as would have been the case if the government owned the facilities. Where no adequate facilities exist, new facilities should be constructed, owned, and controlled by the federal government.[25]

Chapman then listed seven standards to be followed in negotiating contracts when existing non-federally owned transmission facilities had to be used. Among these were the following: (1) The rights of preference customers must be completely protected: (2) the terms of the agreement must not result in monopolization of the power at the bus bar; (3) payment for the use of such lines must be reasonable but never more than the "cost to the Government of its own required transmission capacity"; and (4) the contract in each case must include provision for cancellation privileges.[26]

The department officials who were asked to give their opinions concerning revision of the Ickes memorandum had Chapman's July 14 directive on wheeling contract requirements on their desks while considering their replies. Of the seven consulted, only the Bureau of Reclamation felt that any substantial change should be made in the Ickes statement.[27]

As he had five years earlier, the commissioner objected to Paragraph II-a, which implied an aggressive government role in helping establish public agencies and cooperatives. His proposed revision merely required that "informative assistance" be made available to public agencies and cooperatives in each project area. The reclamation draft also altered the provision for government steam plants "where necessary to independent operation on an economical and efficient basis" by adding that this should be the case only if such supplemental fuel could not be supplied economically by "coordination with other electric systems in the area."[28]

When he reported to Chapman on October 4, 1950 that only the Bureau of Reclamation had submitted proposed changes to the Ickes memorandum, Assistant Secretary Warne added his own opinion. Although originally an opponent of its promulgation, he now said that the Ickes statement, along with the secretary's July 14 directive concerning requirements for wheeling contracts, constituted "sufficient guide posts" for the secretary to carry out his responsibilities in marketing federally generated power.[29]

Public power advocates outside the government were pressing the department to declare openly its power policy. They now believed such action necessary because private power spokesmen more frequently were charging that federal power policy aimed for the nationalization of the entire electric power industry. The managing director of the American Public Power Association, for example, pleaded with Chapman to enunciate the department's policy in order to answer such advertising slogans. However, the secretary said he doubted if such a statement, even if made to the Congress, the press and the people, would arouse much public interest.[30]

This lack of interest, coupled with the opposition or disinterest shown by most of the departmental agency heads, convinced Chapman to abandon revision of the Ickes memorandum. The 1946 statement remained the "current policy" of the Interior Department throughout the Truman presidency.[31]

IV

The establishment of the President's Water Resources Policy Commission on January 3, 1950 represented another of the administration's efforts to formulate a federal power policy.

During the preceding year, several bills intended to amend the Reclamation Act, and thus change certain aspects of power policy, had been introduced in Congress. One of these proposals, H.R. 1770, would have added costs of various functions, such as recreation, sediment control, and improvement of public transportation, to the category of non-reimbursable expenses on multiple-purpose projects so that they would no longer have to be repaid by those who gained irrigation and power benefits from them.[32] In opposing this bill, the Budget Bureau proposed that it be allowed to work out a broad definition of the administration's land and water resources policies. This suggestion later led to the Budget Bureau's proposal that a Water Resources Policy Commission be formed.[33]

Both Secretary Krug and Assistant Secretary Warne were opposed to budget's initial plan. Warne advised his chief in June 1949 that, "with its personnel and facilities," the Budget Bureau was not up to the task. Warne recommended that Krug either push ahead with his "current programs," which included H.R. 1770, or make certain that if such a study were undertaken, interior would be "the leader rather than the collaborator."[34]

Lacking favorable reception of his original plan, Budget Director Frank Pace, Jr., on October 4, suggested to the secretary that a seven-man commission be created to study and "make recommendations to the President on major policy questions involved in the administration of Federal water resources programs."[35]

Although he opposed the idea, Krug realized he would have to cooperate so as not to lose the initiative. The secretary feared that the Army Engineers and the Department of Agriculture wanted to establish a committee sympathetic with their points of view. These suspicions deepened when Krug discovered that the Tennessee Valley Authority, the agency that usually teamed up with interior in its budget requests, had not been consulted about the plans for the commission. Krug confided to TVA Manager George Gant that together they could oppose the choice of members who were prejudiced against their agencies.[36]

At the same time, Warne and Straus conveyed their misgivings to Krug. Warne thought the task should be carried out by the executive branch itself, and Straus felt that Krug's hands would be tied in "handling the Interior program while waiting for the views of this commission."[37]

Although he agreed with much of what his staff members said, Krug had decided by October 13 to cooperate with the Budget Bureau. He pledged to the director that he would do all in his "power to assist the proposed commission." Fearing that if the commission took a year to make its report, it would "merely delay settling the unresolved policy questions concerning water resources," Krug suggested that the body be directed to give priority to certain major policy issues and to report to the president on them within six months of its establishment.[38]

On January 3, 1950, President Truman named a temporary Water Resources Policy Commission consisting of seven members. As chairman he appointed Morris L. Cooke, the New Dealer who had helped pioneer the Rural Electrification Administration. Truman asked the commission to make a "comprehensive study and review" of "all existing water resources legislation" and make recommendations based on "national needs and objectives." Ignoring Krug's advice that he get the commission's views on important policy issues in time for Congress to consider them, the president requested a deadline of December 1, 1950, for completion of the final report.[39]

The president directed the group to consider particularly the "extent and character of Federal Government participation in major water resources programs; an appraisal of the priority of water resources programs from the standpoint of economic and social need; criteria and standards for evaluating the feasibility of water resources projects; and desirable legislation relating to the development, utilization, and conservation of water resources." He specifically asked the commission to omit consideration of organizational issues because they had already been studied by the Hoover Commission, and to confine itself to "questions of policy . . . together with related legislation."[40]

In addition to Cooke, Truman appointed as members of the commission two economists, R. R. Renne, president of Montana State College, and Lewis W. Jones, president of the University of Arkansas; a geographer, Gilbert White, president of Haverford College; an engineer, Samuel B. Morris, general manager of the Los Angeles Department of Water and Power; a biochemist, Paul S. Burgess, dean of the College of Agriculture at the University of

Arizona; and a former FPC commissioner, Leland Olds. With Olds and Cooke, both avid New Dealers, on the commission, the public power viewpoint was strongly represented.[41]

Three months later, the body was just getting organized. In early April, the commission created twelve committees, made up of its own staff as well as employees loaned from federal agencies, to study major topics.[42]

The committee on power policy as related to water resources was assigned the task of reviewing existing federal power policy as "embodied in various acts of Congress and administrative determinations." In addition to Leon Jourolmon, Jr., the chairman, and Leland Olds, commissioner in charge of studies, this committee was composed of representatives from the Department of Commerce, Federal Power Commission, Department of the Interior, Corps of Engineers, Department of Agriculture and Tennessee Valley Authority. Beginning with the fourth meeting, a representative from the Bonneville Power Administration also attended.[43]

Even though private power had been critical of the commission from the beginning, Cooke felt no compulsion to provide for its official representation. The *Electrical World*, in its March 29 issue, criticized the PWRPC for having ignored private industry in its first round of solicitations and for having held only three meetings. Commission member R.R Renne tried to persuade the chairman to appoint a private industry representative to the Power Policy Committee in order to "prevent public criticism later on," and a possible "general rejection of our entire report."[44]

Cooke decided to take his chances with such an eventuality. He further alienated private power interests by refusing an invitation from Purcell L. Smith, president of the National Association of Electric Companies, to discuss federal power policy with his organization. The chairman explained that it would be impractical due to the "short time available" before the PWRPC would have to report and that it would establish a precedent that could lead the commission "far afield."[45]

The commission did, however, invite the opinion of the NAEC, as well as that of the Edison Electric Institute. The submission of the National Association of Electric Companies in May contained few surprises. It recommended that when constructing a multiple-purpose project, the government should allow private utilities to build the power house and install the generating equipment and then pay the government for the falling water; and when no private company wanted to build these facilities, the government should try to lease transmission lines to municipal or private utilities and sell the power it generated at wholesale, "without preference as to customers." (The submission described "preference" as "a polite name for discrimination.") The association advised that the federal government should build transmission lines when non-federal distributors did not want to, but only when the lines were found necessary by

Congress and when they did not duplicate existing lines. It also asked that Congress prohibit the Rural Electrification Act from making loans for acquiring or building any generating plant or transmission line unless approved by a state regulatory agency of the FPC, and recommended that the Southwestern Power Administration be eliminated.[46]

In the same month, the commission announced plans to gather public opinion in various areas of the country that were vitally affected by the availability of water resources. Meetings were held in Sioux City, Iowa; Spokane, Washington; Berkeley, California; Denver, Colorado; Fayetteville, Arkansas; Springfield, Massachusetts; Columbus, Ohio and Atlanta, Georgia. They were attended by over 2,000 people, 500 of whom expressed their opinions on water resources policy.[47]

In its efforts to tap a wide range of technical and non-technical opinion, the PWRPC also consulted the faculties of various colleges and universities, state and federal government departments, authorities in the physical and social sciences, engineers, public and private power associations, business and trade associations, farm groups, members of Congress and governors and attorneys general in each of the states.[48]

In the meantime, the general counsel for the commission, Bernard A. Foster, Jr., aided by two young lawyers, Sherman Poland and Harry Van Cleve, all of whom were on leave from the Federal Power Commission, began work on a review of federal water power policy for the Power Policy Committee. Although there were many points of similarity, traceable to the 1946 memorandum, among the power views submitted by representatives of the various agencies, the committee agreed that no uniform federal power policy existed.[49]

Interior's principles intended to guide staff members in carrying out the objectives contained in the Ickes memorandum differed from the 1946 statement in that some of them pertained to wheeling arrangements. One of these rules stated that the government should try to make such contracts with private companies when they "are in the public interest, . . . economical, and when they will result in Federal power being brought to customers at an earlier date or at more remote points." Another specified that preference customers must be provided "full opportunity to secure the benefits of Federal power." These standards, as reported to the committee by the Interior Department representative, were essentially the same as those Chapman would include in his July 14 directive.[50]

The acting director of interior's Branch of Power Utilization, "emphatically" pointed out the widely differing concepts regarding cost-allocation determination and repayment requirements under which the Reclamation Bureau and the Corps of Engineers operated. The law did not call for reimbursement of investments in corps projects but did require it in bureau projects. One result, he said, was opposition by local interests to federal development of the Kings River. Since plans called for bureau construction, direct beneficiaries would have to pay more than if the engineers had been designated to build the project.[51]

Another example of inconsistent power policy concerned Federal Power Commission jurisdiction over energy rates at federal hydro projects. The FPC was charged by law with approving rate schedules for power produced at Corps of Engineers controlled projects, at the Bonneville Project and at the Fort Peck project. However, the commission had no responsibility for approving rates for power produced at the Boulder Canyon project, the Tennessee Valley Authority projects or the many Bureau of Reclamation projects. Chairman Wallgren pointed out that even in the cases where the FPC was required to give its confirmation or approval, its powers were "very limited," compared to those it had over rates of private utilities. It had "no authority to prescribe rates, to initiate rate investigations or to order the removal of discrimination." The FPC recommended that it be relieved of all responsibility of approving rates at federal projects, or, if Congress did not agree, that it be granted "adequate, effective and complete" control over these rates.[52]

After sifting through the findings and recommendations of its various committees, the PWRPC prepared a general report in the late summer of 1950. Released on December 17, its recommendations included a recognition that the federal government had to play an increasing role in developing and marketing power because of the "characteristics of modern power supply systems and of river basin programs." The report called for continuing the preference policy for public bodies and cooperatives and for making the provision of sufficient power at the lowest possible rates the final goal of all power ownership. The PWRPC recommended that the Federal Power Commission's authority over rates of federally generated power be revoked and that the FPC not be allowed to license a private power project if it interfered with the "full accomplishment" of river · basin comprehensive development. The report recognized the country's mixed system of public and private power and advised that the growing electrical energy requirements of the country could best be met if the two systems cooperated.[53]

This publication, entitled "A Water Policy for the American People," comprised Volume One of what was to be a three-volume report. Volume Two, containing details of the ten river basin studies, and Volume Three, consisting of a review of existing law that applied to water resources policy, were to be submitted to the president later. The commission also promised to present legislative proposals for implementing its recommendations.[54]

Many private power sympathizers were outraged at the report. James W. Parker, president of the Detroit Edison Company and a spokesman for other private electric companies, described its findings as "an extension of 'Government from Washington' despite overwhelming testimony urging water development and supervision by local administrators." The *Electrical World* warned that if the recommendations of the commission were adopted, "national-ization of the power industry" would be furthered, claimed that nowhere in the report was there a suggestion that private power should build or operate a hydroelectric plant, and charged that the recommendations of the private power industry had been totally ignored.[55]

Private power also had harsh criticism for a recommendation on adminis-trative organization of federal water resource activities. The *Electrical World* misleadingly began its article: "More TVA-type river basin developments are the major recommendation of President Truman's Water Resources Policy Commission."[56]

In fact, the commission said that in order for its recommendations to be carried out, federal water resources activities should be reorganized in a Department of Natural Resources, as advised in the Hoover Commission's minority report. If this recommendation were not carried out, the commission advised, "as an absolute minimum," that a system of congressionally approved river basin commissions based on the inter-agency approach should be put in place. As an alternative to both of these methods, it suggested "regional or valley administrations."[57]

By dealing with the thorny problem of water resources organizational arrangements, the President's Water Resources Policy Commission had exceeded its authority. Not only had Truman instructed the commission to steer clear of this issue, but the report itself recognized that the commission was not authorized to deal with it.[58]

In early January, commission member Leland Olds urged the president to ask Congress in his State of the Union Message to create a mechanism for dealing with the "unified organization of Federal river basin activities, with the greatest possible local participation." The matter should be considered, he said in light of the PWRPC's recommendations. The president, however, was preoccupied with the defense emergency that had been heightened by the entry of Chinese Communist forces into the war in North Korea. He did mention the report in his Annual Budget Message, but only to say that the administration would study it. Avoiding the organizational issue entirely, he said it was important to emphasize those aspects of river basin development that "primarily support the national defense."[59]

On February 11, 1951, Cooke sent Volume Three, "Water Resources Law," to the White House, and the following day submitted a summary of a "Draft of a Water Resources Act of 1951." With this draft of proposed legislation, the commission had again ignored the president's wishes by including a provision for the "establishment of not more than 15 River Basin Commissions to coordinate activities of existing Federal agencies."[60]

Now that Cooke had made this explicit organizational legislative proposal, Truman appeared anxious to terminate the commission's work. He granted

Cooke an appointment on the day after receiving the report and told him to come back when he had completed the draft legislation. But the president apparently also indicated that he preferred not to receive the final version if it contained the river basin commission proposal. The PWRPC released Volume Two, entitled "Ten Rivers in America's Future," on February 26, and on the next day informed the press that it had finished its job and gone out of business.[61]

When Truman officially announced on March 14 that the body had completed its work, he said nothing about his instructions to the commission to suggest legislative changes. Nor did he mention the draft of water resources law that Cooke had submitted. Instead, the president said that after carefully reviewing the report, he would "submit to the Congress such legislative recommendations as seem appropriate from time to time."[62]

Now that the work of the commission had dramatically exposed the political difficulties involved in attempts to establish a national water resources policy, the president seemed in no hurry to bring the results of the study to fruition. To help him determine what steps the executive branch should take "in light of the Commission's recommendations," he directed the Bureau of the Budget to establish the Inter-Agency Water Policy Review Committee. Thus began another long, detailed study that would take as long to complete as had the PWRPC report itself.[63]

Not only were the interested agencies and departments asked to participate in this study of a study, but "comments, recommendations and expressions of opinion" also were solicited from "Interstate River Basin Commissions, Associations of State and Municipal governments, Reclamation groups [and] professional organizations."[64]

As could be expected, a split developed in a subcommittee charged with reviewing the commission's recommendations on electric power. While agency representatives could agree unanimously on four of the eight recommendations, a rift occurred over the wording of the remaining four. Interior and agriculture subcommittee members supported the commission's suggestions in each case, whereas the Federal Power Commission and the Corps of Engineers opposed them and offered revisions. The Bureau of the Budget, for the most part, sided with interior and agriculture.[65]

E. C. Weitzell, the Agriculture Department representative, reported to REA officials that he and Ed Eardley, of the Department of the Interior, had faced "strong opposition" from the Federal Power Commission and the Corps of Engineers. Their proposed revisions, he charged, would "for all practical purposes destroy the progress that has been made in Federal power policy during the last twenty years."[66]

The two agencies wanted to change the PWRPC recommendation that full development of the country's undeveloped water power should be regarded as a major responsibility of the federal government. Their revision called for allowing "local non-Federal public and private agencies" to assume a large part of the responsibility for building the power facilities of projects under FPC license.[67]

The FPC and the Corps of Engineers suggested another significant change that involved the recommendation that federal agencies concerned with developing the water resources of a river basin should cooperate with public and cooperative bodies and that all generating capacity should achieve "the best possible regional integration" in accord with preference principles. The dissenters wanted to add "private agencies" to the non-federal public bodies the federal government should cooperate with and to delete the reference to the preference principle.[68]

They also disagreed with the PWRPC recommendation that Congress repeal any legislation that required the Federal Power Commission to approve rates for federally generated power. They wanted the FPC to have the power to revise and approve these rates and, if necessary, prescribe them.[69]

While this inter-agency review committee was going about its task during the spring and summer of 1951, Cooke pressed the president to release the PWRPC's legislative recommendations. Truman refused on the ground that the recommendations on organizational issues might make it more difficult to gain acceptance from Congress for the rest of the proposals. However, increasing criticism of the commission by such organizations as the United States Chamber of Commerce, Engineers Joint Council and the National Reclamation Association, along with the desire of the administration to retain the PWRPC's support for legislation it might propose, influenced Truman finally to allow the commission members to release Volume Four on their own cognizance on February 18, 1952.[70]

In May, the Inter-Agency Water Policy Review Committee drafted a bill and sent it to the interested departments for comments. The proposals on electric power differed in several respects from those in the PWRPC report and suggested legislation. First, because of the differences of opinion among agencies represented on the subcommittee on power, the draft contained no general power policy statement, while the Water Resources Policy Commission report contained a full chapter relating to the subject and made several policy recommendations. Second, the inter-agency draft provided for river basin commissions, as did the Cooke proposal, but it included a provision for more state representation. Third, a large portion of this bill was devoted to "reimbursement policy and other substantive aspects of a water resources policy," while the Cooke plan dealt only "briefly and generally" with these matters.[71]

In this instance, Truman allowed only a brief time for the agencies to submit comments on this draft of the proposed "Water Resources Policy Act of 1952," saying he wanted to send the recommendations to Congress as soon as possible. Despite this call for urgency, the suggested legislation still had not been introduced on January 19, 1953, when the president sent Congress a special message on the nation's land and water resources as he was leaving office. Not until that day—two years after having first received it—did he formally transmit to Congress the report of the Water Resources Policy Commission. Truman's explanation that this report had "been under careful and detailed study by the executive branch agencies since then," was hardly adequate to account for the long delay.[72]

V

In January 1951, about a month after the Cooke Commission presented him the major portion of its report, Truman created the President's Materials Policy Commission, which also contributed to the discussion of hydroelectric power policy. Suggested in late 1950 by Stuart Symington, chairman of the National Security Resources Board, this body was charged with making a broad survey of the nation's raw materials. Truman's decision to set up the inquiry likely was influenced by the general concern during the Korean War about possible exhaustion of nonrenewable resources. The president said the purpose of the commission would be to review the long-range prospects, "as distinct from . . . immediate defense needs," for supply and demand of the nation's resources. The idea was to plan for the future so that the country would not be caught with a shortage of materials that could threaten national security or throttle economic expansion.[73]

Truman appointed William S. Paley, president of the Columbia Broadcasting System, to chair the commission and included on it businessmen George Rufus Brown and Arthur Bunker, as well as a Harvard economist, Edward S. Mason, and an author and editor, Eric Hodgins.[74]

The president directed the commission to inquire into the problem of "assuring an adequate supply of production materials" for the country's long-range needs and to make recommendations that would help him formulate "a comprehensive policy on such materials."[75] Energy constituted just one aspect of this broad survey, and electric power one part of that subject.

As in the case of the President's Water Resources Policy Commission, government agencies provided information and personnel to the Paley Commission. The Interior Department lent staff to assist the commission in the preparation of reports, one of which concerned electric power. Assigned to help on this particular study was BPA economist Samuel Moment. Also a Bonneville Power Administration official, but, unlike Moment, a regular staff member of the commission, Dr. Herschel F. Jones not only helped write the first drafts but also collected most of the data for the section on energy that went into the final report. The chief of staff of the electrical energy section was Robert Blum of the National Security Resources Board. Perhaps because of a desire to avoid the criticism that had been leveled at the Water Resources Policy Commission, top private power executives, including Edward W. Morehouse, vice-president of General Public Utilities, were called in as consultants.[76]

A public versus private power controversy soon developed among those charged with writing this portion of the report. The first two drafts showed the influence of public power sympathizers. The second draft stated that the "vast majority" of voters supported the federal government's role in river basin development for the purposes of flood control, navigation and irrigation, and "no longer opposed" its development of hydroelectric energy. It acknowledged opposition from private power companies to the federal government's preference policy but found that subject outside the purview of the commission.[77]

This version of the report also delved into a controversial subject by observing that federal river basin programs were "handicapped by inadequate administrative organization." It noted that both the Hoover Commission and the last two presidents had recognized this deficiency by recommending, respectively, a single department that would deal with natural resources and regional administrative mechanisms modeled on the TVA.[78]

After objections from the private power consultants and other private power sympathizers working on the electrical energy section, the third draft sought a more balanced approach between the two views. Both sides were still unhappy, however, with the result. Dr. Arthur Maass, a Harvard professor, consultant to the Interior Department and a member of the commission staff, was so disturbed by the anti-public power bent of the third draft that he went to Leland Olds for suggestions. Maass endorsed Olds's comments and sent them to the commission.[79]

Olds, who was then serving as interior's representative on the New England-New York Inter-Agency Committee, warned the commission not to ignore the "sensitive and explosive" situation in which private utilities had embarked on "an all-out campaign" to destroy federal power policy. He criticized the draft for failing to recognize that private enterprise was unable to undertake comprehensive multi-purpose enterprise programs, for failing to explain that private power could not meet the nation's power needs because it refused to lower rates, and for implying that the federal government in the future would build hydro plants to meet the needs of private utilities rather than its preference customers.[80]

The efforts by Maass and Olds were largely unsuccessful. The fourth draft emerged as a document to which some private power sympathizers no longer objected. These included Rolande C. Widgery, an executive of the Gulf Oil Corporation who was a member of the staff working on this section of the report, and Eugene Ayres of Gulf Research and Development Company. The Department of the Army also expressed approval.[81]

The Federal Power Commission and E. W. Morehouse, however, were among those still dissatisfied. The FPC opposed the report's recommendation that multiple-purpose river development projects be carried out mainly by the federal government. Reminding the committee that it was receiving over one hundred applications a year from private companies and other non-federal interests to develop hydro sites, the FPC also objected to the inclusion of a statement that publicly-owned, and especially federal systems, would provide nearly all future additional hydroelectric capacity. Morehouse complained that the draft implied a public demand for multi-purpose projects which had been promoted only by the government and that was biased in favor of government development of hydroelectric energy.[82]

The final report, presented to the President in June 1952, met with considerable approval from the private utility industry because it emphasized cooperation between private power companies and the federal government. The *Electrical World* found this approach to be "in sharp contrast to the recommendations of the President's Water Resources Policy Commission," which, it said, "leaned much more heavily on the all-out federal development of hydroelectric sites."[83]

Gone from the final report were the sections that had acknowledged the conflict between public and private power interests over public acceptance of federal electric power development, marketing policy and river basin organization. Instead, a statement that private industry produced 85 per cent of the electric energy supply and was responsible for most of the technical advances in the past seventy years headed a section titled "A Joint Public-Private Responsibility." While the PMPC found that federal policies and programs appeared to be well-established in some areas, it recognized that questions about such matters as the government's right to acquire and build steam plants and transmission lines still needed clarification. The report asserted as a "basic principle" that government and private industry both had important roles to play and that "there was a need for close coordination."[84]

Also absent in the final version was the statement indicating a nearly exclusive role for the federal government in future hydro expansion. The Paley Commission recognized that the federal government would have to continue developing hydroelectric sites, especially where a multi-purpose approach seemed best, but it also recommended that private industry be allowed to handle "part or all of the job" in certain instances, "particularly where a site can be developed best on a single-purpose basis, or where private industry and Government can collaborate in a multi-purpose development."[85]

Truman sent the Paley Commission's report to Congress on July 1. At the same time, he announced that he was asking several interested government agencies to review its recommendations.[86]

In December, the evaluation of the President's Materials Policy Commission report by the National Security Resources Board, along with individual comments from the interested government agencies, was presented to the president. The board reported that the Paley group had not been "alarmist" in stating that the United States economy no longer produced more raw materials than it consumed as it had for decades. Among recommendations for solving this problem, the board advised that multi-purpose projects on the nation's rivers be speeded up and that the president again ask Congress for funds for constructing new power projects under both "private and public sponsorship."[87]

But by this time, Dwight Eisenhower had been elected president, and Harry Truman would leave the White House a month later. For this reason, no action was taken on the electric power recommendations of this commission. This failure marked the last of several unsuccessful efforts by the Truman Administration to clarify and promulgate a broad national power policy.

9

Victory or Defeat:
Tallying Up

President Harry S. Truman presided over a great struggle between a powerful private electric power industry and liberals intent on extending New Deal public power programs.

The public power policies of the Truman Administration were an important, if flawed and incomplete, expression of mid-century American liberalism. As his presidency approached its end, Truman summed up this liberal perspective and the goal of his own efforts: "Our resources should be used for the benefit of all the people, not just a few. . . . When electric power is produced with the people's money it ought to be used for the benefit of the people and not for the benefit of the private power companies." This policy, he said, was "entirely in accord with the American tradition."[1]

The administration's policy, the president said, provided for "multiple purpose river-basin programs, including the development of hydroelectric power," assured that the power would be used widely by preventing private utilities from monopolizing it, encouraged the growth of rural electric cooperatives to make electric power available to rural families at reasonable rates, granted preference to rural cooperatives and public bodies and assured that the power would be transmitted as economically as possible to the points of wholesale delivery.[2]

In accord with this policy, the Truman Administration sought to establish effective organization of federal water resource activities through structures similar to the Tennessee Valley Authority; to protect the government's power marketing policy, including the preference principle, as set down in various acts of Congress; to build steam plants, transmission lines and interconnections between federal systems for efficient service of cooperatives and public bodies; to save the remaining key power sites for federal development; and to enunciate a broad, national power policy.

The Populist-progressive inheritance present in the New Deal was evident in this program and the administration's efforts to carry it out. A strong selling point was Truman's favorite "people versus special interests" theme, and elements of the two major Progressive Era approaches could be discerned in Fair Deal public power policies.

The first of these was illustrated in the administration's support for federal ownership of large projects where comprehensive river basin development was required and of transmission lines and steam facilities where needed to serve preference customers. The second approach was evident in its position on government regulation of private power—that the Federal Power commission should grant licenses and set rates in the public interest.

The Truman Administration's public power philosophy and program were consistent with the "new liberalism" of the late New Deal. Seeking economic growth within the capitalistic system, and a fair share of the increased income for all Americans, the administration justified low-cost federal power in terms not only of lightening the load of farmers, workers and housewives, but also of providing opportunities for tradesmen and industrialists. Organizational structures similar to the Tennessee Valley Authority, increased federal generation of power at comprehensive river development projects, and additional government transmission lines and steam plants would all contribute to the nation's economic growth.

Assistant Secretary of the Interior C. Girard Davidson summed up this view for the Economic Action Conference in 1949: "The proper role of the Federal Government is to smooth the road so that all the competitors in free enterprise will have an equal opportunity to move forward."[3] Along with this philosophy went a recognition of the necessity for certain types of cooperation between public and private power. Contrary to the accusations of private power proponents, none of the administration liberals advocated nationalization of the power industry, but instead stressed that there was room for both public and private power in the U.S. economic system.[4]

II

In the struggle with private power, the Truman Administration could claim some victories, but it failed to win the war.

A few battles ended in clear triumph. The administration won congressional approval of steam plants for the Tennessee Valley Authority and the establishment of the Southeastern Power Administration. It withstood the efforts by private power advocates to demolish the Southwestern Power Administration, and it advanced the Rural Electrification program to the point that 85 percent of the nation's farms were electrified.

The results of some clashes were mixed. Despite effective steps by Congress to force the Interior Department to conclude wheeling contracts with private companies rather than build transmission lines, Secretary Chapman succeeded in getting appropriations for some lines. These funds also strengthened interior's bargaining position when negotiating wheeling agreements, and in some instances helped Chapman obtain terms that protected liberal power principles.

Although the generating and transmission loans principle was not definitively settled, the Rural Electrification Administration proceeded with several of these loans to federated cooperatives which in turn executed contracts with the Southwestern Power Administration, with the result that low-cost power was brought to 100,000 customers. These loans continued in the Southeast as well, where the Santee Cooper loan went ahead despite a vigorous and costly publicity campaign by a large private utility, pressure from the state legislature and opposition from elements of organized labor.[5]

The federal government increased its generating capacity, production of electrical energy and transmission lines to a significant degree during the Truman years. Federal generating capacity nearly doubled, from nearly 4.9 million kilowatts to almost 9.7 million kilowatts; over 85 per cent of this growth occurred in Truman's second term. Federal production of electric energy grew from about 29 billion kilowatts to nearly 53 billion kilowatts. Of this increase, approximately 70 per cent came between 1949 and 1953. Furthermore, during the Truman era, the federal government built over 13,000 miles of transmission lines as compared with the approximately 11,000 miles it had constructed over the previous four decades.[6]

However, it is misleading to measure the Truman Administration's success in advancing public power interests primarily in terms of these statistics. The figures for generating capacity and production are not particularly surprising since by 1949, the concept of federal comprehensive river basin development, which included hydroelectric power, was well accepted. Although their rate of growth was not as great as that of public power, private generating capacity and production increased considerably during the Truman years. The private power industry logged a healthy 62 percent increase in capacity, going from almost 40 million kilowatts to 64 million kilowatts and raised its production from about 186 billion kilowatts to 322 billion kilowatts. Approximately 70 percent of this growth occurred during Truman's second term.[7]

In terms of percentage of the total generating capacity in the country, the federal government strengthened its position at the expense of private power during the Truman years, but did so only by less than 2 percent. Federal capacity went from nearly 10 percent to almost 12 percent, while private capacity decreased from just under 81 percent to almost 78.5 percent. The federal government's share of electric power production grew only slightly, going from 12.7 percent to 13.2 percent, while private power's decreased to a similar degree, from 81.4 percent to 80.7 percent. Other state and local public power entities accounted for the remainder.[8]

The increase in federal transmission lines is somewhat more impressive than are the production and capacity figures. However, with private power sympathizers in Congress successfully blocking a number of appropriation requests, the trend toward the end of the Truman years was toward fewer lines.

The public power defeats were numerous and significant. The Truman Administration failed in its one serious attempt to establish a valley authority, never came seriously to grips with the river basin organizational problem, and failed to promulgate a broad national power policy. It was unable to win congressional approval of the Bonneville-Central Valley inter-tie, steam plants for the Central Valley and the Pacific Northwest and a number of planned transmission systems.

Private power companies still tried to purchase federally generated power at the bus bar on their own terms whenever the government built a new project in areas where private power was well established. In an important move, Congress, with the Keating Amendment and similar restrictions, virtually forced the administration to enter into negotiations with these utilities for wheeling contracts before allowing appropriations for transmission lines to be used, thus curtailing government expansion of public power into new areas. Congress continued to appropriate funds for some transmission lines because power companies didn't always want to enter into wheeling contracts or because they refused terms that would protect government power policies, but the Keating type proviso signalled an era of increased government cooperation with private power.

In the Southwest, REA loans to cooperatives for steam and transmission facilities and contracts between the SWPA and the cooperatives allowing the power administration to lease the facilities and purchase power were cut back by a congressional limitation on the amount that could be used from SWPA's continuing fund, and the legality of the agreements was kept in question by a pending court case.

The administration also failed to achieve its objectives in the struggle for four remaining choice power sites. All four cases were still undecided when Truman left office, but in none did a victory seem likely. The most serious failure was the administration's inability to establish the principle that a site contained in a congressionally approved federal comprehensive river basin plan had been reserved for government development, the main issue in the contests for Kings River, Roanoke Rapids and Hells Canyon. Another vital unresolved question involved whether private power should be allowed to "skim the cream" from hydroelectric projects in which the government, using tax-payers' funds, had invested large sums of money. The federally built Buggs Island Dam and Pine Flat Dam made saving the Roanoke Rapids and Kings River sites especially important to the government.

Nor was the administration able to establish the principle that the government could develop a site for the primary purpose of producing electric power, and not merely as a purpose "incidental" to other functions of government more clearly spelled out in the Constitution. Interior implied the right by claiming to be an affected party in the Roanoke Rapids case and first openly advocated it in connection with the Niagara site.

III

Some of the reasons for the Truman Administration's failures in the public power field lay with the president himself and certain of his officials.

The push for a Columbia Valley Administration in 1949 stands out as Truman's one great public power effort. Few liberals could find fault with the way Truman handled the attempt: He set up a committee to draft a bill, made sure the final draft contained the liberal Mitchell bill features despite lack of unanimity among the framers and opposition from groups in the Pacific Northwest itself; assigned the secretary of the interior, a valley authorities advocate, the job of presenting the bill to Congress; made the request of Congress in a special message and when the Newell-Weaver plan threatened the success of the bill, delayed transmission of the reports.

The president made a number of other serious but less vigorous attempts to further his public power program. He asked Congress for steam plants for the Tennessee Valley Authority, the Pacific Northwest and the Central Valley, and he tried to fashion a more liberal minded Federal Power Commission with his renomination of Leland Olds and the reorganization plan that required the chairman to be appointed by the president. He urged Congress to appropriate funds for the Hells Canyon project, pushed for federal redevelopment of the Niagara River project, and backed Chapman in his appeal of the Roanoke Rapids case. One of his most consistent efforts was his support for the rural electrification program.

In more instances, however, Truman failed to make strong, straightforward and concerted attempts to achieve immediate public power goals. He made no genuine effort to solve the water resource organization problem after 1949. He paid only lip service to the Columbia Valley Administration idea, remained ambiguous regarding a Missouri Valley Authority and made no serious attempt to establish valley authorities in other river basins. Despite his talk about the dangers of failing to enact the entire Hoover reorganization plan, Truman neglected to include a proposal for consolidating water resource activities functions in the plans he sent to Congress. In fact, he showed practically no interest in the idea at all until early 1952 when he suddenly sent up a trial balloon to test its support in Congress and then just as quickly abandoned the plan. When his Water Resources Policy Commission made an unauthorized recommendation for an alternative river basin organizational device that called for more local participation than the valley authority, Truman refused for an entire year to allow the body to release its legislative proposal that included the plan. He then turned the job of drafting legislation over to an inter-agency committee but failed to send its suggestions for solving the organizational problem to Congress.

Most serious of all, Truman made few genuine attempts to effect unanimity within his own branch of government on public power policies, even though he insisted at the end of his presidency that he and agency heads were "in constant communication" with him on policy.[9] He did nothing, for example, to persuade the Corps of Engineers to cooperate with interior on the Roanoke Rapids case, even though the corps, with a stake in the outcome, could have been helpful.

Leaving aside the problems with the corps, whose entrenched position of relative independence from the executive branch he had inherited, Truman failed to bring other government bodies into line. His efforts to transform the Federal Power Commission into a body more concerned with the public interest were weak or ill advised. The fact that Monrad Wallgren proved a disappointment is perhaps best explained by Truman's lack of judgment when it came to rewarding old friends. However, when he had another chance, Truman neglected to replace Commissioner Nelson Smith with someone more sympathetic to public power. In another instance, the president made no effort to persuade the Defense Department to side with Southeastern Power against the Virginia Electric and Power Company on the Buggs Island-Langley Field transmission line.

Some of Truman's actions regarding power policy seemed not only tentative, ambiguous and shifting but also contradictory and at times devious. Rather than face the politically hot issues of creating river basin organizational machinery and of setting down a clear national power policy, for example, Truman appointed *ad hoc* presidential commissions in an apparent attempt to divert public attention to other issues. Because they are temporary and their members prestigious, these commissions cannot easily be identified with one competing group or the other. The presidents who appoint them want "endorsement, not advice."[10]

Truman chose members for his Resources Policy Commission who were likely to come up with recommendations favorable to public power, but the commission's final report evoked strenuous criticism from private power and only stiffened its opposition to the liberal program. In an apparent effort to balance off the criticism, the president chose members for the Materials Policy Commission who obviously would be more sympathetic to private power.

After both of these commissions reported, Truman appointed inter-agency committees to study the studies, tasks so lengthy that he could further avoid coming to grips with the problem of formulating a broad national power policy.

At the same time that he was delaying sending to Congress the PWRPC report and the legislative recommendations of the inter-agency committee he had set up to study it, Truman went on the offensive in 1952 by vigorously denouncing the private power industry.[11] But his liberal rhetoric often appeared to be a facade for public consumption and a tactic to help the Democrats in the November election. In its July 14 issue, the *Electrical World* noted the striking difference between Truman's powerful pro-public power speech at Bull Shoals Dam, which was intended to set out Democratic campaign policy, and the recently released recommendations of the President's Materials Policy Commission, which urged government cooperation with private power. On the basis of the PMPC recommendations, the private power journal reassured its readers not to worry about a drastic strengthening of public power policy.[12]

The men who ran the department charged with the most responsibility for electric power worked diligently to advance public power. Although his record was less liberal than that of his successor, Interior Secretary Julius Krug, who continued at his post for most of the first year of Truman's second administration, made substantial efforts on behalf of liberalism. Shortly after the president was reelected in 1948, the secretary directed his staff to "devise procedures" for carrying out the liberal policies to which Truman had committed himself during the campaign.[13]

Although he did little to persuade his subordinate Michael Straus to back Truman's plan for a CVA, Krug at least resisted pressure from the Bureau of Reclamation commissioner, as well as from the secretary of the army and the chief of the Corps of Engineers, to release the Newell-Weaver report while the administration's draft legislation was before Congress, and he testified convincingly in favor of the bill. In another area, he held firm in protecting preference customers in negotiations between the Southwestern Power Administration and the eleven Southwest companies for wheeling contracts. His testimony before the House Appropriations Committee helped convince that group to approve the entire amount requested in the budget for 1950 for SWPA construction and contract authority. This authorization led to the offer by the two Oklahoma companies to sign contracts similar to the one executed with the Texas Power and Light Company. While not representing a complete triumph for electric power liberalism, this kind of agreement at least meant that private power would not insist on the old bus bar stance but would agree to protect the government's preference customers.

Krug filed petitions to intervene and presented interior's case to the Federal Power Commission against granting licenses to private companies to develop the Kings River and Roanoke Rapids sites. In the case of Kings River, the secretary tried to convince the commission chairman that FPC staff attorneys involved in the hearings should refrain from arguing against the interests of public power.

Krug sensed that a study commission would delay the solution of the many pressing matters on water resources policy and administration, among which was the organizational problem which he wanted solved on the lines of the Hoover Task Force recommendation. However, he went along with the idea of the President's Water Resources Policy Commission so as not to lose departmental initiative, and he urged the president to speed up the process by asking the commission to make reports on major policy issues within six months.

Oscar Chapman, who commanded the Interior Department during most of the struggles with private power, stands out as the administration official who most assiduously battled for the liberal program. Convinced of the need for government-built steam plants in the Pacific Northwest, he labored diligently, though unsuccessfully, to win congressional approval for them. In 1951 Chapman ruled that defense plants could be located in the area and would have sufficient electric power for their requirements, despite opposition from private power and the Defense Electric Power Administration. He then tied to the defense emergency the need for steam plants to help firm the hydroelectric power, and again urged Congress to authorize such facilities.

When he took over Krug's task of negotiating with the Southwestern power companies, Chapman insisted, as Krug had, that the preference customers and the government's rights be protected. He refused to sign contracts with the two Oklahoma companies, the first to negotiate seriously, until he was satisfied that the contracts contained such guarantees. Despite pressure from Congress, Chapman, with the partial exception of the Pacific Gas and Electric agreement, continued this policy of refusing to execute a contract that would not adequately protect the public power policy as contained in the Ickes memorandum and the statutes. Examples include the Georgia Power Company offer and the Virginia Electric and Power Company negotiations regarding transmission of Buggs Island power.

Chapman also fought to preserve the Kings River, Roanoke Rapids and Hells Canyon sites for federal comprehensive river basin development. When his efforts before the FPC failed to block private power's attempts to obtain licenses for building hydroelectric projects at Kings River and Roanoke Rapids, the secretary continued his battle in the courts. In the case of Hells Canyon, Chapman testified extensively in 1952 before the House subcommittee considering a bill to authorize its construction. When the struggle shifted to the Power Commission, he filed a petition to intervene in the hearings to argue against granting a license to the Idaho Power Company for the Oxbow project, which called for a series of small dams on the Snake River. Chapman worked just as untiringly to obtain public development of the Niagara River. He urged the president to stand firm on federal development and fought the New York Power Authority scheme when he realized that the power generated would be sold to private companies at the bus bar.

Secretary Chapman was concerned that there was no clearly enunciated federal power policy. During negotiations for wheeling contracts, he tried to safeguard liberal principles that were scattered in laws and departmental statements, while Congress eyed him closely to ascertain if he was sincerely trying to avoid having to use funds appropriated for transmission lines. In 1950, he struck a committee to update interior's basic policy document, and while he felt compelled to abandon that effort, he did promulgate some departmental guidelines for making wheeling agreements that would help protect government power principles.

Although he failed to achieve victory in several of the crucial conflicts with private power, Chapman was able in some instances at least to delay a final decision, as he did by appealing to the courts the FPC decisions on Kings River and Roanoke Rapids.

Despite his generally positive record on behalf of the administration's public power program, the secretary contributed to some of its failures. Chapman has been criticized for weakness as an administrator and a "gentle crusader" who failed to vigorously express his beliefs. However, most agreed that he was genuinely devoted to liberal causes and was politically shrewd.[14]

Chapman's political skill, as well as his administrative style, may have inclined him toward deviousness.[15] Years later, he professed to admire Michael Straus for his openness in opposing departmental goals, such as the CVA, but the secretary himself sometimes appeared underhanded in his disinclination to confront subordinates. Chapman was accused of forcing Assistant Secretary Davidson to resign in December 1950 by assigning him tasks outside his interests and experience. By losing Davidson, whose ambitions he distrusted, Chapman lost a strong advocate of public power and the only superior who seriously tried to rein in Commissioner Straus.[16]

The secretary also employed less than straightforward methods when dealing with the private power industry, a tactic that merely made the opposition more determined to prevail. He waited three months before responding to an offer for a wheeling agreement from the two Oklahoma companies, and still had not signed the contracts with the other twelve Southwest companies that had been tentatively agreed upon in February 1952 when he left office nearly a year later. His failure to inform the South Carolina Electric and Gas Company immediately of his determination that it would not be an "affected company" by the Clark Hill-Greenwood transmission line smacked of trickery.

During the struggles with private power in the Central Valley, Chapman's department failed to inform the Pacific Gas and Electric Company of its objections to the company's counter proposals for a wheeling contract before giving them out to the press and Congress. And Straus's beginning a survey on the tie-line contrary to a directive from Congress was a notable example of Chapman's failure to keep the commissioner in line. The secretary's reluctance to keep a closer eye on Straus can be chalked up not only to his inclination to avoid confrontation but also to his awareness, gained from sixteen years in the department before reaching the top, that Straus was well entrenched as head of his own fiefdom.[17] In this case, Chapman's ambiguous directive to Straus regarding the start of work on the interconnection suggests that the secretary was as willing as Straus to circumvent Congress in his eagerness to make the Bonneville-Central Valley inter-tie a reality. Such actions irritated even pro-public power members of Congress and merely made it more difficult for interior to win appropriations.

Jealous of their respective areas of responsibilities, other government department heads involved in hydroelectric power activities were less devoted to advancing public power liberalism.[18] Secretary of Agriculture Charles Brannan was supportive, but not strongly so, especially if his department's vested interests were threatened. He feared the president's Columbia Valley Administration would be too powerful, but he did testify before Congress in favor of the bill when requested to do so by Secretary Krug, and he gave a positive written recommendation to the committee.

Interested in clearly defining federal power policy, agriculture's representatives often sided with interior against the FPC and Corps of Engineers on committees dealing with this problem. Brannan's representative on the interagency committee studying the PWRPC report teamed up with interior to oppose efforts by the army and Federal Power Commission representatives to weaken the public power recommendations of the study group. However, the opposing agencies succeeded in excluding a power policy statement from the proposed legislation.

Brannan strongly supported the program of the Rural Electrification Administration. He backed Administrator Wickard in his successful fight with the Defense Electric Power Administration over allocation. Agriculture's success allowed the Rural Electrification Administration program to go forward during the Korean conflict.

The secretaries of the army, Kenneth Royall, Gordon Gray and Frank Pace, Jr., contributed to the failure of the administration to solve the river basin organizational problem, mainly by allowing the Corps of Engineers nearly free rein to pursue its own policies. Royall pressured Krug to release the joint reclamation-engineers plan immediately, knowing it probably would hurt chances for the president's Columbia Valley Administration proposal in Congress. Secretary Gray testified in favor of the administration bill, but reluctantly. And, when asked by the chairmen of the congressional committees to submit his opinion in writing, Gray gave no definite recommendation.

Among Interior Department officials responsible for electrical energy, assistant secretaries C. Girard Davidson and William E. Warne stand out as champions of public power.[19] A consistent supporter of extending the TVA model, Davidson worked diligently for the president's Columbia Valley Administration plan in presentations to Congress and in speaking engagements around the Northwest. He kept a close watch on Straus, who was quietly trying to wreck the proposal, and insisted that the commissioner follow departmental orders regarding the announcement of the Newell-Weaver plan. With interior counsel Gregory Hankin, Davidson developed the department's position in the Roanoke Rapids case, and he strived to persuade the people of the Northwest of the advantages of a federally built dam at Hells Canyon.

Warne battled for congressional approval of government built steam plants for the Northwest and fought Defense Electric Power Administrator McManus' proposal to keep new industries out of the area until they could be assured of sufficient electric power. Warne was a key figure in the effort to sell federal development of Hells Canyon to the citizens of the Northwest. Although he opposed revision of the Ickes memorandum in 1950, Warne can hardly be accused of defecting from power liberalism. He obviously felt that given the climate that existed in Congress, the public interest could better be advanced by relying on that statement, along with Chapman's July 14, 1950 directive on wheeling contracts, than on a specifically declared public power policy that private power could attack.

Although the commissioner of the Bureau of Reclamation, Michael Straus, was a firm believer in many of the tenets of public power liberalism, his primary interest lay in preserving and extending the powers and functions of the agency that he headed. Straus was opposed to establishing the Southeastern Power Administration because he wanted the bureau to be the marketing agent for Corps of Engineers projects in the area. He tried to thwart his own department's efforts to obtain a Columbia Valley Administration because he feared such an organization would mean the end of the bureau.

Straus fought James Black, president of Pacific Gas and Electric Company, who he believed was trying to gain a monopoly over electric power in the Central Valley of California, which would eliminate the bureau's power operations. Thus, Straus labored hard to get federally built transmission lines and steam facilities for the project in order to strengthen his agency's position. For the same reason, the commissioner began survey work on the Bonneville Power Administration-Central Valley inter-tie without specific congressional authorization.

In 1950, as he had in 1945, Straus opposed the promulgation of an aggressive public power policy, partly on the ground that the authority for it must be spelled out in the statutes. However, in his eagerness to attain his own objectives, Straus attempted to evade departmental orders and congressional directives.

Of the men who headed the three Interior Department power administrations during this period, only Ben Creim and Charles Leavy, who served as Southeastern Power Administration heads, remained steadfast in their devotion to the public power program. They followed their superiors' orders and, in negotiations with private utilities for wheeling contracts, drove hard bargains to uphold the preference and other power principles to which liberals were devoted.

Dr. Paul Raver of the Bonneville Power Administration, whose reputation as a liberal was well recognized in 1949, was so concerned about threats to public power in the Pacific Northwest in January 1952 that he prepared and sent to the secretary of the interior an eighteen-page memorandum. In it, he attacked the failure of the executive branch to persuade the Federal Power Commission to rule promptly and in the public interest on the Idaho Power Company application so that construction of Hells Canyon could proceed, as well as the failure to solve the problem of river basin organization in the Pacific Northwest. Raver strongly supported the proposals for steam plants in his area and the California-Oregon inter-tie.[20]

However, his sincerity was called into question when the administrator proposed in December 1952 that the federal government be taken out of the power business completely. Raver suggested the creation of an Interstate Power Commission to take over the functions of the Bonneville Power Administration. While liberals were stunned, private power proponents hailed the idea, and some newspapers speculated that his motive was to keep his job under the incoming administration. So incredible was the whole affair to Chapman that he refused at a farewell news conference to confirm that Raver advocated such an approach.[21]

Southwestern Power Administrator Douglas Wright talked a good deal about his devotion to the farmer and the common man but in practice appeared more interested in his own prestige than in advancing a liberal power program. He praised a draft contract with private power companies that he had worked out even though Secretary Chapman had called its subsidy feature contrary to the law and opposed to established power policy. Wright then disobeyed the secretary's orders to work on a straight interchange and wheeling agreement and instead submitted an even more objectionable draft. These actions undercut Chapman's efforts to protect liberal power principles.

In other departments, some officials not only opposed the administration's public power program, but came close to subverting it. Prominent among these were General Lewis A. Pick and his entire Army Corps of Engineers. With its history of near independence from the president's office, its close association with Congress and its zealous protection of its public works functions, the corps lacked any real interest in the philosophy of public power liberalism. Going back as far as the Theodore Roosevelt Administration, the corps had opposed most progressive electric power goals. From 1946 on, the engineers worked to counteract support for a valley authority for the Columbia River Basin, as they had done earlier with regard to the Missouri Valley. They pushed their own comprehensive plans for the basins, and when forced to combine them with interior's, backed the combined plans and the inter-agency committee device as a preferred approach. The engineers offered no support to interior in its efforts to save power sites for comprehensive river basin development. This was true in the case of Roanoke Rapids, for example, even though the corps was the agency that would build the project.

Although neither Roosevelt nor Truman thought much of his administrative skills, Rural Electrification Administrator Claude R. Wickard was devoted to the goal of completing the job of rural electrification and worked diligently to achieve it.[22] He could boast in 1952 that nearly 85 per cent of the farms had been electrified as opposed to about 50 per cent when he took office in 1945 and 70 per cent at the beginning of Truman's second term. Despite pressure from private power and a lawsuit aimed at getting an injunction to prevent their use, Wickard continued the practice of granting loans to federated cooperatives for the construction of transmission facilities where sufficient power was unavailable or obtainable only at unreasonable rates. In some cases, these facilities were integrated with those of the Southwestern Power Administration, which resulted in additional power going to areas where it was needed, lower costs for the cooperatives in generating power and ultimately lower rates for the consumer.

In other strong and successful moves, Wickard fought attempts by the South Carolina Electric and Gas Company to block a similar loan to a group of distribution cooperatives for a transmission system to carry low cost power from the Santee Cooper project in South Carolina. Furthermore, when the program for allocation of strategic materials by the Defense Electric Power Administration threatened to slow up the work of his agency during the Korean emergency, Wickard insisted that rural electric cooperatives be allowed to pool their share of construction materials through the Rural Electrification Administration.

IV

There is no doubt that the president was committed to the New Deal and to public power liberalism in particular. His energetic efforts to keep that agenda before the public during the 1952 campaign when he had nothing to gain is convincing evidence of his deeply felt beliefs.[23]

Truman could have worked more diligently and consistently for public power liberalism, but at times he had good reasons for not doing so. And even if he had acted more positively, the outcome probably would have been similar, since other forces and circumstances over which he had little control operated to lessen the chances for success in a number of the phases of the struggle with private power.

The makeup of Congress played an important part. Americans had become more conservative in that they wanted to preserve economic gains made during the war. That sentiment was reflected in Congress, where the leaders and average member were little concerned with extending liberalism. Therefore, it is difficult to see how Truman could have led Congress in a liberal direction. Moreover, his legislative liaison operation was rudimentary, resembling, as Alonzo L. Hamby has pointed out, earlier ones rather than the complex apparatus that developed after 1952.[24]

Truman understood that he never had a real working majority for electric power liberalism in Congress. The Eighty-First was the best for the program, but even then the Democratic majority in both Houses did not assure support. Liberal Democrats and liberal Republicans usually voted for such measures, while conservative Democrats often lined up with most Republicans to vote against liberal power proposals.

Thus, when it became apparent in early 1950 that the Columbia Valley Administration plan could not command sufficient backing in Congress, Truman realistically tried to salvage what he could by urging that the joint army-interior plan be adopted.

Truman was a devoted party man and practical politician. He had to consider the split in the Democratic party, which he hoped to heal; how certain policies might affect party members' chances in the next election; and whether pushing for liberal power programs would jeopardize other parts of the Fair Deal.

It was with an eye to the elections of 1952 that Truman kept in abeyance the question of Niagara redevelopment. Concern about these elections probably also explains his reluctance to come to grips with enunciating a power policy and solving the organization issue. By appointing commissions, he could appear to be grappling with the problem and by appointing other groups to study their reports, he could delay the outcome and help the party avoid a controversial issue in the election campaign.

Government agency and departmental friction played a significant role in the failures of the administration to implement a more liberal power policy. It took various forms. The chief executive and the Interior Department often found themselves pitted against the Department of the Army and the Federal Power Commission. With its close association with Congress, the army's Corps of Engineers proved a formidable enemy in any reorganization plan that would threaten its civil functions. Its interests often coincided with those of private power proponents. The corps sided with the FPC against interior and agriculture to promote a point of view more favorable to private power both on the President's Water Resources Policy Commission's Committee on Power Policy and on the inter-agency committee that reviewed the PWRPC report.

Other examples of bureaucratic in-fighting found agencies within a department working at cross purposes, as the Bureau of Reclamation did with Bonneville Power and the Office of the Secretary in the effort to establish valley authorities in the Columbia and Missouri River basins. And, of course, an agency in one department often clashed with an agency of another department. The most important example was the traditional rivalry between the Bureau of

Reclamation and the Corps of Engineers. Determined to retain their vested interests, these agencies often frustrated liberal power proposals.

Local area sentiment also worked against the administration's goals in the public power struggle. It played a role in blocking a Columbia Valley Administration and in thwarting serious presidential consideration of a Missouri Valley Authority. Although public opinion in the Northwest appeared to favor the proposal for federal development of Hells Canyon, opposition by governors, chambers of commerce and other influential individuals and groups contributed to congressional inaction.

Withdrawal of support for parts of the liberal electric power program by segments of organized labor played a small though psychologically effective part in some of the Truman administration's failures to attain its goals. A representative of the International Brotherhood of Electrical Workers testified before congressional subcommittees in opposition to appropriations to the Southeastern Power Administration for construction of transmission lines on the ground that the preference clause was anti-labor. His charge that public systems often violated the Davis-Bacon Act by letting contracts to non-union contractors called into question the sincerity of the liberalism of this aspect of the public power program. Perhaps it was pay-back time since Truman had long been equivocal about supporting organized labor.[25]

In 1952, the Congress of Industrial Organizations' Utility Workers' Union of America joined the Brotherhood of Electrical Workers in backing private utility executives in their opposition to federal development of the Niagara River and expansion of transmission lines. This attitude influenced men like House Interior Appropriations Subcommittee Chairman Michael J. Kirwan, an Ohio Democrat closely associated with organized labor, and Representative Ben F. Jensen of Iowa, ranking minority member, to look for cuts in appropriations for transmission facilities.[26]

Finally, the campaign by private power to discredit public power liberalism was effective. It won allies in Congress and in various sectors of society through its extensive media campaign. Private power's use of scare phrases to describe liberal power objectives probably helped sway a number of citizens. Especially effective during the McCarthy anti-Communist crusade, these phrases included "creeping socialism," "state socialism," "crushing of private industries and individual rights," "ruination of initiative," and "vicious paternalism."[27]

Other efforts to link the administration's public power program, as well as Interior Department personnel, to communism and socialism put the administration on the defensive. Especially insidious were the unsubstantiated charges by the "Kansas McCarthy," Republican Senator Andrew Schoeppel, that Oscar Chapman and Michael Straus had been members of Communist front organizations. Congress held an investigation, and the men had to defend themselves.[28] After a report that a district manager for the Bureau of Reclamation in Wyoming had said at an open meeting that the federal power program was "socialistic," an investigation ensued, going up through the echelons of the bureau to the Interior Department and then to Congress. Chapman felt compelled to place in the record of the hearings held by the House Committee on Interior and Insular Affairs a categorical denial that the federal power program was in any way "socialistic."[29] SWPA Administrator Douglas Wright felt constrained in nearly every public speech he made in 1950 and 1951 to defend himself and his agency against charges of socialism and communism. A favorite defense he used was to call the Mayflower Compact and even the original thirteen colonies "cooperative ventures." The United States, he would say, was "the biggest cooperative arrangement that ever happened."[30]

These smear techniques played a role in the defeat of public power supporters running for Congress in 1950. Both Representative Helen Gahagan Douglas of California and Senator Glen Taylor of Idaho fell before this attack.

The Korean War, which began in the summer of 1950, served to lessen the public versus private power struggle in some of its aspects, but in others had little effect. For example, Congress approved government construction of steam plants in the Tennessee Valley to fill the power needs of federal atomic energy plants and for defense related industries and gave the nod to three new hydroelectric projects that Truman recommended in 1951. But it turned down a number of important projects that the administration requested in the name of defense, including steam plants for the Northwest, the California-Oregon inter-tie, Hells Canyon, and the Niagara River power development project.

The defense emergency engendered an increase in production of both public and private power, but not at the rate expected. The Interior Department announced an accelerated electric power program, calling for 7.4 million kilowatts installation by 1955 and then revising it downward to 6.4 million kilowatts. However, in October 1950, Straus complained that no speed-up program worthy of the name existed. In April 1951, Chapman predicted to the president that the expansion, which had been "justified strictly" on national defense, would increase all public power generating capacity by 46 percent over the next three years. But one month later, he was still protesting that the power program was not being allocated sufficient materials.[31]

With the administration thus defeated, checked or forced to compromise on nearly every aspect of the liberal electrical energy program, a trend toward a stronger position for private power emerged, signalling a turning point in the relationship between public and private power.

The signs were clear—in the defunct status of the valley authority idea and the talk of inter-state compacts, in the Keating Amendment and other congressional directives intended to pressure the Interior Department into signing wheeling contracts, in the Federal Power Commission's pro-private power rulings on the remaining choice sites, in the Paley Commission's emphasis on cooperation between public and private power, and in the newly elected Republican president and Congress. The new order seemed at hand when President Eisenhower announced in his State of the Union Message on February 2, 1953 that the principle of "partnership" would be applied to federal water resources development. This partnership, he said, would involve "the States and local communities, private citizens and the Federal Government all working together."[32]

The advent of a stronger position for private power was further demonstrated in March by a court decision on the Roanoke Rapids case. In a major setback for federal power development, the Supreme Court agreed with the Court of Appeals that Congress had not withdrawn the site from the FPC's licensing jurisdiction.

In May, the secretary of the interior, Douglas McKay, informally announced his department's new policy when he withdrew opposition to the Idaho Power Company's application to build three small dams on the Snake River. That the new administration intended to foster a much larger role for private power in building hydroelectric projects and transmission lines was confirmed on August 18 by the Department of the Interior's first formal statement on electric power, described as the "heart" of its policy. Revealing a clear break with two decades of federal river basin development policy based on the national interest was its assertion that "the Department does not assume that it has exclusive right or responsibility for the construction of dams or the generation, transmission and sale of electric energy in any area, basin or region." Instead, interior now declared that, wherever possible, local interests, both private and public, should construct and operate hydroelectric power projects.[33]

Truman and even the most liberal of his administrators concerned with hydroelectric power favored substantial private participation in order to encourage the economic growth essential for carrying out the administration's programs. But they had sought a much greater expansion of public power than they were able to accomplish. As it turned out, the Truman Administration unwittingly presided over a crucial transition to a more conservative era in American public power policy.

Notes

Chapter 1. The Progressive-New Deal Legacy

1. The term "navigable" was applied ultimately to nearly all fairly large streams, and "interstate commerce" came to include a river entirely inside a state; see Thomas K. McCraw, *TVA and the Power Fight*, 16.

2. U.S. Congress, *Congressional Record*, 57th Cong., 2d sess., 1903, 36: 3071. See also Judson King, *The Conservation Fight*, 4-5; Samuel P. Hays, *Conservation and the Gospel of Efficiency*, 114-15; Gifford Pinchot, *Breaking New Ground*, 327.

3. Hays, *Conservation and the Gospel of Efficiency*, 115-16.

4. *Ibid.*, 109-114.

5. Twentieth Century Fund, *Electric Power and Government Policy*, 481; William Warne, *The Bureau of Reclamation*, 13; address, H.F. McPhail, "The Development of Power by the Federal Government," Office File of C. Girard Davidson, Records of the Department of the Interior, Record Group (hereafter cited as RG) 48, National Archives, Washington, D.C. (hereafter cited as NA). Sufficient head and flow of water to allow generation of electricity usually resulted from the dams required to store water, so it was more economical to generate power for construction at the site than to bring it in from existing facilities many miles away across rugged terrain.

6. Specific legislation was required for actual generation of such power. The amount of power developed incidentally to flood control by the federal government has not been great, partly because of the question of whether design of facilities for maximum generation of power makes flood control less effective. See Twentieth Century Fund, *Electric Power and Government Policy*, 485-88.

7. Composed of the secretaries of war, interior and agriculture, the Federal Power Commission was empowered to issue licenses for the use of water resources over which the federal government had control. In 1930, it was transformed into an independent five-member body; in 1935, it was given authority to regulate the sale of electricity meant for resale across state lines and by acts in 1937 and 1938, it was authorized to regulate rates of electric power generated at Bonneville and Fort Peck.

8. Electricity is a secondary form of energy; that is, it is generated from waterpower or from other fuels. Progressives considered it a natural monopoly because the cost to transmit and distribute it was so high that duplication of services rendered competition impractical and because electric power so obviously affected the public interest. See David Howard Davis, *Energy Politics*, 142-43; Twentieth Century Fund, *Electric Power*, 45, 144; McCraw, *TVA and the Power Fight*, 13; John Bauer and Nathaniel Gold, *The Electric Power Industry and Government Policy*, 11; James C. Bonbright, *Public Utilities and the National Power Policies*, 5-9.

9. A problem that began with an 1898 Supreme Court decision, *Smyth v. Ames*, plagued these commissions as it would later trouble the TVA. The court said that utilities must be given the opportunity to earn a "fair return on the fair value of the property being used." Fair return, which came to be set at between 5 and 10 percent of the fair value of the property being used, could mean any number of things, depending on what was included in the computation; hence, interpreting this rule made for huge problems in administration. Utility companies, in fact, called on the "fair value" doctrine of the courts to avoid any real control of their rates. See McCraw, *TVA and the Power Fight*, 14; Bonbright, *Public Utilities*, 15-18, 28.

10. McCraw, *TVA and the Power Fight*, 15, 53. See also Richard Lowitt, "A Neglected Aspect of the Progressive Movement: George W. Norris and Public Control of Hydro-electric Power, 1913-1919," *The Historian* 27 (1964-65): 350-65.

11. Herbert Hoover, *Memoirs: The Cabinet and the Presidency, 1920-1933* (New York, 1952), 228; McCraw, *TVA and the Power Fight*, 17, Richard Lowitt, *George W. Norris*, 454-55; Arthur M. Schlesinger, Jr., *The Politics of Upheaval*, 376-77; John D. Hicks, *Republican Ascendancy*, 123-34. The Boulder Dam bill was fashioned during the time when the "associational" approach to dealing with problems created by business concentration was dominant. This "new capitalism" strain of progressivism, which aimed to create a stable economic order and at the same time maintain collective organization and democracy, runs through American twentieth century liberal programs.

12. See Preston J. Hubbard, *Origins of the TVA*, 2-30, 143; Jerome G. Kerwin, *Federal Water-Power Legislation*, 268-73; George W. Norris, *Fighting Liberal*, 249-59; Mario Einaudi, *The Roosevelt Revolution*, 160-61; McCraw, *TVA and the Power Fight*, 19-20; Alfred Lief, *Democracy's Norris*, 244-70; Twentieth Century Fund, *Electric Power*, 574.

13. King, *The Conservation Fight*, 256; Davis, *Energy Politics*, 145-46.

14. Norris, *Fighting Liberal*, 26-67; Einaudi, *Roosevelt Revolution*, 162-65.

15. The Boulder Canyon Project Act of 1928 had led the way by allowing the use of power revenues to finance repayment of the cost of building Boulder Dam.

16. See Craufurd D. Goodwin, "Truman Administration Policies toward Particular Energy Sources," in *Energy Policy in Perspective*, ed. Craufurd D. Goodwin, 168-69.

17. Responsibility for administrative decisions was vested in a three-person board of directors appointed by the president, with confirmation by the Senate.

18. Samuel I. Rosenman, ed., *The Public Papers and Addresses of Franklin D. Roosevelt, 1933*, 123; McCraw, *TVA and the Power Fight*, 46-55, 155-59; David E. Lilienthal, *TVA: Democracy on the March*, xiv-xv; David E. Lilienthal, *The Journals of David E. Lilienthal*, vol. 1: *The TVA Years, 1939-45*, 125-38; Einaudi, *Roosevelt Revolution*, 188; Harold L. Ickes, *Secret Diary*, vol. 2: *The Inside Struggle, 1936-1939*, 632; idem, *Secret Diary*, vol. 3: *The Lowering Clouds, 1939-1941*, 400.

19. Roosevelt failed to act decisively partly because he wanted to avoid an open break within his administration over national resource planning and administrative powers and because he wanted to allow room for compromise by Congress. See William E. Leuchtenburg, "Roosevelt, Norris and the 'Seven Little TVA's,' " *The Journal of Politics* 14 (1952): 428-33; Lilienthal, *Journals 1:*, 253; Ickes, *Secret Diary* 2: 80-81; Edwin Vennard, *Government in the Power Business*, 109-10; McCraw, *TVA and the Power Fight*, 158; Ellis W. Hawley, *The New Deal and the Problem of Monopoly*, 339-40.

20. John R. Ferrell, "Water in the Missouri Valley: The Inter-Agency River Committee Concept at Mid-Century," *Journal of the West* 7 (January 1968): 96-98; Alfred R. Golzé, *Reclamation in the United States*, 207-13.

21. *Annual Report of the Tennessee Valley Authority for the Fiscal Year Ended 1934* (Washington, D.C., 1934), 22-24; Einaudi, *Roosevelt Revolution*, 180-81; McCraw, *TVA and the Power Fight*, 57-59.

22. McCraw, *TVA and the Power Fight*, 80.

23. Letter, Franklin D. Roosevelt to Harold Ickes, July 9, 1934, National Power Policy Committee, General File, RG 48. Agencies represented on the group were the Rural Electrification Administration, the Securities and Exchange Commission, the Bureau of Reclamation, the Federal Power Commission, the War Department, the Forest Service and the Tennessee Valley Authority.

24. McCraw, *TVA and the Power Fight*, 81-82; Arthur Maass, *Muddy Waters*, 198-99; Schlesinger, *Politics of Upheaval*, 378-79.

25. Maass, *Muddy Waters*, 198-99; Edwin Vennard, *Government in the Power Business*, 115-16; Schlesinger, *Politics of Upheaval*, 378-79.

26. McCraw, *TVA and the Power Fight*, 147; Edward Eyre Hunt, ed., *The Power Industry and the Public Interest,* 195.

27. Maass, *Muddy Waters*, 199-201.

28. *Statutes at Large* 58 (1944): 890; Craufurd D. Goodwin, "Energy Policy in Perspective," in *Energy Policy in Perspective*, ed. Craufurd D. Goodwin, 173; *Congress and the Nation* 1: 800-801.

29. Morris Cooke, "Early Days of Rural Electrification," *American Political Science Review* 42 (1948): 438-45; Kenneth E. Trombley, *The Life and Times of a Happy Liberal*, 144-45; M.S. Childs, *The Farmer Takes a Hand*, 54-55.

30. Trombley, *Life and Times*, 146-47; Childs, *Farmer Takes a Hand*, 56-58; U.S. Department of Agriculture, *Rural Lines, USA*, 7; H.S. Person, "The Rural Electrification Administration," *Agricultural History* 24 (1950): 71-73. Person, consulting economist for the agency, has described this change to a lending agency as "probably the most far reaching fundamental policy decision in the history of REA" because it "established promotion of rural electrification as an orderly lending program on an interest-bearing, self-liquidating basis," made rural electrification "a national business investment" and made it possible for the number of electrified farms to increase within fifteen years from 10.9 percent to approximately 78 percent of all farms; see *ibid.*, 73.

31. Person, "The Rural Electrification Administration," 74; Trombley, *Life and Times*, 149; Childs, *Farmer Takes a Hand*, 60-63; Schlesinger, *Politics of Upheaval*, 382-83.

32. Trombley, *Life and Times*, 251-52; Childs, *Farmer Takes a Hand*, 65-66; Person, "The Rural Electrification Administration," 75; Ernest R. Abrams, *Power in Transition*, 32; U.S. Department of Agriculture, *Rural Lines*, 33-34.

33. Schlesinger, *Politics of Upheaval*, 306-07; Hawley, *New Deal* 336-37; Twentieth Century Fund, *Electric Power*, 279-80.

Chapter 2. Public Power Liberalism, 1945-1948

1. During the war years, private power companies increased their generating capacity by more than 4 million kilowatts and their production by about 37 billion kilowatt hours. The federal government's generating capacity went up by about 3 million kilowatts and its production by about 17 billion kilowatt hours. See *Electrical World*, January 25, 1954, 167, 177. See also *Annual Report of the Federal Power Commission*, 1946, 71; "Summary of Federal Power Development from the Fiscal Years 1932, 1946, and 1951," Records Concerning Electric Power and Submerged Lands, 1946-1952, Oscar L. Chapman Papers, Harry S. Truman Library (hereafter cited as HSTL).

2. "The Power Policy Fight," undated, File 1-310, Administrative General, Power Development-General, RG 48.

3. Seymour E. Harris, "Public Spending and Resources," in *Saving American Capitalism*, ed. Seymour E. Harris, 150.

4. Congress had already authorized, in the Flood Control Act of 1944, a program of multiple-purpose projects that included hydroelectric energy production. One of the major reasons was to help deal with the depression that was expected to return with conversion to a peacetime economy.

5. Carleton L. Nau, "Electric Power," in *Saving American Capitalism*, ed. Seymour E. Harris, 118-129; Memorandum on Power Policy to All Staffs of the Department of the Interior, January 3, 1946, Federal Power Policy File, Joel D. Wolfsohn Papers, HSTL. See also *Congress and the Nation*, 5.

6. Memorandum on Power Policy, January 3, 1946, Federal Power Policy Folder, Wolfsohn Papers. The legislation containing these policies were the Reclamation Act of 1906, Act of July 25, 1912; the Raker Act of 1913; the Federal Water Power Act of 1920; the Boulder Canyon Act of 1928; The Tennessee Valley Authority Act of 1933; the Rural Electrification Act of 1936; the Bonneville Act of 1937; the Fort Peck Act of 1938; the Reclamation Project Act of 1939; and the Flood Control Acts of 1938, 1944 and 1945.

7. Although not publicly owned, the REA cooperatives favored federally built power facilities because they benefited from the public power preference policy.

8. "167 Electric Companies Announce Stand in Federal River Projects," *Edison Electric Institute Bulletin*, 13 (August 1945): 236; John R. Waltrip, "Public Power During the Truman Administration" (Ph.D. diss., University of Missouri, 1965), 28; Vennard, *Government in the Power Business*, 144-86; *Congressional Quarterly Almanac* 4 (1948): 281.

9. Vennard, *Government in the Power Business,* 130-31; Memorandum on Power Policy, January 3, 1946, Federal Power Policy File, Wolfsohn Papers; "Chronological Highlights of Southwestern Power Administration's Development," undated, File 1-310, Administrative General, Power Development-General, RG 48. According to law, rates of power from multiple-purpose developments had to be high enough to cover costs of building the power project over a reasonable period, plus 3 percent interest; costs of operating and maintaining the project; and, when involved, a portion of irrigation costs.

10. In the 1920s, when private utilities were forming great holding companies, the National Electric Light Association successfully worked to convince the public of the industry's substantial public service and great engineering feats. This reputation plummeted, however, with the stock market crash and the subsequent collapse of the empire of Samuel Insull, who symbolized the success of private utilities. An extensive investigation of the industry by the Federal Trade Commission in the late 1920s brought private power and the NELA into further disrepute by revealing that a great organization of utility corporations centered in the electric power industry had been waging a massive propaganda campaign to indoctrinate the public about the evils of government ownership. The FTC concluded that the campaign was being financed by the public since the companies were charging its costs to operating expenses. By 1933, the NELA's reputation had been damaged to such an extent that the industry replaced it with the Edison Electric Institute whose symbol became the "Reddy Kilowatt" and which for a time kept its promise to be apolitical.

11. Lee Metcalf and Vic Reinemer, *Overcharge*, 94-95; Merrill J. Collett, "Utility Lobbies at Work," a digest of four articles from the *Chicago Sun*, March 31, April 1, 2 and 3, 1946, Speech and Article File, Julius A. Krug Papers, Library of Congress (hereafter cited as LC); memorandum, David D. Lloyd to Charles Murphy, August 25, 1950, David D. Lloyd folder, Box 10, Charles S. Murphy Papers, HSTL.

12. Merrill J. Collett, "Utility Lobbies at Work," Speech and Article File, Krug Papers.

13. Alonzo L. Hamby, *Man of the People*, 288.

14. *Public Papers of the Presidents: Harry S. Truman, 1945*, 10.

15. For example, he endorsed expansion of social security in press conferences on May 2 and June 1 but not the specific legislation that lay before Congress. See *ibid.*, 38, 82.

16. Harry S. Truman, *Memoirs*, vol. 1: *Year of Decisions*, 481-86; *Public Papers, 1945*, 263-309.

17.*Public Papers, 1945*, 300-02, 385.

18. *Ibid.*, 389-92; *Public Papers, 1946*, 61, 472, 473. See also letter from Truman to Ora Bundy, November 10, 1945, Columbia Valley Authority folder, Box 21, Charles S. Murphy Files, Harry S. Truman Papers (hereafter cited as HST Papers), HSTL; clipping, *St. Louis Post Dispatch*, July 15, 1947, White House Central Files, Official File (hereafter cited as OF) 201, HST Papers. For Truman's failure to push the Missouri Valley Authority during this period, see Larry Allen Whiteside, "Harry S. Truman and James E. Murray: The Missouri Valley Authority Proposal" (M.A. thesis, Central Missouri State College, 1970).

19. Ickes, who had supported Roosevelt loyally and had served as his secretary of the interior since 1933, resigned after a disagreement with Truman over the president's nomination of Ed Pawley to be under secretary of the navy, while Wallace was dismissed over a disagreement on Soviet-American relations. See Alonzo L. Hamby, *Beyond the New Deal*, 71-74, 127-34; "Secretary of the Interior," undated, Longhand Notes, 1953 folder, Box 334, President's Secretary's Files (hereafter cited as PSF), HST papers.

20. Ironically, it was this division in the party that had enabled Truman to be nominated for the vice-presidency in 1944 and hence to become president in 1945. By creating a need for compromise, it had allowed a "border state" politician to be chosen. But during his first administration, the schism worked to frustrate his attempts to fulfill Roosevelt's promise of a New Deal revival after the war. See Samuel Lubell, *The Future of American Politics*, 30, which describes such Democrats as not necessarily coming from border states (although Truman did) but primarily as representing a certain "state of mind." The border state Democrats supported Roosevelt's foreign policy but were "middle of the roaders on domestic issues."

21. Harry S. Truman, *Memoirs*, 1: 9-13; quoted in William E. Leuctenburg, *In the Shadow of FDR*, 12.

22. Hamby, *Man of the People*, Chapter 24; Susan M. Hartmann, *Truman and the 80th Congress*, Chapter 4.

23. Robert H. Ferrell, ed., *Off the Record*, 122; quoted in Irwin Ross, *The Loneliest Campaign*, 55-56; Clark M. Clifford oral history, by Jerry N. Hess, 192, HSTL.

24. "Annual Message to the Congress on the State of the Union," January 7, 1948, *Public Papers, 1948*, 1-10. Charles Murphy recalled that during the spring of 1948, the White House sent special messages to Congress every Monday morning based on the president's requests, but it expected little response. See Charles Murphy, Richard Neustadt, David Stowe and James Webb joint oral history, by Hugh Heclo and Anna Nelson, 42, HSTL.

25. Address in Kansas City at the 35th Division Reunion Memorial Service, June 7, 1947, *Public Papers, 1947*, 269-71; memorandum, Krug to Vernon Northrop, December 20, 1947, Subject File, Krug Papers.

26. *Public Papers, 1948*, 4, 48, 278, 388, 390, 461.

27. *Public Papers, 1948*, 420-21.

28. Ferrell, *Off the Record*, 389.

29. Harry S. Truman, *Memoirs*, vol. 2: *Years of Trial and Hope*, 178; David McCullough, *Truman*, 653-55.

30.See, for example, *Public Papers, 1948*, 505, 531-35; 539-41. See also Ross, *Loneliest Campaign*, 263, 266.

31. *Public Papers, 1948*, 539, 534.

32. Quoted in Hamby, *Beyond the New Deal*, 268.

33. The followers of these methods, who were influenced by the Harvard economist, Alvin Hansen, had gained ascendancy over those who preferred direct and detailed governmental social and economic planning as inspired by John Dewey and Thorstein Veblen. World War II, which liberals saw as a struggle between democracy and fascism, affected their attitudes toward overly centralized planning, which they feared would bring totalitarianism. Fear of totalitarianism, if deflation were to recur with the conversion to a peace-time economy, and high unemployment also played a part in liberals' advocating a full employment program at the end of the war. Roosevelt had appeared to embrace this philosophy when he used the Hansen-influenced National Resources Planning Board's report as a basis for the Economic Bill of Rights in his 1944 State of the Union Message and when he insisted that Henry A. Wallace, who figured prominently in this group, be his running mate in 1940. For a discussion of these two approaches and their respective advocates, see *ibid.*, 9-12.

34. Hamby, *Man of the People*, 372; Margaret Truman, ed., *Where the Buck Stops*, 16; Ferrell, ed., *Off the Record*, 379, 68. Clark Clifford reportedly told David Lilienthal that Truman liked neither "progressive" nor "liberal" but

preferred "forward looking" to describe his policies and beliefs; see David E. Lilienthal, *Journals of David Lilienthal*, vol. 2: *The Atomic Energy Years*, 434.

35. Ferrell, ed., *Off the Record*, 35; Robert Underhill, *The Truman Persuasion*, 182-83. See also Clark Clifford, *Counsel to the President*, 77; William E. Pemberton, *Harry S. Truman*, 65. For an interpretation of Truman's personality, which traces the president's feelings of insecurity to a number of negative experiences going back to his childhood, see Alonzo L. Hamby, "An American Democrat: A Reevaluation of the Personality of Harry S. Truman," *Political Science Quarterly* 106, no. 1 (199): 33-55.

36. Letter to Jonathan Daniels, November 7, 1951, Personal File, Box 309, PSF.

37. Rear platform remarks, Marfa, Texas, September 25, 1948, *Public Papers, 1948*, 571; *ibid.*, 504, 505.

38. *Ibid.*, 504.

39. Clinton Rossiter, *The American Presidency*, 163; Alonzo L. Hamby, *Liberalism and its Challengers*, 63; Alonzo L. Hamby, "Vital Center, Fair Deal, Liberal Political Economy" in *Harry S. Truman and the Fair Deal*, ed. Alonzo L. Hamby, 148-49; Clifford oral history, by Hess, 194-198.

40. Clifford, *Counsel to the President*, 195. See also Charles Murphy, et al. joint oral history, 41-42.

41. Truman, Memoirs, 1: 484; Gale Peterson, "Truman and the Independent Regulatory Commissions, 1945-1952" (Ph.D. diss., University of Maryland, 1973), 15-16.

42. Charles S. Murphy oral history, by Jerry N. Hess, 536, HSTL; Clifford, *Counsel to the President*, 77. See also Harvard Sitkoff, "Years of the Locust," in ed. Richard S. Kirkendall, *The Truman Period As a Research Field*, 99; Alonzo L. Hamby, *Liberalism and Its Challengers*, 71; Alonzo L. Hamby, "The Mind and Character of Harry S. Truman," in ed. Michael J. Lacey, *The Truman Presidency*, 51.

43. Clifford oral history, by Hess, 203. For the genesis and work of this group, which began meeting in January 1947, see Clifford oral history, 186-92, 197-98; Cabell Phillips, *The Truman Presidency*, 162-65; Ken Hechler, *Working with Truman*, 60-61; Pemberton, *Harry S. Truman*, 108-109; Patrick Anderson, *The Presidents' Men*, 116. Clifford, who had recently become Truman's chief executive advisor, was chosen to pass along the group's ideas to the president.

44. Murphy oral history, 47-48. Clifford, who became Truman's chief speech writer for the campaign, rewrote and discussed with other members ideas for a 43-page memorandum outlining predictions and suggesting tactics for winning. Among its recommendations that were followed were making "Winning the West" the top priority, vigorously attacking the Republican controlled Eightieth Congress for failing to act in the interests of the people, stressing pocketbook issues and pushing a strong liberal program to woo Wallace

supporters. Most of the ideas in the memo came from an earlier one written by James G. Rowe, a Washington lawyer and former administrative assistant to Franklin Roosevelt. The memo has been regarded as having strongly influenced Democratic strategy in 1948; however, Charles Murphy believes it had little importance and that Truman would have followed the same course in any case. See Hechler, *Working with Truman*, 61-63; Clark Clifford, "Annals of Government," *The New Yorker*, March 25, 1991, 54; Clifford, *Counsel to the President*, 189-94; Ferrell, *Harry S. Truman*, 274-75; Allen Yarnell, *Democrats and Progressives*, 28-61; Murphy et al. joint oral history, 57-58.

45. Truman, *Memoirs*, 1:226-27; see also Hamby, "Mind and Character of Harry S. Truman," 44.

46. Ferrell, ed., *Off the Record*, 29; Hamby, Man of the People, 298; Hamby, "Mind and Character of Harry S. Truman," 42-43.

47. Richard E. Neustadt, *Presidential Power*, 172; Murphy oral history, 110-11; Ferrell, *Harry S. Truman*, 187.

48. Ferrell, *Harry S. Truman*, 188-192; Hamby, *Man of the People*, 305; Murphy et al. joint oral history, 61.

49. Francis H. Heller, ed., *The Truman White House*, xxi; Clifford oral history, by Hess, 202; Murphy oral history, 538-39.

50. Quoted in Neustadt, *Presidential Power*, 177. See also Murphy oral history, 253-54.

51. Murphy oral history, 112-17. See also Ferrell, *Harry S. Truman*, 291; Harold F. Gosnell, *Truman's Crises*, 546; Neustadt, *Presidential Power*, 173.

52. The Corps of Engineers had begun river and harbor improvement construction in 1824 under the Rivers and Harbor Act and had been involved in flood control work before the federal government claimed responsibility with the 1936 Flood Control Act.

53. Maass, *Muddy Waters*, 188-90, 215; *The Hoover Commission Report on Organization of the Executive Branch*, 280; U.S. Army Corps of Engineers, "The History of the U.S. Army Corps of Engineers" (Washington, D.C., January 1986), 53-54.

54. The secretary of the army was not a member of the cabinet.

55. See Robert de Roos and Arthur A. Maass, "The Lobby that Can't Be Licked," *Harper's Magazine* 99 (July-December 1949): 214-25, 29-30.

56. Arthur A. Maass, "Congress and Water Resources," *The American Political Science Review* 44 (1950): 580-81; Maass, *Muddy Waters*, 62-102, 215.

57. Quoted in Maass, *Muddy Waters*, 46-48.

58. Stephen K. Bailey and Howard D. Samuel, *Congress at Work*, 168-69; Maass, *Muddy Waters*, 21-30; Golzé, *Reclamation in the United States*, 135-40.

59. Golzé, *Reclamation in the United States*, 297.

60. David Arlin Kathka, "Bureau of Reclamation in the Truman Administration" (Ph.D. diss., University of Missouri, 1976), 114-15.

61. *Annual Report of the Secretary of the Interior, 1946*, 77.

62. Quoted in Kathka, "Bureau of Reclamation," 26.

63. See de Roos and Maass, "The Lobby that Can't Be Licked," 21-30.

64. Golzé, *Reclamation in the United States*, 139-40; memorandum, Frederick N. Ferguson to James C. Bradley, Reclamation: Jones Subcommittee to Study Civil Works folder, Office Files of Under Secretary Richard Searles, RG 48.

65. Maass, "Congress and Water Resources," 581.

66. "Where Is Our Power Coming from?" address delivered before the Region VIII Meeting of the National Rural Electric Cooperative Association, Tulsa, Oklahoma, October 20, 1949, Box 1, Douglas G. Wright Papers, HSTL; *Annual Report of the Secretary of the Interior, 1946*, 16; "United States Department of the Interior Code of Federal Regulations," Organization and Methods, General, 1937-1953, RG 48; untitled draft report, February 12, 1949, Box 9, C. Girard Davidson Papers, HSTL.

67. Kathka, "Bureau of Reclamation," 116-121; Waltrip, "Public Power During the Truman Administration," 35-36.

68. Memorandum for the President of the United States, Longhand Notes, undated, 1953 folder, PSF; Ferrell, ed., *Off the Record*, 233; Hamby, *Beyond the New Deal*, 73.

69. Waltrip, "Public Power During the Truman Administration," 36; Speech, for Public Ownership League of the State of Washington, October 12, 1946, Speech and Article File, Krug Papers; Kathka, "Bureau of Reclamation," 116-121.

70. Ferrell, ed., *Off the Record*, 233; memorandum for the President of the United States, Longhand Notes, undated, 1953 folder, PSF. See newspaper clippings, Department of the Interior Subject File, Oscar Chapman, Dale E. Doty Papers, HSTL; *The New York Times*, November 11, 1949, 1:2.

71. Ferrell, ed., *Off the Record*, 233; In 1946, Truman had been about to tell Secretary Krug that he was going to make Chapman under secretary when Krug recommended the promotion. See *ibid.*, 87.

72. Truman had passed over Chapman to appoint Krug in 1946. Chapman is thought by some historians to have been a member of the "Monday Night Group." See, for example, Underhill, *The Truman Persuasion*, 178 and Bert Cochran, *Harry Truman and the Crisis Presidency*, 216-17. But Clifford said in 1971 that Chapman's office of under secretary made him a "little too high up" for the group. He said there had been no effort to bring in leading liberals like Chapman because the participants wanted to keep their meetings secret and because they felt they could work effectively together; see Clifford oral history, by Hess, 192-93. See also newspaper clipping, *Washington Star*, November 20, 1949, Department of the Interior Subject File, Oscar Chapman, Doty Papers.

73. Oscar L. Chapman, "Movie Tone News statement," November 15, 1949, Department of the Interior Subject File, Oscar Chapman, Doty Papers.

74. *New York Times*, November 12, 1949, 1:6; 26:2; Thomas Sancton, "Gentle Crusader," *The Nation*, March 5, 1949, 267-68; newspaper clipping, *The Anderson Independent*, (Anderson, SC), May 17, 1951, Administrative General, Power Development-General, RG 48.

75. William E. Warne oral history, by Niel M. Johnson, 11-14, HSTL; Kathka, "Bureau of Reclamation," 114. Chapman finally appointed an under secretary in April 1951.

76. Richard L. Neuberger, "Daring Young Man from the West," *The Nation*, January 29, 1949, 129-30.

77. *Ibid.*; letter to Theodore T. Wing from C. Girard Davidson, June 29, 1949, File 1-310, Administrative General, Power Development-Administrative, RG 48.

78. Department of Agriculture, *Rural Lines*, 35-36; Truman, *Memoirs*, 1: 326. In an unsent 1950 letter to Jonathan Daniels, who was then finishing his book, *The Man of Independence*, Truman wrote critically of Roosevelt's cabinet. He called Secretary Wickard "a nice man who never learned how his department was set up." See Ferrell, ed., *Off the Record*, 174.

79. Undated, "Longhand Notes," 1953 folder, PSF; Ferrell, *Harry S. Truman*, 188.

80. Murphy et al. joint oral history, 36-37.

81. *Ibid.*, 1-3, 56; Ferrell, *Harry S. Truman*, 192-93.

82. David B. Truman, *The Governmental Process*, 428-31; Maass, *Muddy Waters*, 14-15, 109-10, 114; Bailey and Samuel, *Congress at Work*, 171-73.

83. Peterson, "President Harry S. Truman and the Independent Regulatory Commissions," 25-26.

84. Twentieth Century Fund, *Electric Power and Government Policy*, 68-76; Charles S. Rhyne, "Municipal Interest in the Work of the Federal Power Commission," *The George Washington Law Review* 14 (December 1945): 247-53; *Annual Report of the Federal Power Commission, 1946*, 26, 32-33, 37; Maass, *Muddy Waters*, 189-90.

85. Burton K. Wheeler, "The Federal Power Commission as an Agency of Congress," *The George Washington Law Review* 14 (December 1945): 1-4.

86. Peterson, "Truman and the Independent Regulatory Commissions," 168-71.

87. *Ibid.*, 171-74; Federal Power Commission Files, Subject File-Personnel, Doty Papers, HSTL.

88. Peterson, "Truman and the Independent Regulatory Commissions," 8.

89. Quoted in *Congress and the Nation*, 812.

90. *Congressional Quarterly* 4 (1948): 30, 34; Waltrip, "Public Power During the Truman Administration," 50-76.

91. Kirk H. Porter and Donald Bruce Johnson, comps., *National Party Platforms, 1840-1956*, 434-52.

92. These committees were the House and Senate Committees on Public Works and the House and Senate Committees on Interior and Insular Affairs, for authorization of projects, and the Appropriations Committees of both Houses, together with their Interior and Civil Functions Subcommittees, for the granting of monies.

93. See David R. Mayhew, *Party Loyalty Among Congressmen*, 128-45.

94. Ferrell, ed., *Off the Record*, 168, 201

95. Letter, George A. Dondero to Herb M. Moffen, December 6, 1951, File 310, Administrative General, Power Development-General, RG 48; *Congressional Quarterly* 5 (1949): 26-34, 90-91, 94-95; Maass, *Muddy Waters*, 46.

96. Maass, *Muddy Waters*, 46; Arthur Morgan, *Dams and Other Disasters: A Century of the Army Corps of Engineers in Civil Works* (Boston, 1971), 69-76.

97. Schoeppel charged that Chapman had belonged to subversive organizations until 1946 when he signed the oath. Chapman denied such membership and said it was common for his department personnel to cross out the anti-communist section since they had already taken a "basic loyalty oath." See Department of the Interior, Subject File, Oscar Chapman, Doty Papers.

98. Memorandum, William Warne to Acting Director, Program Staff, "President's Economic Report," December 20, 1950, Division of Power Files, General Power Policy File, RG 48; *Public Papers, 1951*, 61, 86. Alonzo Hamby points out that the Korean War contributed to reform in other areas, including forcing the army to implement its integration policy; see "Vital Center," 156-59.

99. *Public Papers, 1949*, 1-7; memorandum, The Director of Programs and Finance to the files, November 9, 1948, Administration and Planning Conferences and Visits, Records of the Bureau of Reclamation, RG 115, NA.

Chapter 3. The Opening Battle: The Valley Authority Question

1. *Public Papers, 1948*, 322. The Seattle speech to the Washington State Press Club was given on June 10, at the beginning of Truman's "non-political, non-partisan" western tour; see also Kathka, "The Bureau of Reclamation in the Truman Administration," 123.

2. *Public Papers, 1949*, 5.

3. "Statement on the Federal Inter-Agency Committee and Its Associated Committees," Natural Resources folder, Box 25, Murphy Files, HST Papers; Maass, *Muddy Waters*, 101, 107-109; *Annual Report of the Federal Power Commission, 1946*, 111-12.

4. Ferrell, "Water in the Missouri Valley," 98; *Annual Report of the Federal Power Commission, 1946*, 109.

5. *Annual Report of the Federal Power Commission, 1946*, 110.

6. *Annual Report of the Federal Power Commission, 1949*, 150-51.

7. *Hoover Commission Report*, 282-83.

8. Letter, Straus to Acting Secretary Chapman, February 23, 1946, File 8-3, Administrative General, Columbia Basin, RG 48.

9. Straus had at first planned to make an even stronger attack on valley authorities in his speech, but changed his mind after Assistant Secretary of the Interior Warner W. Gardner cautioned him that it was all right to say that valley authorities would be necessary if inter-agency cooperation failed, but Straus should not "either attack the proponents of valley authorities or indicate that this would be a disastrous result." See memorandum, Gardner to Straus, August 27, 1946 and report, "Bureau of Reclamation, Department of the Interior, No. 44," September 13, 1946, File 8-1, Organization and Methods-General, RG 48.

10. Letters, Weaver to Brigadier General R.A. Wheeler, December 31, 1947, Wheeler to Weaver, January 28, 1948, File 800-92, Records of the Office of the Chief of Engineers, RG 77, NA.

11. Senate, *Hearings before the Subcommittee of the Committee on Appropriations on H.R. 3734 (Civil Functions) for Fiscal 1950*, 514-15, 751-52, 774; Senate, *Hearings before the Subcommittee on Appropriations, Making Appropriations for Civil Functions . . . for the Fiscal Year 1951*, 501-02.

12. Report, "Organizing for the Development of the Columbia Valley," undated, Natural Resources, Columbia Valley Administration folder, Stephen J. Spingarn Files, HST Papers.

13. Letter, Truman to Beauford H. Jester, February 26, 1949, OF 284, HST Papers.

14. Letters, James E. Webb to Truman, December 30, 1948, Truman to Krug, January 13, 1949, OF 360A, HST Papers; memorandum, Truman to Krug, March 21, 1949, Subject File, Congressional correspondence re secretary's visits to Pacific Northwest, 1950, Box 11, Davidson Papers; letter (unsent), Chapman to Senator Harry P. Cain, March 31, 1950, *ibid*.

15. *New York Times*, January 25, 1949, 3.

16. *Ibid.*, February 17, 1949, 33; February 14, 1949, 35; March 30, 1949, 6.

17. *New York Times*, January 25, 1949, 3, February 14, 1949, 35; report, "Who Finances C.V.A. Opposition?" undated, Office Files of C. Girard Davidson, RG 48.

18. Teletype, J. W. Rupley to J. Otis Garber, February 14, 1949, CVA: Legislative Drafts, Memoranda Re Columbia Valley Administration folder, Spingarn Files, HST Papers.

19. Letter, Truman to Lew Wallace, January 31, 1949, OF 360A, HST Papers.

20. Richard L. Neuberger, "Daring Young Man from the West," *The Nation*, January 29, 1949, 129-30.

21. Memorandum, Davidson to Murphy, January 28, 1949, Columbia Valley Authority folder, Murphy Files, HST Papers; *New York Times*, February 14, 1949, 35; memorandum, C. Girard Davidson to Charles S. Murphy, January 28, 1949, Murphy Files, HST Papers; letter, Hugh B. Mitchell to Truman, January 26, 1949 and telegram, Earl Cole, Secretary of State, Washington, to Truman, January 25, 1949, OF 360A, HST Papers; various letters and telegrams to the president from labor organizations, rural electric cooperatives, Farmers' Union, Granges and Democratic Party Organizations, *ibid.* and in Columbia Valley Administration folder, Chapman Papers.

22. Letter, Truman to Krug, January 13, 1949, File 1-12, Administrative General, Instructions and Orders, RG 48; memorandum, David E. Bell to Truman, March 28, 1949, CVA: Legislative Drafts, Memoranda Re Columbia Valley Administration folder, Spingarn Files, HST Papers.

23. David E. Lilienthal, *The Journals of David E. Lilienthal*, vol. 1: *The TVA Years*, 493-94; draft of letter, Paul Raver to Secretary Ickes, February 12, 1946, File 1-310, Administrative General, Power Development, Bonneville Project-General, RG 48.

24. Memorandum, Bell to Truman, March 28, 1949, CVA: Legislative Drafts, Memoranda Re Columbia Valley Administration folder, Spingarn Files, HST Papers.

25. Memorandum, Michael Straus to Herbert J. Slaughter, February 28, 1949, Office Files of the Secretary of the Interior, Bureau of Reclamation, 1946-49, RG 48.

26. Memoranda, Bell to Murphy, February 1, 1949 and February 15, 1949 and William R. Davlin to Bell, February 11, 1949, Columbia Valley Authority folder, Murphy Files, HST Papers; memorandum, Bell to Truman, March 28, 1949, CVA: Legislative Drafts, Memoranda Re Columbia Valley Administration folder, Spingarn Files, HST Papers.

27. Memorandum, Davlin to Bell, February 11, 1947, Columbia Valley Authority folder, Murphy Files, HST Papers; letter, Brannan to Frank Pace, Jr., March 14, 1949, Office Files of Riggs Sheppard, Records of the Rural Electrification Administration, RG 221, NA. See also memorandum, Bell to Truman, March 28, 1949, CVA: Legislative Drafts, Memoranda Re Columbia Valley Administration folder, Spingarn Files, HST Papers.

28. Letter, Mitchell to Truman, March 28, 1949, OF, 360A, HST Papers.

29. *Congressional Quarterly* 5 (1949): 763; *Congressional Record*, 81st Cong., 1st sess., 1949, 95: 4827.

30. *Congressional Record*, 81st Cong., 1st sess., 1949, 95: 4740, 4742.

31. The change in name had been suggested by Arthur M. Piper a staff scientist for the Department's Geological Survey in Oregon, to R.F. Bessey of the Pacific Northwest Field Committee. Piper argued that the proposed agency should be "designated by almost any other word" so that it would have a better chance to be "considered on its merits." In recommending the change to his superior, C. Girard Davidson, Bessey cited Piper's "psychological reasons"; see memorandum, March 1, 1949, Subject File, CVA unclassified material, Davidson Papers.

32. "Special Message to the Congress Recommending Establishment of a Columbia Valley Administration," April 13, 1949, *Public Papers, 1949*, 208-13; Lilienthal, *TVA: Democracy on the March*, xiv-xviii; letter, David Bell to John J. Doherty, March 18, 1950, Columbia Valley Administration folder, David E. Bell Files, HST Papers.

33. While the administration's version provided for Civil Service coverage of employees, these bills exempted personnel from it, but provided similar protection. See letter, Bell to Robert Greenleaf, April 27, 1949, Columbia Valley Administration folder, Bell Files, HST Papers.

34. Joint Press Release, Department of the Interior and Department of the Army, April 19, 1949, Press Releases, RG 48.

35. The Corps of Engineers plan was named for Colonel Theron D. Weaver, division engineer, while the bureau plan carried the name of R. J. Newell, regional director.

36. Letter, Davidson to Straus, December 22, 1948, File 8-3, Administrative General, Projects-Columbia Basin folder, RG 48.

37. Memoranda, Straus to Krug, January 1, 1949, Davidson to Straus, January 14, 1949, Office Files of the Secretary of the Interior, Bureau of Reclamation 1946-49, RG 48.

38. Letter, Robert P. Patterson, Secretary of War, to Krug, June 10, 1947, File 800.92, Columbia River, Oregon, Washington, RG 77; identical letters, Truman to Krug, Truman to Royall, June 1, 1948, Floods-Pacific Northwest, OF 83, HST Papers; Maass, *Muddy Waters*, 119-21; memorandum, Acting Commissioner of Reclamation to Krug, July 1, 1948, File 8-3, Administrative General, Bureau of Reclamation Projects-Columbia Basin, RG 48.

39. Memorandum, Truman to Krug, April 12, 1949, Columbia Valley Authority folder, Murphy Files, HST Papers; letters, Truman to Royall, April 18, 1949, Truman to Krug, April 18, 1949, Floods-Pacific Northwest, OF 83, HST Papers.

40. Speech and Press Conference of March 2, 1949, Speech and Article File, Krug Papers.

41. U.S. Senate, Committee on Public Works, *Hearings, Bills Dealing with the Development of the Water Resources of the Columbia River Basin and the*

Establishment of a Columbia Valley Administration, and for Other Purposes, 81st Cong., 1st sess., Part 1, 271-75.

42. Senate Committee on Public Works, *Hearings, Bills Dealing with the Establishment of a Columbia Valley Administration*, 81st Cong., 1st sess., Part 1, 339-44. See also *New York Times*, January 25, 1949, 1; memorandum, Krug to Heads of Bureaus and Offices, January 19, 1949, File 1-12, Administrative General, Instructions and Orders, RG 48; *Congressional Quarterly* 5 (1949): 764.

43. House of Representatives, Committee on Public Works, *Hearings, Bills to Reorganize and Consolidate Certain Federal Functions and thereby Secure More Effective Administration by Establishing a Columbia Valley Administration.*, 81st Cong., 1st sess., Part 1, 655-63, 771, 776; Senate, Committee on Public Works, *Hearings, Bills Dealing with the Establishment of a Columbia Valley Administration*, 81st Cong., 1st sess., Part 1, 1045-48.

44. *Ibid.*, 257, 263, 376, 381, 422, 440; Senate Committee on Public Works, *Hearings, Bills Dealing with the Establishment of a Columbia Valley Administration*, 81st Cong., 1st sess., Part 1, 426, 504, 579, 788; Elmo Richardson, *Dams, Parks & Politics*, 32.

45. House Committee on Public Works, *Hearings, Bills for Establishing a Columbia Valley Administration*, 81st Cong., 1st sess., Part 1, 305.

46. *Ibid.*, 717-24, 289-92, 324-38, 362-564; Senate Committee on Public Works, *Hearings, Bills Dealing with the Establishment of a Columbia Valley Administration*, 81st Cong., 1st sess., Part 1, 622-43, 752, 943-44.

47. Letters, Charles Sawyer to Dennis Chavez, May 27, 1949, Sawyer to William M. Whittington, May 27, 1949, General Correspondence File, Records of the Department of Commerce, RG 40, NA; House Committee on Public Works, *Hearings, Bills for Establishing a Columbia Valley Administration*, 81st Cong., 1st sess., Part 1, 31-35, 747, 749-50. Senate Committee on Public Works, *Hearings, Bills Dealing with the Establishment of a Columbia Valley Administration*, 81st Cong., 1st sess., Part I, 945, 1045-48.

48. Davidson sent Peet a copy of Brannan's testimony and pointed out that the secretary had "made his position quite clear that he and the Department of Agriculture are for CVA." Letter, Davidson to Peet, August 2, 1949, CVA Unclassified Material, Box 9, Davidson Papers; newspaper clipping, *The Oregonian*, July 21, 1949.

49. Memorandum, Elmer Staats to Murphy, December 8, 1949, Natural Resources folder, Correspondence and General File, Murphy Files, HST Papers; memoranda, W. G. Hoyt, to Warne, June 30, 1949, Luce to H. B. McCoy, June 1, 1949, John D. Davis for Norman A. Stoll to W. G. Hoyt, October 17, 1949, File 1-318, Administrative General, River Valley Authorities-General, RG 48.

50. Memoranda, Straus to Krug, July 1, 1949; Walton Seymour to Krug, July 18, 1949, File 8-3, Administrative General, Bureau of Reclamation Projects-Columbia Basin, RG 48.

51. Letter, Krug to Truman, July 20, 1949, File 8-3, Administrative General, Bureau of Reclamation Projects-Columbia Basin, RG 48; telephone call, Krug to Davidson, April 12, 1949, Conference File, Krug papers; memorandum, Straus to Krug, July 1, 1949, File 8-3, Administrative General, Bureau of Reclamation Projects-Columbia Basin, RG 48; letter, Krug to Lewis A. Pick, June 16, 1949, File 800.92, Columbia River, RG 77; memorandum, Krug to Straus, July 20, 1949, *ibid.* Under the Flood Control Act of 1944, the secretary of the interior was required to comment on the army's report before it was sent to Congress, and the secretary of the army was likewise required to comment on interior's.

52. Memorandum, Bell to Murphy, June 29, 1949, Bell Files, HST Papers.

53. *Congressional Quarterly* 6 (1950): 609.

54. Senate, Committee on Public Works, *Hearings, Bills Dealing with the Establishment of a Columbia Valley Administration,* 81st Cong., 1st sess., Part 1, 939; memorandum, Straus to Krug, July 1, 1949, File 8-3, Administrative General, Bureau of Reclamation Projects-Columbia Basin, RG 48; letter, Murphy to Dr. J. R. Binijon, September 14, 1949, OF 360, HST Papers; letters, Truman to Krug, August 30, 1949, Warne to Senator Dennis Chavez, August 31, 1949, *ibid.*

55. Letter, Kirby Billingsley to Chapman, December 8, 1949, Office Files of Secretary of the Interior Oscar Chapman, 1933-53, Bureau of Reclamation, RG 48.

56. January 4, 1950, *Public Papers, 1950,* 8; *Electrical World,* February 13, 1950, 6; Interior Department Press Release, February 2, 1950, File 800.92, Columbia River folder, RG 77.

57. *Congressional Quarterly,* VI (1950), 609-11.

58. "Special Message to the Congress Following the Signing of the Rivers and Harbors Bill," May 22, 1950, *Public Papers, 1950,* 429-30.

59. Address at the Dedication of the Grand Coulee Dam, May 11, 1950, *Public Papers, 1950,* 373; letter, Chapman to Taylor, May 19, 1950, Reading File, 1950, Chapman Papers.

60. *New York Times,* May 13, 1950, 4, August 11, 1950, 27.

61. Letter, Truman to Martin C. Smith, April 5, 1945, Senatorial Papers, TVA-1945 folder, HST Papers; *Congressional Record,* 79th Cong., 1st sess., 1945, 91: 1126.

62. *Public Papers, 1946,* 34, 61; letter, Murray to Truman, April 24, 1945, Missouri Valley Authority, OF 201A, HST Papers; *Public Papers, 1945,* 386-87, 391-92.

63. Letter, Steelman to Richard Shipman, August 22, 1947, Box 768, OF 201A, HST Papers; President's News Conference of July 10, 1947, *Public Papers, 1947*, 330, 334; Special Message to Congress on Flood Control in the Missouri River Basin, *ibid.*, 334; *New York Times* clipping, July 11, 1947, Records of the President's Water Resources Policy Commission, Box 61, HST Papers; St. Louis *Post Dispatch* clipping, July 13, 1947, OF 201, HST Papers.

64. Pencilled notation by Truman, Ickes to Truman, November 23, 1945, Columbia Valley Authority, OF 360A, HST Papers; The President's News Conference at Tiptonville, Tennessee, October 8, 1945, *Public Papers, 1945*, 386; St. Louis *Post Dispatch* clippings, July 13, 15, 1947, OF 201, HST Papers.

65. Letter, Senator Harry S. Truman to G. L. DeLapp, March 6, 1944, Flood Control folder, Senatorial Files, HST Papers; Murphy et al. joint oral history, 39.

66. Whiteside, "Harry S. Truman and James E. Murray," 35-40; *Congressional Record*, 81st Cong., 1st sess., 1949, 95: 1707; The President's News Conference of April 14, 1949, *Public Papers, 1949*, 215; Address in Casper, Wyoming, May 9, 1950, Speech at Pasco, Washington, May 10, 1950, Address at the Dedication of the Grand Coulee Dam, May 11, 1950, Speech at Fort Peck Dam, May 13, 1950, *Public Papers, 1950*, 323-24, 357, 372, 392-93.

67. Letter, Murray to Truman, July 23, 1951, OF 201, HST Papers.

68. Letter to the President, C.I.O., on the Flood Control Problem in the Missouri River Basin, August 3, 1951, *Public Papers, 1951*, 444-46.

69. Draft, letter, Truman to Murray, undated, OF 201, HST Papers.

70. Letter, Murray to Truman, July 23, 1951, OF 201, HST Papers; memorandum, Bell to Murphy, October 10, 1951, OF 201B, HST Papers.

71. Memorandum, Bell to Murphy, October 10, 1951, OF 201B, HST Papers.

72. Statement by the President Upon Signing Executive Order Establishing the Missouri Basin Survey Commission, January 3, 1952, *Public Papers, 1952-53*, 7-9; Statement by the President Upon Appointing the Members of the Missouri Basin Survey Commission, February 9, 1952, *ibid.*, 144; letter, H. M. Shooshan, Jr. to Richard Searles, January 8, 1952, Office File of Under Secretary Searles, RG 48.

73. See Whiteside, "Harry S. Truman and James E. Murray." Whiteside argues that Truman demonstrated his shrewdness as a politician by managing to get rid of the Missouri Valley Authority idea; keeping Murray's friendship; and retaining the Pick-Sloan Plan, which he had wanted to do all along.

74. U.S. Missouri Basin Survey Commission, *Missouri: Land and Water*, 8-9, 229, 241-42, 250.

75. *Hoover Commission Report*, 271, 265.

76. *Hoover Commission Report*, 271, 252-53; Maass, *Muddy Waters*, 113.

77. *Hoover Commission Report*, 285; *New York Times*, April 18, 1949, 18:1; Maass, *Muddy Waters*, 112-13.

78. Comments of the Department of the Interior on the recommendations of the Commission on Organization of the Executive Branch of the Government Concerning the Department of the Interior, May 26, 1949, Department of the Interior Files, Hoover Commission Report, Box 8, Doty Papers, HSTL; memorandum, the Secretary to Bureaus and Offices, June 14, 1949, Subject File, Krug Papers.

79. Senate, *Hearings on Appropriations for Civil Functions for Fiscal 1951*, 514-515.

80. *New York Times*, April 18, 1949, 18:1.

81. Quoted in Maass, *Muddy Waters*, 117; see also *New York Times*, March 22, 1950, 4:3, *Electrical World*, April 21, 1952, 113.

82. *New York Times*, April 9, 1949, 28, May 27, 1949, 1.

83. "The President's News Conference of April 17, 1952," *Public Papers, 1952-53*, 275-76; *New York Times*, April 15, 1952, 7, April 24, 1952, 22.

84. *Electrical World*, April 21, 1952, 113; *ibid.*, April 24, 1952, 22; Waltrip, "Public Power During the Truman Administration," 126-27. Margaret Truman has called her father's devotion to the Democratic Party and Missouri his "cardinal virtue"; Margaret Truman, *Harry S. Truman*, 121; see also Mary H. Hinchey, "The Frustration of the New Deal Revival" (Ph.D. diss., University of Missouri, 1965), 61.

85. *A Water Policy for the American People: The Report of the President's Water Resources Policy Commission*, 1: 49.

86. *Ibid*.

87. House of Representatives, Committee on Interior and Insular Affairs, *Hearings before the Subcommittee on Irrigation and Reclamation on an Interpretation of the Recommendations of the President's Water Resources Policy Commission*, 82nd Cong., 1st sess., 65-66.

88. *Public Utilities Fortnightly*, March 13, 1952, 373; *New York Times*, February 18, 1952, 37.

89. Memorandum, Lawton to Truman, April 4, 1951, President's Water Resources Policy Commission folder, OF 2393A, HST Papers; letter, Truman to N.T. Veatch, July 26, 1951, Folder 1949-53, OF 201, HST Papers; memorandum, Northrop to Warne, May 7, 1951, File 1-318, Administrative General, River Valley Authorities, RG 48; memorandum, J. C. Bradley to Joel D. Wolfsohn, September 12, 1951, *ibid.*; letter, Chapman to Frederick J. Lawton, July 31, 1951, File 1-246, Administrative General, Administrative Committees-Water Resources, RG 48.

90. Letters, Cooke to Truman, August 1, 1951 and October 24, 1951, Truman to Cooke, August 1, 1951, President's Water Resources Policy Commission folder, OF 2393A, HST Papers.

91. Letter, Cooke to Truman, August 1, 1951, *ibid.*

92. Letter, Cooke to Truman, August 13, 1951, *ibid.*

93. Letter, Truman to Cooke, November 19, 1951, *ibid.*; Press Release, February 18, 1952, Commission Report and Recommendations, 1950-51, President's Water Resources Policy Commission Records (hereafter cited as PWRPC Records), HSTL.

94. Draft of letter, Lawton to Truman, August 8, 1952, OF 2393, HST Papers; memorandum, Melvin E. Scheidt to Staats, February 12, 1952, Unit 943, Review of the President's WRPC Report, General, 1952, Division of Fiscal Analysis, 1939-52, Records of the Bureau of the Budget, RG 51, NA.

95. Memorandum, Lawton to Truman, May 21, 1952, OF 2393, HST Papers.

96. Missouri Basin Survey Commission, *Missouri: Land and Water*, 9, 11-12.

97. *New York Times*, December 2, 1952, December 31, 1952, 7.

98. Newspaper clippings, *Oregon Journal*, December 23, 1952, *Oregonian*, December 28, 1952, *Astorian Evening Budget*, December 18, 1952, *Seattle Times*, December 21, 1952, all in File 1-310 Administrative General, Power Development-Pacific Northwest, RG 48; *Electrical World*, January 19, 1953, 5, December 29, 1952, 52.

99. Special Message to the Congress on the Nation's Land and Water Resources, January 19, 1953, *Public Papers, 1952-53*, 1208-15.

100. *Ibid.*, 1213.

Chapter 4. Major Campaigns: Steam Plants and Transmission Lines

1. Carl D. Thompson, *Public Ownership*, 371; Vennard, *Government in the Power Business*, 37-38.

2. Vennard, *Government in the Power Business*, 35-40.

3. *Annual Report of the Secretary of the Interior, 1946*, 17-18.

4. *Ibid.*, 20.

5. *Electrical World*, January 16, 1950, 43; see also *ibid.*, February 14, 1948, 69, November 20, 1948, 75; Vennard, *Government in the Power Business*, 139.

6. C. Herman Pritchett, *The Tennessee Valley Authority*, 78.

7. Glaeser, *Public Utilities*, 553; Vennard, *Government in the Power Business*, 198; Pritchett, *The Tennessee Valley Authority*, 78.

8. Lilienthal, *TVA: Democracy on the March*, 18-19; *Electrical World*, January 10, 1948, 13, February 7, 1948, 5-6, 79; Pritchett, *The Tennessee Valley Authority*, 76-78.

9. *Congressional Quarterly* 4 (1948): 111.

10. *Ibid.*, 110-12.

11. "Statement by the President Upon Signing the Government Corporations Appropriations Act, June 30, 1948," *Public Papers, 1948*, 389; *Congressional Quarterly* 4 (1948), 354; *Congressional Record*, 80th Cong., 2d sess., 1948, 94: 8282; Hartmann, *Truman and the 80th Congress*, 143-45.

12. *Electrical World*, November 13, 1948, 11.

13. *Congressional Quarterly* 5 (1949): 233.

14. *Congressional Record*, 81st Cong., 1st sess., 1949, 95: 1220-22, 1246-50, 1257.

15. *Ibid.*, 1247, 1222.

16. *Ibid.*, 4456, 4458.

17. *Ibid.*, 4458.

18. *Congressional Record.* 81st Cong., 2d sess., 96: 1750; *Congressional Quarterly* 6 (1950): 110-11; *Electrical World*, February 13, 1950, 65, February 27, 1950, 74.

19. *Electrical World*, March 27, 1948, 65, February 27, 1950, 74.

20. *Public Utilities Fortnightly*, February 2, 1950, 168; *Congressional Quarterly* 7 (1951): 115-19, 139-41; "Annual Budget Message to the Congress, Fiscal year 1951," January 9, 1950, *Public Papers: Truman, 1950*, 90; Press Release, President's Office, August 28, 1950, OF 42, HST Papers.

21. *Congressional Record*, 82d. Cong., 2d sess., 1952, 98: 2669, 2673, 6462-73.

22. *Ibid.*, 6464, 6473.

23. *Ibid.*, 8356; U.S. Senate, *Appropriations, Budget Estimates, etc.*, 82d Cong., 2d sess., *Senate Document 169*, 577; Public Law 547, *Statutes at Large* 66 (1952): 645.

24. *Congress and the Nation*, 783, 798.

25. Vennard, *Government in the Power Business*, 121, 198-200; letter, Warner W. Gardner to Charles D. Curran, November 16, 1945, File 1-310, Administrative General, Power Development-Southwestern General, RG 48.

26. Letter, Willis T. Batcheller to C. Girard Davidson, February 17, 1951, File 1-310, Administrative General, Power Development- Pacific Northwest, RG 48.

27. Memorandum, McManus to Secretary of the Interior, February 1, 1951, *ibid.*; Craufurd D. Goodwin, ed., *Energy Policy in Perspective*, 189; House of Representatives, *Hearings before the Subcommittee of the Committee on Appropriations, Interior Department Appropriations for 1952*, 82d Cong., 1st sess., 20; *Electrical World*, January 15, 1951, 48; *New York Times*, April 1, 1950, 1, December 17, 1950, II, 1; House of Representatives, *Hearings on H.R. 5743* (Hells Canyon Project), 82d Cong., 2d sess., 125.

28. *House, Hearings on H.R. 5743*, 82d Cong., 2d sess., 125; *New York Times*, October 20, 1950, 24; *Electrical World*, October 23, 1950.

29. Memorandum, Warne to Chapman, February 12, 1951; letter, Magnuson to Batcheller, February 12, 1951, File 1-310, Administrative General, Power Development-Pacific Northwest, General, RG 48.

30. Memorandum, Marlett to Chapman, February 6, 1951, *ibid.*

31. Memorandum, Chapman to McManus, March 1, 1951, *ibid.*; *Electrical World*, March 12, 1951, 79.

32. Letter, Chapman to Representative Norris Poulson, November 21, 1951, File 1-310, Administrative General, Power Development-Pacific Northwest General, RG 48; letter, Chapman to Senator Dennis Chavez, October 5, 1951, Reading File, Chapman Papers.

33. Letter, Willis T. Batcheller to Charles E. Wilson, October 10, 1951, File 1-310, Administrative General, Power Development- Administrative, RG 48; *New York Times*, September 29, 1951, 23, October 3, 1951, 49, November 2, 1951.

34. *New York Times*, October 25, 1950, 57; see also October 19, 1949, 19, October 31, 1949, 33, May 23, 1950, 43, May 27, 1950, 24, July 21, 1950, 26, July 27, 1950, 35, August 15, 1950, 37, October 29, 1950, II, 1, January 30, 1951, 32, October 7, 1951, 29, October 9, 1951, 46.

35. Annual Budget Message to the Congress: Fiscal year 1953, January 31, 1952, *Public Papers, 1953-53*, 89; House, *Hearings on Interior Department Appropriations for 1952*, 82d Cong., 1st sess., 178-79.

36. *Statutes at Large* 58 (1944): 890.

37. Edwin Vennard, *Government in the Power Business*, 121-23, 130-31.

38. Memorandum, Secretary Ickes to All Staffs of the Department of the Interior, January 3, 1946, Federal Power Policy File, Wolfsohn Papers; report, "Power Transmission," undated, Correspondence File, General, 1949-53, Power-Information, Chapman Papers.

39. *Annual Report of the Secretary of the Interior, 1946*, 20.

40. "Wheeling Contracts," July 1, 1950, Policy on Wheeling Arrangements File, Division of Power Files, RG 48.

41. Memorandum, Warne to Chapman, "Power Wheeling Contract Requirements," July 14, 1950, Policy on Wheeling Arrangements File, Division of Power Files, RG 48; R. C. Price, "Power Marketing Problems in Central Valley California," September 25, 1952, Natural Resources folder, Box 3, Ken Hechler Files, HST Papers.

42. Memorandum, Secretary Ickes to All Staffs of the Department of the Interior, January 3, 1946, Federal Power Policy File, Wolfsohn Papers; memorandum, Secretary of the Interior to the Administrators of Bonneville, Southeastern and Southwestern Power Administrations; Acting Director,

Division of Power and Commissioner, Bureau of Reclamation, July 14, 1950, File 1-310, Administrative General, Power Development, RG 48.

43. Letter to Senator Hayden on the Effect of Certain House Amendments on Hydroelectric Power Policy, June 11, 1951, *Public Papers, 1951*, 327; memorandum, Warne to Chapman, "Power Wheeling," July 14, 1950, Division of Power Files, RG 48.

44. Report, "Power Transmission," undated, Correspondence File, General, 1949-53, Chapman Papers; letter, Chapman to Senator George Smathers, March 4, 1952, Miscellaneous Records, Reading File, *ibid.*

45. Charles M. Coleman, *P.G. and E. of California*, 324-326; report, Robert B. Head, Consultant to the Central Valley Project Conference, September 8, 1945; letter, George Sehlmeyer, Chairman, Central Valley Project Conference to Truman, September 17, 1945, OF 620, HST Papers; *New York Times*, April 4, 1951, 45, July 16, 1951, 28.

46. Folsom Dam and Reservoir constituted a key unit in the Central Valley project; Department of the Interior Press Release, August 30, 1949, Reclamation, 1949-50 folder, General Office Files of Assistant Secretary C. G. Davidson, 1946-50, RG 48; memorandum, Frank Pace, Jr. to the President, August 5, 1949, Budget Bureau Memoranda and Letters on Water Policy Issues folder, Roundup of Information and Opinion, 1950-51, PWRPC Records; transmittal letter, Secretary Krug to Harry S. Truman, July 29, 1948, OF 620, HST Papers.

47. Senate, *Interior Department Appropriations Bill for 1949, Hearings before a Subcommittee of the Committee on Appropriations on H.R. 6705*, 80th Cong., 2d sess., 14-15, 19, 28, 916-17; Senate, *Interior Department Appropriations Bill for 1950, Hearings before a Subcommittee of the Committee on Appropriations on H.R. 3838*, 81st Cong., 1st sess., 2511.

48. Newspaper clipping, *San Francisco News*, March 30, 1949, Bureau of Reclamation, 1946-49, Office Files of Secretary of Interior Oscar Chapman, 1933-53, RG 48.

49. Senate, *Interior Appropriations Bill for 1948, Hearings before a Subcommittee of the Committee on Appropriations*, 80th Cong., 1st sess., 14.

50. Statement by the President on the Interior Department Appropriations Act, June 30, 1948, *Public Papers, 1948*, 390-91; Senate, *Hearings on Interior Department Appropriations Bill for 1949*, 80th Cong., 2d sess., 28, 917; House of Representatives, *Interior Appropriations Bill for 1950, Hearings before a Subcommittee of the Committee on Appropriations*, 81st Cong., 1st sess., 298-99, 1091.

51. Memoranda, Truman to Krug, February 25, 1949; Krug to Truman, March 2, 1949, OF 620, HST Papers.

52. Senate, *Hearings on Interior Department Appropriations Bill for 1950*, 81st Cong., 1st sess., 1815, 2509-10; Coleman, *P.G. and E. of California*, 329.

53. Senate, *Hearings on Interior Department Appropriations Bill for 1950*, 81st Cong., 1st sess., 2513, 2515; see also 2512, 2514.

54. Statement by the President on the Interior Department Appropriation Act, June 30, 1948, *Public Papers*, 1948, 390-91; House, *Hearings on Interior Department Appropriations Bill for 1950*, 81st Cong., 1st sess., 298.

55. Senate, *Hearings on Interior Department Appropriations Bill for 1950*, 81st Cong., 1st sess., 1148; *Congressional Quarterly* 5 (1949): 209-11, 761; Senate, *Appropriations Budget Estimates, Etc.*, 81st Cong., 1st sess., *Senate Document 125*, 107.

56. *Congressional Quarterly* 5 (1949): 209-12, 761.

57. Telephone call, Oscar Chapman to Secretary Krug, October 6, 1949, Conference File, Krug Papers.

58. *New York Times*, August 26, 1949, 3, August 28, 1949, III, 1.

59. House of Representatives, *Interior Department Appropriations for 1951, Hearings before a Subcommittee of the Committee on Appropriations*, 81st Cong., 2d sess., 698-99; telephone call, Davidson to Krug, October 8, 1949, Conference Record, Subject File, Krug Papers.

60. Federal Power Commission, "Statement Regarding Status of Investigation, Work, Surveys, Design, etc., on Proposed California Northwest Intertie," in House, *Hearings on Interior Department Appropriations Bill for 1952*, 81st Cong., 2d sess., 501-03; memoranda, Krug to Straus, March 25, 1949, Otis Beasley, Director of Budget and Finance, and Harry W. Rice, Finance Examiner, to Chapman, June 12, 1951, File 1-310, Administrative General, Power Development-Bonneville Project, RG 48.

61. Memorandum, Beasley and Rice to Chapman, June 12, 1951, File 1-310, Administrative General, Power Development-Bonneville Project, RG 48; Senate, *Appropriations, Budget Estimates, Etc.*, 81st Cong., 1st sess., *Senate Document 125*, 107.

62. Memoranda, Beasley and Rice to Chapman, June 12, 1951, Commissioner, Bureau of Reclamation to Secretary of the Interior, March 3, 1950, File 1-310, Administrative General, Power Development-Bonneville Project, RG 48.

63. Memoranda, Chapman to Straus, February 28, 1950; Straus to Chapman, March 3, 1950, *ibid*.

64. Memorandum, John D. Davis, Manager, Bonneville Power Administration, Washington, D.C. Office, to Joel Wolfsohn, Assistant to the Secretary, August 2, 1950; memorandum, Beasley and Rice to Chapman, June 12, 1951, *ibid*.

65. House of Representatives, *House Report 1797*, 81st Cong., 2d sess., March 21, 1950, 171.

66. Senate, *Interior Department Appropriations Bill for 1951, Hearings before a Subcommittee of the Committee on Appropriations*, 81st Cong., 2d sess., 467; letter, Secretary Chapman to Robert H. Gerdes, General Counsel,

Pacific Gas and Electric Company, May 8, 1950, Reading File, Chapman Papers.

67. Letter, Secretary Chapman to Robert H. Gerdes, May 8, 1950, Reading File, Chapman Papers; Senate, *Hearings on Interior Department Appropriations Bill for 1951*, 81st Cong., 2d sess., 1193-94.

68. Senate, *Hearings on Interior Department Appropriations Bill for 1951*, 81st Cong., 2d sess., 29-30.

69. *Ibid.*, 814.

70. *Ibid.*, 1187-93; see also 1184-86.

71. *Ibid.*, 1193, 1196, 1709-10.

72. Letter, Chapman to Gerdes, May 8, 1950, Reading File, Chapman Papers.

73. Report, "California Transmission Lines," undated, File 110, Administration and Planning Authorization and Policies, RG 115; House, *Hearings on Interior Department Appropriations Bill for 1952*, 82d Cong., 1st sess., 313, 536-37.

74. *New York Times*, April 4, 1951, 45.

75. Letter, Boke to Ickes, February 20, 1951, Box 46, Harold L. Ickes Papers, LC.

76. *Ibid.*; Coleman, *P.G. and E. of California*, 330; report, "California Transmission Lines," File 110, Administration and Planning, Authorization and Policies, RG 115; memorandum, Acting Commissioner, Bureau of Reclamation to Chapman, August 31, 1951, Miscellaneous Reading File, 1951-52, Chapman Papers; *Electrical World*, April 9, 1951, 85. Some disadvantages for the Bureau in this wheeling agreement were corrected in another contract signed by both parties in October 1951. It provided for integration of Central Valley generating plants with those of Pacific Gas and Electric by spelling out in detail the amount of energy that had to be delivered for each kilowatt of capacity sold as firm by the private utility. See *Electrical World*, October 15, 1951, 12.

77. Memorandum, Secretary of Interior to Commissioner, Bureau of Reclamation, and Administrator, Bonneville Power Administration, January 17, 1951; letter, Assistant Secretary William E. Warne to Representative Clair Engle, January 19, 1951, File 3-10, Bonneville Project, Administrative, RG 48.

78. House, *Hearings on Interior Department Appropriations Bill for 1952*, 82d Cong., 1st sess., 1346-47, 1358-59.

79. *Ibid.*, 1342-45; *Electrical World*, February 9, 1951, 6; *New York Times*, March 18, 1951, III, 1.

80. House, *hearings on Interior Department Appropriations Bill for 1952*, 82d Cong., 1st sess., 500-10.

81. Memorandum, Chapman to Goodrich W. Lineweaver, Acting Commissioner, Bureau of Reclamation, February 20, 1951, File 1-310, Administrative General, Power Development-Bonneville Project, RG 48.

82. House, *Hearings on Interior Department Appropriations Bill for 1952*, 82d Cong., 1st sess., 513-15, 540.

83. Memorandum, Chapman to Lineweaver, February 20, 1951, Miscellaneous Records, Reading File, 1950-51, Chapman Papers; memorandum, Acting Commissioner to Chapman, February 27, 1951, File 1-310, Administrative General, Power Development-Bonneville Project, RG 48.

84. Memorandum, Assistant Secretary Northrop to Chapman, April 20, 1951, Miscellaneous Papers, Reading File, 1950-51, Chapman Papers.

85. Memorandum, Chapman to Straus, May 18, 1951, File 1-310, Administrative General, Power Development-Bonneville Project, RG 48.

86. Financial reports had been sent at the time to the Washington office of the bureau showing these expenditures, but no action had been taken to stop them; memorandum, Beasley and Rice to Chapman, June 12, 1951, *ibid*.

87. Letters, Chapman to Representative Michael Kirwan and Senator Carl Hayden, August 1, 1951, Miscellaneous Papers, Reading File, 1951, Chapman Papers.

88. Senate, *Hearings on Interior Department Appropriations Bill for 1952*, 82d Cong., 1st sess., 516-17, 4645-47; *Congressional Quarterly* 7 (1951): 121-22, 516; "Development and Marketing of Hydroelectric Power under Multiple-Purpose Projects Authorized by Congress," January 6, 1953, Reports and Recommendations on Departmental Programs File, Office Files of the program Staff, RG 48.

89. *Congressional Record*, 82nd. Cong., 1st sess., 1951, 97: 4645-47; *The Charlotte Observer*, May 10, 1951, 20-21; *Electrical World*, November 20, 1950, 96; *Congress and the Nation*, 827.

90. Letter to Senator Hayden on the Effects of Certain House Amendments on Hydroelectric Power Policy, June 11, 1951, *Public Papers, 1951*, 326, 328.

91. *Statutes At Large*, 65 (1951), 255; letter, Chapman to Truman, June 26, 1951, Reading File, Chapman Papers; *Public Utilities Fortnightly*, August 2, 1951, 168-69; *Congressional Quarterly* 7 (1951): 122-24.

92. *Conference Report 888 on H.R. 3790, Appropriations Bill for 1952* in *Congressional Record*, 82d Cong., 1st sess., 1951, 97: 10205.

93. Memoranda, Administrator, Bonneville Power Administration, to Assistant Secretary Warne, August 24, 1951, Straus to Chapman, September 26, 1951, File 1-310, Administrative General, Power Development-Bonneville Project, RG 48.

94. Senate, *Hearings on Interior Department Appropriations Bill for 1953*, 82d Cong., 2d sess., 14-15; Public Law, 470, *Statutes at Large* 67 (1953): 451; Senate, *Appropriations, Budget Estimates, Etc.*, 82d Cong. 2d sess., *Senate Document 169*, 148.

95. Letters, James Fairman, Administrator, Defense Electric Power Administration, to Thomas Buchanan, Chairman, Federal Power Commission, May 9, 1952, Buchanan to Fairman, July 30, 1952, File 1-310, Administrative General, Bonneville Project, RG 48; memorandum, Assistant Administrative Secretary Beasley to the Under Secretary of Interior, October 17, 1952, *ibid.*; *Electrical World*, April 28, 1952, 10; *Congressional Record*, 82d Cong., 2d sess., 1952, 98: 9191.

96. Memorandum, Straus to Chapman, November 4, 1952, File 1-310, Administrative General, Power Development-Bonneville Project, RG 48.

Chapter 5. Compromises and Unholy Alliances: The Southwest

1. *Electrical World*, March 6, 1950, 20.

2. *Statutes at Large* 50 (1937): 732; *ibid.* 54 (1939-1941): 47.

3. Address, H. F. McPhail, "The Development of Power by the Federal Government," Office File of C. Girard Davidson, RG 48; Vennard, *Government in the Power Business*, 225-26; *Annual Report of the Secretary of the Interior, 1946*, 41; Departmental Order No. 2136, November 1945, File 1-12, Administrative General, Instructions and Orders, Office of the Secretary, RG 48.

4. Vennard, *Government in the Power Business*, 116; see also 226; Ickes, *Secret Diary*, 3: 228; Ickes, *Secret Diary*, 2: 42, 53.

5. Report, "Chronological Highlights of Southwestern Power Administration's Development," undated, File 1-310, Administrative General, Power Development-Southwestern, RG 48; *Annual Report of the Secretary of the Interior, 1947*, 41.

6. Department of the Interior Release, Order No. 2135, November 21, 1945, File 1-310, Administrative General, Power Development-Southwestern General, RG 48; "Chronological Highlights," undated, File 1-310, Administrative General, Power Development-Southwestern, RG 48; "Directions to the Administrator in Carrying Out His Orders," November 21, 1945, File 1-12, Administrative General, Instructions and Orders-Interior, RG 48.

7. Memoranda, Arthur Goldschmidt to Reginald Price, October 23, 1947, William Warne to Krug, November 25, 1947, Michael Straus to Krug, October 2, 1947, File 1-310, Administrative General, Power Development-Southeastern General, RG 48.

8. Letters, Krug to Gordon R. Clapp, Chairman, Tennessee Valley Authority, February 10, 1947 and Krug to Senator Styles Bridges, February 18, 1945, *ibid.*; *Annual Report of the Secretary of the Interior, 1947*, 42; *Annual Report of the Secretary of the Interior, 1948*, 135.

9. *Public Utilities Fortnightly*, April 13, 1950, 497; telephone call, George Brady, Boston-American Company, to Krug, February 4, 1949, Conference File, Krug Papers; *New York Times*, May 26, 1949, 45.

10. *New York Times*, March 19, 1950, III, 1.

11. Departmental Order No. 2558, March 21, 1950, File 1-12, Administrative General, Instructions and Orders, RG 48; *Congressional Quarterly* 5 (1949): 209-14, 792; *Public Utilities Fortnightly*, April 13, 1950, 497.

12. Report, "Chronological Highlights," File 1-310, Administrative General, Power Development-Southwestern RG 48.

13. Letter, Chapman to Tom Clark, March 7, 1946, *ibid*.

14. Letters, Wright to the eleven power companies, March 8, 1946, Clark to Krug, October 23, 1946, *ibid*.

15. "Chronological Highlights," *ibid*.

16. Senate, *Hearings on Department of the Interior Appropriations Bill for 1949*, 80th Cong., 2d sess., 1434, 1436.

17. House of Representatives, *Interior Department Appropriations Bill for 1948, Hearings before a Subcommittee of the Committee on Appropriations*, 80th Cong., 1st sess., Part 2, 414; Senate, *Hearings on Interior Department Appropriations Bill for 1948*, 80th Cong., 1st sess., Part 2, 198; House of Representatives, *Interior Department Appropriations Bill for 1949, Hearings before a Subcommittee of the Committee on Appropriations*, 80th Cong., 2d sess., Part 3, 400; Senate, *Hearings on Interior Department Appropriations Bill for 1949*, 80th Cong., 2d sess., 1418.

18. Letter, Ellis to Monroney, November 10, 1948, Office Files of Claude Wickard, Records of the Rural Electrification Administration, RA 221, NA; "Chronological Highlights" File 1-310, Administrative General, Power Development-Southwestern, RG 48.

19. "Chronological Highlights," File 1-310, Administrative General, Power Development-Southwestern, RG 48.

20. Letters, Rayburn to Truman, November 12, 1948, Albert to Truman, Kerr to Truman, September 24, 1948, Southwestern Power Administration, OF 6LL, HST Papers.

21. House, *Hearings on Interior Department Appropriations Bill for 1950*, 81st Cong., 1st sess., Part 2, 18-21.

22. *Ibid.*, Part 1, 33.

23. *Ibid.*, Par 1, 25; *ibid.*, Part 2, 554-55.

24. *Congressional Quarterly* 5 (1949): 210; "Chronological Highlights," File 1-310, Administrative General, Power Development-Southwestern, RG 48; Senate, *Hearings on Interior Department Appropriations Bill for 1950*, Part 1, 1366-67.

25. Senate, *Hearings on Interior Department Appropriations Bill for 1950*, Part 1, 1566-67.

26. Senate, *Report No. 661*, July 13, 1949, 4; *Congressional Quarterly*, 5 (1949), 211-12; "Chronological Highlights," File 1-310, Administrative General, Power Development-Southwestern, RG 48.

27. *Congressional Quarterly* 5 (1949): 213.

28. *Congressional Record*, 81st Cong., 1st sess., 1949, 95: 14389.

29. Letter, Krug to Senator Thomas, November 17, 1949, File 1-310, Administrative General, Power Development-Southwestern, RG 48.

30. Memorandum, Administrator, Southwestern Power Administration to Chapman, February 2, 1950, *ibid*. Under these agreements certain transmission facilities were leased to the SWPA to enable it to deliver electric power to the load centers of the federated cooperatives as called for in power exchange contracts between the two parties. Southwestern had the option of buying the lines if it paid the amount of the REA loan. The generating facilities were not leased nor was an option to buy them given the SWPA. The cooperatives sold the output from such plants to the agency, which could then better supply the member cooperative because its hydro-electric power was firmed up.

31. Memorandum, Walton Seymour, Director, Division of Power, to Chapman, February 21, 1950, *ibid*.

32. Memoranda, Ben Creim to Seymour, February 10, 1950, Paul Raver to Seymour, February 1, 1950, *ibid*.

33. Speech, Douglas Wright at Annual Meeting of the Missouri State Rural Electrification Administration, Jefferson City, Missouri, February 9, 1950, File 1-310, Administrative General, Power Development-Southwestern, RG 48.

34. *Congressional Quarterly* 6 (1950): 115; *New York Times*, January 22, 1950, III,1; "Chronological Highlights," File 1-310, Administrative General, Power Development-Southwestern, RG 48.

35. House, *Hearings on Interior Department Appropriations Bill for 1951*, 81st cong., 2d sess., 96; *Electrical World*, January 30, 1950, 95, March 6, 1950, 6.

36. Letter, Chapman to Wright, April 3, 1950, Reading File, Chapman Papers; letter, Chapman to Wright, April 24, 1950, File 1-310, Administrative General, Power Development-Southwestern, RG 48.

37. *Tulsa World*, May 4, 1950, 33; *Public Utilities Fortnightly*, May 25, 1950, 688-89.

38. Letters, Chapman to Wright, April 24, 1950, June 13, 1950, File 1-310, Administrative General, Power Development-Southwestern, RG 48; identical letters, Chapman to Senators Estes Kefauver, Carl Hayden and Lister Hill and Congressmen Sam Rayburn and Michael J. Kirwan, June 13, 1950, Reading File, Chapman Papers.

39. Letter, Wright to Chapman, June 14, 1950, Reading File, Chapman Papers; memoranda, Chapman to Northrop, June 15, 1950, Northrop to

Chapman, June 28, 1950, File 1-310, Administrative General, Power Development-Southwestern, RG 48.

40. *Public Utilities Fortnightly*, July 6, 1950, 29.

41. Letter, Chapman to Representative Clarence Cannon, July 11, 1950, press release, Southwestern Power Administration, July 13, 1950, File 1-310, Administrative General, Power Development-Southwestern, RG. 48; *Tulsa Daily World*, July 14, 1950, 1.

42. *The Daily Oklahoman*, July 14, 1950; *Arkansas Gazette*, July 14, 1950, 2.

43. *Tulsa Daily World*, July 14, 1950, 1; *The Daily Oklahoman*, July 14, 1950, 1.

44. Memorandum, Clyde Ellis to C. Girard Davidson, January 18, 1950, General Office File of Assistant Secretary Davidson, 1946-50, RG 48.

45. Letter, Chapman to Cannon, July 11, 1950, File 1-310, Administrative General, Power Development-Southwestern, RG 48.

46. *Electrical World*, July 31, 1950, 78, September 4, 1950, 13; Senate, *Appropriations, Budget Estimates, Etc.*, 81st Cong., 2d sess., *Senate Document 239*, 153, 887, 915; *Electrical World*, September 4, 1950, 13.

47. Memorandum, Assistant Secretary Warne to Secretary of the Interior, July 14, 1950, Policy on Wheeling Arrangements File, Division of Power Files, RG 48.

48. Letter, Claude R. Wickard to Representative John L. McMillan, January 5, 1949, speech, Claude R. Wickard, prior to a power panel, June 12, 1950, Office Files of Claude Wickard, 1947-49, RG 221; see also *Annual Report of the Department of Agriculture, Administration of Rural Electrification Administration, 1949*, 9.

49. *Electrical World*, February 5, 1950, 6; *New York Times*, March 11, 1950, 18, March 22, 1950, 44.

50. *New York Times*, March 22, 1950, 44.

51. *Congressional Quarterly* 6 (1950): 96; *Electrical World*, November 27, 1950, 13; *Public Utilities Fortnightly*, March 2, 1950, 298, March 16, 1950, 363.

52. *Public Utilities Fortnightly*, August 3, 1950, 163.

53. *Congressional Quarterly* 7 (1951): 120.

54. *Congressional Quarterly* 7 (1951): 120; Senate, *Appropriations, Budget Estimates, Etc.*, 82d Cong., 1st sess., *Senate Document 88*, 593; *Public Utilities Fortnightly*, January 1, 1951, 166; letter, Ludwick Graves, Counsel for Kansas City Power and Light Company, to Chapman, June 4, 1951, File 1-310, Administrative General, Power Development-Southwestern General, RG 48.

55. *Conference Report No. 888*, 82d Cong., 1st sess., 5; letter, Charles Brannan, Secretary of Agriculture to Chapman, August 22, 1951, Power Authorities: SWPA folder, Files of Riggs Sheppard, RG 221.

56. *Congressional Quarterly* 7 (1951): 123.

57. *Congressional Quarterly* 7 (1951): 120-25; *Public Utilities Fortnightly*, August 2, 1951, 168-69; *Electrical World*, July 28, 1951, 73; Public Law 136, *Statutes at Large*, 65 (1951): 249; Senate, *Appropriations, Budget Estimates, Etc.*, 82d Cong., 1st sess., 593. The total amount for construction and maintenance and operation was $4,630,882.

58. *Congressional Quarterly* 7 (1951): 123-24; letter, Brannan to Chapman, August 21, 1951, Power Authorities: SWPA folder, Files of Riggs Sheppard, RG 221; Public Law 136, *Statutes at Large* 65 (1951): 249.

59. *Electrical World*, October 16, 1950, 5, December 11, 1950, 6; *New York Times*, January 23, 1951, 39.

60. Memorandum, Henry W. Blalock, Assistant to the Administrator, to Douglas Wright, August 16, 1951, File 1-310, Administrative General, Power Development-Southwestern General, RG 48.

61. Letter, Brannan to Chapman, August 21, 1951, Power Authorities: SWPA folder, Files of Riggs Sheppard, RG 221; letter, Brannan to Chapman, August 22, 1951, memorandum, Solicitor Mastin G. White to Director, Division of Water and Power, September 14, 1951, File 1-310, Administrative General, Power Development-Southwestern General, RG 48.

62. Address in Arkansas at the Dedication of the Norfolk and Bull Shoals Dams, July 2, 1952, *Public Papers, 1952-53*, 458; see also *Electrical World*, June 2, 1952, 70-71.

63. Letters, H. B. Munsell to Truman, February 4, 1950, Wickard to Matthew J. Connelly, March 20, 1950, Connelly to Munsell, March 23, 1950, 1948-53 folder, OF 375, HST Papers.

64. *New York Times*, October 28, 1952, 46; "Memorandum on the Power Supply Problems in the Southwest Area," March 23, 1953, "Notes of Meeting on Cooperatives Having Contracts with S.W.P.A.," May 18, 1953, Power Authorities: SWPA folder, Files of Riggs Sheppard, RG 221; Senate, *Interior Department Appropriations for 1953, Hearings before a Subcommittee of the Committee on Appropriations*, 82d Cong., 2d sess., 17; *Public Utilities Fortnightly*, January 4, 1951, 36-38; *Electrical World*, January 19, 1953, 5, January 28, 1952, 115; Senate, *Appropriations, Budget Estimates, Etc.*, 82d Cong., 2d sess., 559.

65. Senate, *Hearings on Interior Department Appropriations for 1953*, 82d Cong., 2d sess., 17; *Congressional Quarterly* 8 (1952): 106; *Electrical World*, July 14, 1952, 116; Senate, *Appropriations, Budget Estimates, Etc.*, 82d Cong., 2d sess., 143, 560.

66. Speech, Douglas Wright at Herman, Missouri, February 5, 1952, File 1-210, Administrative General, Power Development-Public Statements by Departmental Officials, RG 48; *New York Times*, February 13, 1952, 43. See also Wright's speech before the Advisory Committee on Power for the

Southwest, September 15, 1952, Speech and Statement File, Box 1, Wright Papers.

67. Senate, *Hearings on Interior Department Appropriations Bill for 1953*, 82d Cong., 2d sess., 67, 68.

68. *Electrical World*, August 4, 1952, 5; Press Conferences, February 13 and April 29, 1952, Public Addresses and Statements, Transcripts of Press Conferences Held by Secretary Chapman, Chapman Papers; speech given before the Advisory Committee on Power for the Southwest, September 15, 1952, Speech and Statement File, Box 1, Wright Papers; "Notes of Meeting on Cooperatives Having Contracts with SPA," May 18, 1953, Power authorities, SWPA folder, Files of Riggs Sheppard, RG 221.

Chapter 6. Advances, Retreats and Holding Actions: The Southeast

1. SEPA, however, was created just to market electric power, while the Bureau of Reclamation not only marketed power but also built and operated irrigation and power projects.

2. See, for example, *New York Times*, March 19, 1950, III, 1; *Electrical World*, March 6, 1950, 4-5.

3. Letter, C. Girard Davidson to Representative James C. Davis, August 20, 1948, File 1-310, Administrative General, Power Development-Southeastern, RG 48; *Electrical World*, March 6, 1950, 4-6; *Public Utilities Fortnightly*, April 27, 1950, 560.

4. Memorandum, Creim to Chapman, February 7, 1951, File 1-310, Administrative General, Power Development-Southeastern, RG 48. The Savannah River separates Georgia from South Carolina.

5. Memorandum, Creim to Warne, November 6, 1950; letter, Creim to Charles A. Collier, October 6, 1950, *ibid*.

6. Memorandum, Creim to Chapman, February 7, 1951, *ibid*.

7. Memorandum, Creim to Chapman, February 7, 1951; letters, Creim to Charles A. Collier, March 2, 1951, November 9, 1951, Warne to Collier, March 13, 1951, *ibid*.

8. Memoranda, Straus to Warne, August 3, 1951, Earley to Leavy, acting administrator, August 1, 1951, Creim to Warne, October 8, 1951, *ibid*.

9. Letter, Chapman to C. B. McManus, January 2, 1953, *ibid*.

10. Letter, Harlee Branch, Jr., President, Georgia Power Company, to Chapman, January 10, 1953, *ibid*.

11. Letter, Ken G. Whitaker to Chapman, January 14, 1953, *ibid*.

12. *Congressional Quarterly* 6 (1950): 142-43; *Electrical World*, December 18, 1950, 72; *Public Utilities Fortnightly*, January 4, 1951, 37; *Richmond Times Dispatch*, December 20, 1950, 1; see also Senate, *Interior Department Supplemental Appropriations Bill for 1951, Hearings before a Subcommittee of the Committee on Appropriations*, 81st Cong., 2d sess., 362, 382.

13. *Congressional Record*, 81st Cong., 2d sess., 1950, 96: 17095, 17097-99; memorandum, Warne to Creim, January 3, 1951, File 1-310, Administrative General, Power Development-Southeastern General RG 48; *Congressional Quarterly* 6 (1950): 142-43; *Electrical World*, January 1, 1951, 42, January 8, 1951, 5; *Public Utilities Fortnightly*, January 4, 1951, 37.

14. Memorandum, Warne to Creim, January 3, 1951, "Significant Votes in House and Senate Pertaining to Public Power in the Southeast," File 1-310, Administrative General, Power Development-Southeastern RG 48; *Congressional Record*, 81st Cong., 2d sess., 1950, 96: 17095-17102; *Congressional Quarterly* 6 (1950): 142-43.

15. Memoranda, Chapman to Warne, Chapman to Creim, January 4, 1951, Miscellaneous Papers, Reading File, Chapman Papers; letter, Chapman to Hayden, January 4, 1951, *ibid.*

16. Minutes, "Water and Power Programs Meetings," January 3, 1951, March 20, 1951, March 27, 1951, April 10, 1951, General Congresses and Conventions, Water and Power Programs, RG 115; House, *Hearings on Appropriations Bill for 1952*, 82d Cong., 1st sess., 93-94, 1161-62.

17. Identical letters, Chapman to the chairmen of the House and Senate Committees on Interior and Insular Affairs and to the chairmen of the House and Senate Interior Subcommittees of the Committees on Appropriations, April 6, 1951, Miscellaneous Papers, Reading File, 1950-51, Chapman Papers.

18. *Congressional Quarterly* 7 (1951): 120-21; House, *Hearings on Interior Appropriations Bill for 1952*, 82d Cong., 1st sess., Part 1, 94-97, 106; Part 2, 1395, 1480-81, 1483.

19. *Congressional Quarterly* 7 (1950): 120-23; "Significant Votes in House and Senate Pertaining to Public Power in the Southeast," File 1-310, Administrative General, Power Development-Southeastern General, RG 48; *Congressional Record*, 82d Cong., 1st sess., 1951, 97: 4282-83, 4292, 7774; Public Law 136, *Statutes at Large* 65 (1951): 249.

20. Senate, *Hearings on Interior Department Appropriations Bill for 1953*, 82d Cong., 2d sess., 160-62.

21. *Ibid.*, 1159, 1157.

22. Letter, Warne to Ellis, May 4, 1951, File 1-310, Administrative General, Power Development-Southeastern, RG 48; *Congressional Quarterly* 7 (1951): 120-24; *Congressional Record*, 82d Cong., 1st sess., 1951, 97: 7774-75.

23. *Congressional Quarterly* 7 (1951): 120-24; *Congressional Record*, 82d Cong., 1st sess., 1951, 97: 7774-75; Senate, *Report No. 499*, 82d Cong., 1st sess., v; letter, N. A. Cocke, vice-president, Duke Power Company, to Senator Clyde R. Hoey, January 25, 1952, File 1-310, Administrative General, Power Development-Southeastern General, RG 48; Senate, *Appropriations, Budget Estimates, Etc.*, 82d Cong., 1st sess., 146.

24. Memoranda, Leavey to Chapman, February 18, 1952, Chapman to SEPA Administrator, January 15, 1952, File 1-310, Administrative General, Power Development, Southeastern General, RG 48.

25. Letter, N.A. Cocke to Hoey, January 25, 1952, *ibid*.

26. Letters, Hoey to Hayden, January 28, 1952, Hayden to Chapman, January 30, 1952, *ibid*.

27. Letter, Chapman to Hayden, March 17, 1952, *ibid*.

28. Senate, *Hearings on Interior Department Appropriations Bill for 1953*, 82d Cong., 2d sess., 47-53; *Congressional Quarterly* 7 (1952): 106-07.

29. Senate, *Hearings on Interior Department Appropriations Bill for 1953*, 82d Cong., 2d sess., 52.

30. *Ibid.*, 1087-1101.

31. *Congress and the Nation* 830; *Statutes at Large* 66 (1952): 445.

32. Telegrams, Leavy to McMeekin, Leavy to E. C. Marshall, Duke Power Company, July 8, 1952, McMeekin to Leavy, July 12, 1952, McMeekin to Leavy, July 14, 1952, Leavy to McMeekin, July 18, 1952, Marshall to Leavy, July 23, 1952, Leavy to Marshall, August 23, 1952, Marshall to Leavy, August 26, 1952; letter, Chapman to Lindsay C. Warren, December 19, 1952, File 1-310, Administrative General, Power Development-Southeastern General, RG 48. Leavy had become administrator in April, following the death of Ben Creim.

33. Memorandum, Administrator, Southeastern Power Administration, to Administrative Assistant Secretary, August 26, 1952, *ibid*.

34. Chapman to Barkley and Rayburn, September 15, 1952, *ibid*.

35. Telegram, McMeekin to Chapman, September 25, 1952, letter, McMeekin to Chapman, August 18, 1952, letter, Hayden to Chapman, October 9, *ibid*.

36. Letter, Chapman to McMeekin, October 10, 1952, telegram, McMeekin to Vernon D. Northrop, Acting Secretary of the Interior, October 14, 1952, telegram, Northrop to McMeekin, October 14, 1952, *ibid*.

37. Telegram, Hayden to Chapman, October 15, 1952, letter, Hayden to Chapman, October 9, 1952, *ibid*.

38. Letter, Comptroller General to Chapman, October 22, 1952, *ibid*.

39. Telegram, Hayden to Chapman, October 31, 1952, letter, Chapman to Hayden, November 18, 1952, memorandum, Administrator, Leavy to Chapman, December 3, 1952, *ibid*.

40. Leavy to Chapman, December 3, 1952, *ibid*.

41. Letter, Warren to Chapman, January 7, 1953, *ibid.*

42. *Electrical World*, January 19, 1953, 9.

43. Memorandum, Solicitor to Chapman, January 12, 1953, letter, Chapman to Comptroller General, January 16, 1953, File 1-310, Administrative General, Power Development-Southeastern General, RG 48; *Electrical World*, February 2, 1953, 5. This line was begun, but during the Eisenhower Administration, Congress mandated, in the Interior Department appropriations bill for 1954, that all federal facilities and parts of the line be sold to the Greenwood County Electric Power Commission. Thenceforth, SEPA delivered its power to its customers by wheeling agreements.

44. *Congressional Quarterly* 7 (1951): 122; House, *Hearings on Interior Department Appropriations Bill for 1952*, 82d Cong., 1st sess., Part 2, 1751-53.

45. House, *Hearings on Interior Department Appropriations for 1952*, 82d Cong., 1st sess., Part 2, 1463, 1478-79.

46. *Congressional Quarterly* 7 (1952): 122; Public Law 136, *Statutes at Large* 65 (1951): 249; *Electrical World*, January 28, 1952, 115; Public Law 470, *Statutes at Large* 66 (1952): 445; Senate, *Appropriations, Budget Estimates, Etc.*, 82d Cong., 1st sess., 446, 533; Senate, *Appropriations, Budget Estimates, Etc.*, 82d Cong., 2d sess., 559.

47. Press release, "REA Approves Loan for New South Carolina Transmission System," S.C. Santee Cooper folder, Office Files of Riggs Sheppard, 1946-53, RG 221.

48. *The News and Courier*, June 2, 1950, 5-A; *New York Times*, June 2, 1950, 5-A.

49. News clipping, letter, Wickard to Editor, *Washington Post*, June 19, 1950, S.C. Santee Cooper folder, Office Files of Riggs Sheppard, 1946-53, RG 221; *New York Times*, June 2, 1950, 16. See also news clipping, letter, Wickard to Editor, *Washington Post*, June 19, 1950, S.C. Santee Cooper folder, Office Files of Riggs Sheppard, 1946-53, RG 221.

50. *Annual Report of the Administrator of the Rural Electrification Administration, 1950*, 21.

51. *The News and Courier*, June 4, 1950, 5-A.

52. *Public Utilities Fortnightly*, July 6, 1950, 21; *The News and Courier*, June 5, 1950, 4; *Public Utilities Fortnightly*, June 22, 1950, 847, July 6, 1950, 31; remarks, Claude R. Wickard, prior to power panel, June 12, 1950, Office Files of Claude R. Wickard, 1947-49, RG 221.

53. *The News and Courier*, June 5, 1950, 4; *Public Utilities Fortnightly*, June 22, 1950, 845-48.

54. *Public Utilities Fortnightly*, June 22, 1950, 847-48.

55. Senate, *Appropriations, Budget Estimates, Etc.*, 81st Cong., 2d sess., 145; Senate, *Appropriations, Budget Estimates, Etc.*, 81st Cong., 1st sess., 27; *Electrical World*, April 3, 1950, 4-5, September 4, 1950, 13; *Congressional*

Quarterly 5 (1949): 186; *Annual Report of the Administrator of the Rural Electrification Administration, 1950*, 3; *Annual Report of the Administrator of the Rural Electrification Administration, 1951*, 6.

56. *Public Utilities Fortnightly*, September 14, 1950, 365-66, May 10, 1951, 629; House of Representatives, *Hearings before the Committee on Agriculture, Activities of the Department of Agriculture*, 82d Cong., 1st sess., 117-48.

57. Annual Budget Message to the Congress: Fiscal year 1952, January 15, 1951, *Public Papers, 1951*, 89; *Electrical World*, January 22, 1951, 4.

58. Letter, Brannan to Chapman, February 2, 1951, Secretary of Agriculture, General Correspondence, Power-1, 1945, 1947-52, *Records of the Office of the Secretary of Agriculture*, RG 16, NA; *Public Utilities Fortnightly*, May 10, 1951, 628-29; *New York Times*, March 30, 1951, 40.

59. *New York Times*, March 30, 1951, 40.

60. "Farmer's Union in Washington," a Weekly Report of the National Farmer's Union, March 2, 1951, Administrative General, Preparedness, 1-188, Controlled Materials, May 22-June 6, 1951, RG 48.

61. Letter, Ellis to Chapman, March 19, 1951, File 1-310, Administrative General, Power Development-Administrative, RG 48; letter, McWhorter to Truman, February 6, 1951, Secretary of Agriculture, General Correspondence, Power-1, 1945, 1947-52, RG 16.

62. Letter, Brannan to Chapman, February 2, 1951, Secretary of Agriculture, General Correspondence, Power-1, RG 16; memo of Agreement between Secretary of Interior and Secretary of Agriculture, April 14, 1951, letter, Wickard to Chapman, March 13, 1951, notes on conversation with Gordon Clapp, March 13, 1951, notes on conversation with Charles Murphy, March 13, 1951, letter, Wickard to Chapman, undated, Office Files of Secretary of the Interior Chapman, 1933-53, RG 48; *Annual Report of the Administrator of the Rural Electrification Administration*, 1951, 19.

63. *Public Utilities Fortnightly*, January 4, 1951, 36-38; Senate, *Agriculture Department Appropriations Bill for 1952, Hearings before a Subcommittee of the Committee on Appropriations on H.R. 3973*, 82d Cong., 1st sess., 784; House of Representatives, *Agriculture Department Appropriations Bill for 1953, Hearings before a Subcommittee of the Committee on Appropriations on H.R. 7314*, 82d Cong., 2d sess., 573; Public Law 135, *Statutes at Large*, 66 (1952): 349; Senate, *Appropriations, Budget Estimates, Etc.*, 82d Cong., 1st sess., 54, 564.

64. *Annual Report of the Administrator of the Rural Electrification Administration, 1951*, 6, 9; *Annual Report of the Administrator of the Rural Electrification Administration, 1952*, 10.

65. United States Department of Agriculture, *Annual Report of the Administrator of the Rural Electrification Administration, 1946* (Washington, D.C, 1947), 13; United States Department of Agriculture, *Annual Report of the*

Administrator of the Rural Electrification Administration, 1947 (Washington, D.C., 1948), 5; *New York Times*, March 11, 1952, 38; "Annual Message to the Congress on the State of the Union," January 7, 1953, *Public Papers, 1952-53,* 1149.

66. Letter, Dr. Harry Field Parker to President Truman, June 6, 1950, President Truman to Parker, June 13, 1950, OF 293, HST Papers.

67. Special Message from the President to the NRECA Annual Meeting, Chicago, March 12, 1952, 1948-53 folder, OF 375, HST Papers.

68. *Ibid.*

Chapter 7. Prizes to Be Won: The Remaining Choice Power Sites

1. David B. Truman, *The Governmental Process*, 412-13; Maass, *Muddy Waters*, 210-21.

2. Truman, *The Governmental Process*, 413-15; Maass, *Muddy Waters*, 221-40.

3. Maass, *Muddy Waters*, 240-50.

4. *Ibid.*, 251.

5. Project No. 175, Pacific Gas and Electric Company, Formal, January 1, 1948 to August 4, 1948, File 100-2, Federal Power Commission Files (hereafter cited as FPC Files), Washington, D.C.; Release No. 3630, January 22, 1948, U.S. Federal Power Commission Press Releases, 1948, *ibid.*; *Annual Report of the Federal Power Commission, 1948*, 34.

6. Letter, Krug to Smith, May 11, 1948, Project No. 175, Pacific Gas and Electric Company, Formal, January 1, 1948 to August 4, 1948, File 100-2, FPC Files.

7. *Ibid.*

8. Brief of Commission Staff Counsel on Projects 1925, 175, 1988 and 1990 before the FPC, August 4, 1948, File 100-2, FPC Files.

9. *Ibid.*

10. Brief of Bureau of Reclamation, U.S. Department of Interior, before the FPC in the Matters of Fresno Irrigation District and Pacific Gas and Electric Company, August 21, 1948, *ibid.*

11. Brief of Commission Staff Counsel of Projects 1925, 175, 1988 and 1990 before the FPC, August 4, 1948, *ibid.*; brief of Bureau of Reclamation, U.S. Department of Interior before the FPC in the Matters of Fresno Irrigation District and Pacific Gas and Electric Company, August 21, 1948, *ibid.*

12. Letter, Krug to Smith, June 2, 1949, FPC Official Record, Correspondence, Project 1925, FPC Files; see also Press Release No. 4056, December 13, 1948, U.S. Federal Power Commission Press Releases, 1948, FPC Files.

13. Letter, Krug to Smith, June 2, 1949, FPC Official Record, Correspondence, Project 1925, FPC Files.

14. "Suggested Statement with Reference to Appointment of Buchanan to Federal Power Commission," October 20, 1948; letter, Truman to Harold L. Ickes, September 18, 1951, 1948-1951 folder, OF 235, HST Papers.

15. Letter, Jerome M. Joffee, Special Utilities and Legislative Counsel, Office of City Counselor, Kansas City, to Truman, May 16, 1949; letter, Truman to Joffee, June 22, 1949, 1948-51 folder, OF 235, HST Papers; *New York Times*, June 7, 1949, 18.

16. Newspaper clippings, *Washington Post*, July 6, 1949, OF 235, HST Papers; *Congressional Record*, 81st Cong., 1st sess., 1949, 95: 14357-87.

17. *Congressional Record*, 81st Cong., 1st sess., 1949, 95: 14359, 14386-87; *New York Times*, October 5, 1949, 1, October 6, 1949, 28, October 7, 1949, 1, October 9, 1949, 34, October 20, 1949; newspaper clipping, October 14, 1949, 1948-51 folder, OF 235, HST Papers; Truman's nomination of Wallgren as chairman of the National Resources Board in early 1949 had shocked liberals because of the nominee's apparent mediocrity. After the Senate Armed Services Committee refused to report his nomination to the full Senate, Truman withdrew Wallgren's name. See Hamby, *Beyond the New Deal*, 335-36.

18. Newspaper clippings, *Washington Evening Star*, November 17, 1949, *Seattle Times*, November 20, 1949, Monrad C. Wallgren Papers, HSTL; Press Releases No. 4501, November 10, 1949 and No. 4056, December 13, 1949, U.S. Federal Power Commission Press Releases, 1949, FPC Files.

19. *The Nation*, November 6, 1949, 502; newspaper clipping, *Washington Evening Star*, November 17, 1949, Wallgren Papers.

20. Press Release No. 4501, November 10, 1949, U.S. Federal Power Commission Press Releases, 1948, FPC Files; *The Nation*, November 6, 1949, 502.

21. Application for Rehearing before the Federal Power Commission in Matters of Fresno Irrigation District and Pacific Gas and Electric Company Formal, October 1949 to December 1949, File 100-2, FPC Files; *Electrical World*, January 23, 1950, 13.

22. Letter, Pace to Chapman, Roundup of Information and Opinion, 1950-51, PWRPC Records.

23. *Christian Science Monitor*, March 21, 1950, 11; *San Francisco Chronicle*, March 23, 1950, 18; *Public Utilities Fortnightly*, April 13, 1950, 496-98, July 6, 1950, 32; letter, Cecil White to Chapman, March 16, 1950, File 100-2, Project 175, FPC Files.

24. *Public Utilities Fortnightly*, April 13, 1950, 498.

25. Executive Order, May 24, 1950, newspaper clipping, *New York Herald Tribune*, December 8, 1949, 1948-1951 folder, OF 235, HST Papers; *Electrical World*, July 3, 1950, 70.

26. *The Nation*, May 13, 1950, 434-35.

27. Newspaper clipping, *Washington Evening Star*, May 26, 1950, Wallgren Papers; *The Nation*, May 13, 1950, 434-35.

28. *Public Utilities Fortnightly*, June 8, 1950, 781, July 6, 1950, 32.

29. *Ibid.*, December 7, 1950, 828; George H. Mayer, *The Republican Party*, 479. In Douglas's case, her opponent's charge that the congresswoman was receiving substantial Communist support gained more attention than did public power issues.

30. *A Water Policy for the American People: The Report of the President's Water Resources Policy Commission, 1950*, 1: 245, 238.

31. Letter, Leland O. Graham to Leon M. Fuquay, Secretary, Federal Power Commission, December 18, 1950; letter, Robert H. Gerdes to Leon M. Fuquay, January 1, 1951, FPC Official Record, File Series P-1925, Correspondence, FPC Files.

32. Opinion No. 183A, December 21, 1951, Projects Nos. 1925, 175 and 1988, Release No. 5795, FPC Press Releases, July-December, 1951, FPC Files.

33. Letter, Thomas C. Buchanan to Philip B. Perlman, February 6, 1952, FPC Official Record, Correspondence, 100-2, Projects Nos. 1925, 175 and 1988, FPC Files; see also *Electrical World*, February 25, 1952, 66.

34. Letter, Truman to Daniels, November 7, 1951, Personal File, Box 309, PSF.

35. Letter, Buchanan to Perlman, February 6, 1952, FPC Official Record, Correspondence, 100-2, Projects Nos. 1925, 175 and 1988, FPC Files.

36. Letter, Perlman to Buchanan, February 7, 1952, FPC Official Record, File Series P-1925, Correspondence, FPC Files; Docket Sheet 175-1, No. 2, FPC Files.

37. Memorandum, Chapman to Truman, June 25, 1952, OF 284, HST Papers.

38. *Ibid.*

39. Gale E. Peterson, "President Harry S. Truman and the Independent Regulatory Commissions," 13-14.

40. Newspaper clipping, *Wall Street Journal*, May 6, 1952, OF 293, HST Papers.

41. Docket Sheet 175-1, No. 2, FPC Files. During the Eisenhower Administration, on November 16, 1953, the petition was dismissed in the United States Circuit Court of Appeals.

42. Licensed Projects, Docket Sheets, Docket Project No. 2009, FPC Files.

43. Report, "Summary of the Main Issues of Fact, Law and Discretion in the Roanoke Rapids Case, and the Position of the Department of the Interior," prepared by Gregory Hankin, undated, General Office Files of C. Girard Davidson, 1946-50, RG 48; letter, Davidson to Fischer S. Black, editor,

Electrical World, July 18, 1949, File 1-310, Administrative General-Power Development, RG 48.

44. Telephone call, Krug to Mastin White, August 11, 1949, Conference File, Krug Papers.

45. Brief of the Secretary of the Interior, Project No. 2009, August 31, 1949, FPC Official Record, File Series P-2009, FPC Files.

46. Report, "Summary of the Main Issues of Fact, Law and Discretion in the Roanoke Rapids Case, and the Position of the Department of the Interior," prepared by Gregory Hankin, undated, General Office Files of C. Girard Davidson, 1946-50, RG 48.

47. FPC Official Record, File Series P-2009, FPC Files.

48. *Congressional Record*, 82d Cong., 1st sess., 1951, 97: 12935; *Electrical World*, March 27, 1950, 76, July 3, 1950, 70.

49. *The Nation*, April 15, 1950, 349; see also *New York Times*, June 14, 1950.

50. *Electrical World*, April 3, 1950, 20.

51. *Electrical World*, November 27, 1950, 13; *Richmond Times Dispatch*, January 29, 1951, 8; *Electrical World*, December 4, 1950, 86.

52. *Richmond Times Dispatch*, December 23, 1950, 1.

53. Opinion No. 24, In the Matter of Virginia Electric and Power Company, Project No. 2009, FPC Official Record, File Series P-2009, FPC Files.

54. *New York Times*, January 31, 1951, 37.

55. Licensed Projects, Docket Sheets, Project No. 2009, FPC Files.

56. *Public Utilities Fortnightly*, February 15, 1951, 235; letter, Secretary Chapman to Henry Ligon, September 12, 1951, Reading File, Chapman Papers.

57. Minutes, Water and Power Programs Meeting, January 17, 1951 and April 10, 1951, File 0.30, General, Congresses and Conventions, Water and Power Programs, RG 115; telephone call, J. A. Krug to Walton Seymour, November 1, 1949, Conference File, Krug Papers.

58. Letter, Secretary Chapman to President Truman, February 18, 1952, Miscellaneous Records, Reading File, 1952, Chapman Papers.

59. *Public Utilities Fortnightly*, September 27, 1951, 429; *Electrical World*, October 15, 1951, 5.

60. *Public Utilities Fortnightly*, September 27, 1951, 429; see also *Electrical World*, October 15, 1951, 5.

61. Letter, Chapman to Philip B. Perlman, Solicitor General, October 17, 1951, Miscellaneous Records, Reading File, Chapman Papers; *Congressional Record*, 82d Cong., 1st sess., 1951, 97: 12935-36.

62. *Public Utilities Fortnightly*, December 6, 1951, 829, March 13, 1952, 375; *Electrical World*, February 11, 1952, 7; letter, Chapman to Truman, November 16, 1951, letter, Chapman to Perlman, October 17, 1951, Miscellaneous Records, Reading File 1951-52, Chapman Papers.

63. Truman to Daniels, November 7, 1951, Personal File, Box 39, PSF.

64. *Electrical World*, March 24, 1952, 103, February 11, 1952, 72.

65. *Ibid.*, October 27, 1952, 10; U.S., *United States* [Supreme Court] *Reports* 345 (October Term, 1952): 153-74.

66. Senate, *Hearings on Interior Department Appropriations Bill for 1953*, 82d Cong., 2d sess., 1130.

67. *Ibid.*; *Electrical World*, October 27, 1952, 10.

68. *United States Reports* 345 (October Term, 1952): 153.

69. *Ibid.*, 155.

70. House of Representatives, *House Document 473*, 81st Cong., 2d sess., 2 vols., 2: 113-19. An acre-foot designates the amount of water required to cover one acre of land with water one foot deep.

71. *Annual Report of the Federal Power Commission, 1947*, 123; *ibid., 1951*, 51; *The Nation*, November 1, 1952, 405; Roy F. Bessey, "The Political Issues of the Hells Canyon Controversy," *Western Political Quarterly* 9 (September 1956): 681-83; *Congress and the Nation*, 950.

72. *House Document 473*, 81st Cong., 2d sess., 1: 1-39.

73. For a fuller treatment of the combined report as it related to the administration's efforts to establish a CVA, see Chapter 3, above.

74. *Congressional Quarterly* 7 (1951): 678, *ibid.* 8 (1952): 345.

75. *Annual Report of the Federal Power Commission, 1951*, 51-52; *The Nation*, November 1, 1952, 405.

76. *The Nation*, November 1, 1952, 405-06; Bessey, "The Political Issues of the Hells Canyon Controversy," 681-83; *Electrical World*, April 7, 1952, 95; *New Republic*, March 17, 1952, 16-17.

77. Memoranda, Warne to Chapman, November 30, 1950, and Davidson to Chapman, February 12, 1951, File 1-310, Administrative General-Power Development, RG 48.

78. Bessey, "The Political Issues of the Hells' Canyon Controversy," 683-85; *New York Times*, June 15, 1952, 33; *A Water Policy for the American People: The Report of the President's Water Resources Policy Commission*, 1: 9, 25-26, 245. *The Nation*, November 1, 1952, 406; letter, Chapman to H. W. Morrison, President, Southwestern Idaho Water Conservation Project, March 20, 1951, Miscellaneous Records, Reading File, 1950-51, Chapman Papers.

79. House of Representatives, *Hearings on H.R. 5743 before the Subcommittee on Irrigation and Reclamation of the House Committee on Interior and Insular Affairs*, 82d Cong., 1st sess., 155-57.

80. *House Document 473*, 81st cong., 2d sess., 1: 53; memorandum, Straus to Chapman, April 11, 1951, Subject File, Columbia River, Krug Papers.

81. Memorandum, Davidson to Chapman, February 12, 1951, Administrative General, Power Development, RG 48; see also memorandum, Chapman to Warne, December 28, 1950, *ibid.*

82. *Electrical World*, March 19, 1951, 13; *New Republic*, March 17, 1952, 17.

83. Annual Budget Message to the Congress: Fiscal Year 1952, January 15, 1951, *Public Papers, 1951*, 86-87.

84. "Statement by Assistant Secretary William E. Warne before Civil Functions Committee of the House Appropriations Committee, May 10, 1951," File 1-310, Administrative General, Power Development-Pacific Northwest, RG 48.

85. "Annual Budget Message to the Congress, Fiscal Year 1953," January 21, 1952, *Public Papers*, 88; *Electrical World*, April 7, 1952, 94.

86. *Electrical World*, April 7, 1952, 94.

87. House of Representatives, *Hearings on H.R. 5743*, 82d Cong., 2d sess., 27. A problem that plagued the federal government in its plans for the comprehensive development of the Columbia River Basin was the issue of "fish versus dams." Any mainstream dam built on the Columbia below the Okanogan River or on the Snake below the Salmon River would harm the salmon run. Residents engaged in the sizable commercial salmon fishing industry in the Northwest, five Indian tribes that were guaranteed their usual fishing places by an 1855 treaty, as well as parties interested in fishing as a sport (including the National Park Service) were concerned about government plans to build eight projects on the Columbia and five on the Snake. However, it was generally agreed that Hells Canyon dam would have no significant effect on the salmon since it would be located above the Salmon River. In fact, one of interior's arguments for proceeding with Hells Canyon, as well as the Boundary and Wolf Creek projects, immediately and ahead of The Dalles, and projects on the lower Snake was that these dams would not impair the salmon run and would allow time for the Fish and Wildlife Service and the Office of Indian Affairs, together with the Bureau of Reclamation and the Corps of Engineers, to solve the problem before more mainstream dams were built below the Okanogan and Salmon Rivers. See memorandum, W. W. Gardner to Krug, March 6, 1947, Warner W. Gardner Papers, HSTL; memorandum, Davidson to Chapman, February 12, 1951, File 1-310, Administrative General Power Development-Pacific Northwest, RG 48.

88. House of Representatives, *Hearings on H.R. 5743 before the Subcommittee on Irrigation and Reclamation of the House Committee on Interior and Insular Affairs*, 82d Cong., 2d sess., 113, 126-27, 49-50, 78.

89. *Ibid.*, 129-130.

90. *Ibid.*, 152-55, 173, 183-83, 186-89, 190-91, 200-02, 211-13, 216-17, 239-41, 250-51, 266-68, 295-96, 300-01; *New York Times*, June 15, 1952, 33.

91. House of Representatives, *Hearings on H.R. 5743 before the Subcommittee on Irrigation and Reclamation of the House Committee on Interior and Insular Affairs*, 82d Cong., 2d sess., 157-58.

92. *Ibid.*, 520-24, 528-37, 577-79; see also Bessey, "The Political Issues of the Hells Canyon Controversy," 687-90.

93. House of Representatives, *Hearings on H.R. 5743 before the Subcommittee on Irrigation and Reclamation of the House Committee on Interior and Insular Affairs*, 82d Cong., 2d sess., 506-09.

94. *Ibid.*, 736; *Electrical World*, June 30, 1952, 62; see also April 7, 1952, 94; *New York Times*, June 15, 1952, 33.

95. Bessey, "The Political Issues of the Hells Canyon Controversy," 682; *New York Times*, June 28, 1952, 23, July 9, 1952, 40.

96. Bessey, "The Political Issues of the Hells Canyon Controversy," 682; *Electrical World*, December 8, 1952, 8; *The Nation*, November 1, 1952, 406.

97. Memorandum, Administrator, Bonneville Power Administration, to Secretary of the Interior, January 31, 1952, File 1-310, Administrative General, Power Development-Pacific Northwest General RG 48.

98. The secretaries of interior and agriculture in the Eisenhower Administration withdrew their respective departments' interventions, and the FPC granted the Idaho Power Company a license to build the three low dams on August 4, 1955. Supporters of the federal high dam initiated a suit against the decision, but the courts upheld it in 1956 and 1957. Its backers continued to try to win congressional approval of the federal Hells Canyon project until 1958, when it became clear that President Eisenhower would veto any authorization bill that was passed, and the private company had already begun work on its project.

99. Report, "Niagara Development and Democratic Power Policy, a Summary," November 12, 1949, Murphy Files, HST Papers.

100. The mouth of the Niagara River is located nearly 200 miles from the St. Lawrence River at the opposite end of Lake Ontario.

101. The politics and diplomacy involved in the creation of the Seaway plan are treated in William R. Willoughby, *The St. Lawrence Waterway, a Study in Politics and Diplomacy*, especially Chapters 14, 15 and 16.

102. Letter, Truman to Governor Thomas E. Dewey, August 19, 1945, OF 156, HST Papers; telegram, Truman to Dewey, September 27, 1945, *Public Papers, 1945*, 349; Special Message to Congress, October 3, 1945, *ibid.*, 359; memorandum, Chapman and Lewis A. Pick to Truman, March 5, 1952, OF 156, HST Papers; Message to Congress, January 21, 1946, *Public Papers, 1946*, 53; letters, Truman to President Pro-Tem of Senate and Speaker of House, January 26, 1948, *Public Papers, 1948*, 107; U.S. Federal Power Commission, Opinion 203, December 22, 1950, FPC Release No. 5160, Project No. 2000, and memorandum Bell to Charles Murphy, November 8, 1949, OF 235, HST Papers; letter, Louis St. Laurent to Truman, May 27, 1949, and letter, Truman to St. Laurent, June 8, 1949, OF 156, HST Papers; Joint Statement Following Discussions with Prime Minister St. Laurent of Canada, September 28, 1951, *Public Papers, 1951*, 546.

103. Special Message to the Congress Urging Action in the St. Lawrence Seaway, January 28, 1952, *Public Papers, 1952-53*, 125-28; *Congress and the Nation*, 958-60.

104. Letter to the President of the Senate and Speaker of the House Regarding the St. Lawrence Seaway and Power Project, July 1, 1952, *Public Papers, 1952-53*, 451-54; memorandum, Chapman to Murphy, June 26, 1952, Murphy Files, HST Papers; letter, Truman to Senator Warren G. Magnuson, August 14, 1952, OF 156, HST Papers.

105. Memorandum, Bell to Eban Ayers, January 15, 1953, Bell Files, HST Papers; Annual Budget Message to the Congress, January 9, 1953, *Public Papers, 1952-53*, 1147; letter, Stanley Woodward to Truman, January 8, 1953, Murphy Files, HST Papers. The license for the project was awarded to the New York State Power Authority on July 15, 1953; see Docket Sheets, Project 2000, FPC Files; Willoughby, *The St. Lawrence Waterway*, 251. The Seaway Act, authorizing the United States to build the seaway with Canada, was finally passed and signed by President Eisenhower in May 1954. It did not call for any federal government participation in the power project, nor did it require the New York State Power Authority to adhere to federal preference policy in disposing of the power. Work on the seaway was completed in 1960.

106. Report, "Niagara Development and Democratic Power Policy, a Summary," November 12, 1949, Murphy Files, HST Papers.

107. Memorandum, Olds to Truman, November 12, 1949, report, "Niagara Development and Democratic Power Policy, a Summary," November 12, 1949, Niagara Falls folder, Murphy Files, HST Papers; memorandum, Murphy to Truman, September 13, 1949, letter, Prime Minister Louis St. Laurent to Truman, May 27, 1949, memorandum, Truman to Secretary of State, September 23, 1949, OF 2396, HST Papers.

108. Report, "Power and Flood Control in the Northeast, 1952," Hechler Files, HST Papers; *Electrical World*, October 8, 1951, 104; U.S., Department of State, *Treaties and Other International Agreements, 1: 1950*, TIAS 2130, 694-98; E. Robert de Luccia, "Report to Federal Power Commission on Possibilities for Redevelopment of Niagara Falls for Power, Niagara River, New York" (Washington, D.C., September 1949), 11-12.

109. Memorandum, Bell to Murphy, March 7, 1950, Niagara Falls Folder, Murphy Files, HST Papers.

110. Special Message to the Senate Transmitting Treaty with Canada Concerning Uses of the Waters of the Niagara River, May 2, 1950, *Public Papers, 1950*, 280; newspaper clipping, *Watertown Daily Times*, July 26, 1950, File 1-310, Administrative General, Power Development-Northeastern General, RG 48; report, "Power and Flood Control in the Northeast, 1952," Hechler Files, HST Papers; *Treaties and Other International Agreements, 1: 1950*, TIAS 2130, 699-700.

111. Newspaper clipping, Thomas L. Stokes, "Private Power Renews Attack," *Washington Evening Star*, February 25, 1952, File 110, Administration and Planning, Authorization and Policies, RG 115; *New York Times*, January 6, 1952, III, 7; *Electrical World*, October 8, 1951, 104.

112. Senate, *Hearings before Senate Committee on Public Works on the Project for Redevelopment of Niagara Falls*, 82d Cong., 1st sess., 163-64; see also 153-62.

113. *Ibid.*, 110, 113; see also 114-37.

114. *Ibid.*, 191, 194; "Statement of Assistant Secretary Warne at Hearings of House Committee on Public Works on the Project for Redevelopment of Niagara Falls," September 20, 1951, File 1-310, Administrative General, Power Development-Northeastern General, RG 48.

115. Annual Budget Message to the Congress: Fiscal year 1953, January 21, 1952, *Public Papers, 1952-53*, 89.

116. Investigation of Private Power folder, Federal Trade Commission File, Stephen J. Spingarn Papers, HSTL.

117. *Electrical World*, February 18, 1952, 6; *New York Times*, January 4, 1952, 11, March 25, 1952, 37, May 30, 1952, 2.

118. Memorandum, Director, Northeast Field Staff to Acting Director, Program Staff, File 1-310, Administrative General, Power Development-Northeastern General, RG 48; *Electrical World*, March 17, 1952, 5.

119. *The Nation*, June 7, 1952, 551-52; *Electrical World*, June 2, 1952, 70-71.

120. Memorandum, Chapman to Truman, February 9, 1952, Correspondence File, General, 1949-1953, Chapman Papers.

121. *Washington Evening Star*, February 25, 1952, in *Congressional Record*, 82d Cong., 2d sess., 1952, 98: 2265; *ibid.*, 2264.

122. *Congressional Record*, 82nd Cong., 2d sess., 1952, 98: 2316. See also Herbert Lee Williams, *The Newspaperman's President* (Chicago: Nelson-Hall, 1984), 138-39. Williams points out that Truman approved of advertising when it backed policies of the Democratic Party; for example, in 1945, he praised sponsors for placing an advertisement favoring national compulsory health insurance in major Eastern newspapers.

123. Address Before the Electric Consumers Conference, May 26, 1952, *Public Papers, 1952-53*, 372.

124. Clipping, *Congressional Record, Senate, 1952*, 7706-07, memorandum, Stephen J. Spingarn to the files, July 9, 1952, letter, James M. Mead to Frederick J. Lawton, July 11, 1952, letter, Mead to Edwin C. Johnson, July 11, 1952, memorandum, Spingarn to Mead, July 15, 1952, Investigation of Private Power folder, Federal Trade Commission File, Spingarn Papers.

125. Memorandum, Spingarn to David Bell, July 16, 1952, memorandum, Spingarn to the files, August 25, 1952, *ibid.*

126. *Electrical World*, May 19, 1952, 123.

127. Memorandum, Chapman to Murphy, June 26, 1953, OF 556, HST Papers.

128. Letter, Chapman to Truman, February 14, 1952, File 1-310, Administrative General, Power Development, Northeastern General, RG 48.

129. *New York Times*, March 14, 1952, 8.

130. The congressional deadlock continued throughout Eisenhower's first administration and into his second. The president then came out in favor of New York State development, and a bill, representing a compromise, finally passed in 1957 which provided that New York State would build the power project, with 50-50 allotments of kilowatts to public and private power.

Chapter 8. War of Words: Efforts to Enunciate a Power Policy

1. Senate, *Hearings on Interior Department Appropriations Bill for 1950*, 81st Cong., 1st sess., 203.

2. Senate, *Hearings on Department of the Army Appropriations Bill for 1950*, 81st Cong., 1st sess., 1149.

3. *Public Utilities Fortnightly*, August 3, 1950, 163.

4. *Congressional Quarterly* 5 (1949): 212.

5. Newspaper clipping, *Wall Street Journal*, June 29, 1950, Wallgren Papers; U.S. Chamber of Commerce, "Business in Action," March 31, 1950, in File 1-310, Administrative General, Power Development, RG 48.

6. Senate, *Hearings on Interior Department Appropriations Bill for 1952*, 82d Cong., 1st sess., 109.

7. Letter, Joel D. Wolfsohn, Executive Secretary, National Power Policy Committee, to Krug. January 10, 1947, File 1-288, Administrative General, National Power Policy Committee, RG 48.

8. Letter, Krug to Wickard, August 26, 1947, memorandum, Carl Hamilton, Assistant Administrator, Rural Electrification Administration, to Wickard, September 10, 1947, Office Files of Claude Wickard, RG 221; memorandum, Arthur Goldschmidt to the files, October 6, 1947, File 1-288, Administrative General, National Power Policy Committee, RG 48.

9. Memorandum, H.S. Person, Consulting Economist to Hamilton, Office Files of C. R. Wickard, 1947-49, Rural Electrification Administration, RG 221; memorandum, Arthur Goldschmidt to the files, October 6, 1947, File 1-288, Administrative General, National Power Policy Committee, RG 48.

10. Memorandum, Hamilton to Wickard, September 10, 1947, Office Files of Claude Wickard, RG 221.

11. *Ibid*.

12. Letters, Krug to Wickard, October 22, 1947, John P. Robertson, Assistant to the Director, Division of Power, to Stephen G. Kelley, Supervisor of the City Record, Manhattan, File 1-288, Administrative General, National Power Policy Committee, RG 48.

13. Robertson to Dr. Ralph R. Reuter, October 11, 1948, *ibid*.

14. Memorandum, Joel D. Wolfsohn to Secretary Chapman, July 27, 1950, Wolfsohn Papers.

15. Memorandum, July 10, 1950, File 1-310, Administrative General, Power Development, RG 48.

16. Memoranda, Fowler Harper, Solicitor, to Secretary Ickes, August 7, 1945, Straus to Ickes, October 22, 1945, *ibid*.

17. Memorandum on Power Policy, January 3, 1946, Federal Power Policy File, Wolfsohn Papers.

18. Memorandum, Straus to Ickes, December 21, 1945, File 1-310, Administrative General, Power Development, RG 48.

19. Memorandum, Warne to Ickes, December 20, 1945, File 1-310, Administrative General, Power Development, RG 48.

20. Memorandum on Power Policy, January 3, 1946, Federal Power Policy File, Wolfsohn Papers.

21. *Ibid*. There had been other efforts in the Roosevelt Administration to coordinate power policy among the various units of the Interior Department and between them and other government divisions that dealt with power. A Division of Power, set up in the Department in 1941, had some success in achieving this aim. Its Branch of Economics and Statistics issued statements on policy on subjects such as river basin development. In 1945, Joel Wolfsohn, then assistant commissioner of the General Land Office, recommended to Secretary Ickes that a Bureau of Power be formed for centralizing all power activities, but nothing came of the proposal. See memorandum, Wolfsohn to Ickes, January 4, 1945, Power Organization File, Wolfsohn Papers; Craufurd D. Goodwin, "Policies toward Particular Energy Sources," 173-74.

22. Memorandum, Secretary of the Interior to Commissioner, Bureau of Reclamation; Administrator, Bonneville Power Administration; Administrator, Southwestern Power Administration; Administrator, Southeastern Power Administration; Assistant Secretary William E. Warne; Director, Division of Power; Solicitor, July 10, 1950, File 110, Administration, Authorization and Policies, RG 115.

23. Memorandum, Warne to Chapman, July 14, 1950, Policy on Wheeling Arrangements File, Division of Power Files, RG 48.

24. Memorandum, Assistant Secretary Warne to Secretary of the Interior, Policy on Wheeling Arrangements File, Division of Power Files, RG 48; memorandum, Secretary of the Interior to Administrator, Bonneville Power Administration; Administrator, Southeastern Power Administration; Administra-

tor, Southwestern Power Administration; Acting Director, Division of Power; and Commissioner, Bureau of Reclamation, July 14, 1950, File 1-310, Administrative General, Power Development, RG 48.

25. *Ibid.*

26. *Ibid.*

27. Memorandum, Warne to Chapman, October 4, 1950, File 1-310, Administrative General, Power Development, RG 48.

28. Memorandum on Power Policy to All Staffs of the Interior Department, September 1, 1950, Bureau of Reclamation, W.O. Draft, *ibid.*; memorandum on Power Policy, January 3, 1946, Federal Power Policy File, Wolfsohn Papers.

29. Memorandum, Warne to Chapman, October 4, 1950, File 1-310, Administrative General, Power Development, RG 48.

30. Letters, Carlton L. Nau to Chapman, July 19, 1950; Chapman to Nau, August 15, 1950, *ibid.*

31. Letter, Kenneth Markwell, Acting Commissioner of Reclamation, to Kenneth G. Whitaker, Electric Power Board of Chattanooga, April 15, 1952, *ibid.* On April 20, 1953, the new Secretary of the Interior in the Eisenhower Administration verified that the Ickes memorandum had been interior's basic power policy statement since 1946; see letters, Secretary Douglas McKay to Congressmen John P. Saylor, Chairman, Subcommittee on Territories, Committee on Interior and Insular Affairs, and Norris Poulson, chairman, Subcommittee on Irrigation and Reclamation, Committee on Interior and Insular Affairs, April 20, 1953, *ibid.*

32. *Congressional Quarterly* 5 (1949): 767-68.

33. Memorandum, Warne to Krug, June 20, 1949, Office Files of Secretary of the Interior Oscar Chapman, 1933-53, Bureau of Reclamation, 1946-49, RG 48.

34. *Ibid.*

35. Letter, Krug to Pace, October 27, 1949, File 8-1, Reclamation Bureau, Organization and Methods, RG 48.

36. Telephone calls, Krug to Gant, Gant to Krug, October 27, 1949, Conference File, Krug Papers.

37. Memoranda, Straus to Krug, October 27, 1949, Warne to Krug, October 27, 1949, File 8-1, Reclamation Bureau, Organization and Methods, RG 48.

38. Letter, Krug to Pace, October 27, 1949, *ibid.*; telephone call, Krug to Pace, October 13, 1949, Conference File, Krug Papers;

39. Letter to the Chairman of the President's Water Resources Policy Commission, January 3, 1950, *Public Papers, 1950*, 1. Krug had resigned in November, and Oscar Chapman was now secretary of the interior.

40. *A Water Policy for the American People,* 1: 307; Letter to the Chairman of the President's Water Resources Policy Commission, January 3, 1950, *Public Papers, 1950,* 2; Press Release, January 3, 1950, President's Water Resources Policy Commission, Administrative, 1950-51, Press Releases, PWRPC Records.

41. Press Release, May 8, 1950, President's Water Resources Policy Commission, Administrative, 1950-51, Press Releases, PWRPC Records.

42. President's Water Resources Policy Commission, Administration Subject File, General, Press Releases, Committees and Subcommittees folder, PWRPC Records; *A Water Policy for the American People*, 1: 309.

43. "Committee on Power Policy as Related to Water Resources, Outline of Work"; "Membership of the Committee on Power Policy," President's Water Resources Policy Commission, Administrative, 1950-51, Press Releases, Committees and Subcommittees Folder, PWRPC Records; *A Water Policy for the American People*, 1: 309.

44. Letter, R. R. Renne to Morris L. Cooke, May 23, 1950, President's Water Resources Policy Commission, Administrative, 1950-51, Press Releases, Committees and Subcommittees folder, PWRPC Records; *Electrical World*, March 29, 1950, 32.

45. *New York Times*, June 22, 1950, 4; *Public Utilities Fortnightly*, July 20, 1950, 101.

46. "Water Resources, Electric Power and National Policy: Recommendations of the National Association of Electric Companies in Response to Inquiries from the Water Resources Policy Commission," May 1950, Power File, PWRPC Files.

47. Press Release, May 8, 1950, Executive Office of the President, Water Resources Policy Commission, Administrative, 1950-51, Press Releases, PWRPC Records; *A Water Policy for the American People*, 1: 308; *Public Utilities Fortnightly*, July 20, 1950, 101.

48. *A Water Policy for the American People*, 1: 308.

49. Memorandum, Sherman S. Poland to Bernard Foster, Jr., May 23, 1950, President's Water Resources Policy Commission, Administrative, 1950-51, Policy folder, PWRPC Records; Minutes, Third Meeting, May 17, 1950, President's Water Resources Policy Commission, Commission Deliberation, 1950-51, Committee on Power Policy as Related to Water Resources Statements . . . by Committee Members folder, *ibid.*; memorandum, Acting Director, Branch of Power Utilization, to Director, Branch of Project Planning, May 12, 1950, File 122, President's Water Resources Policy Commission, RG 115.

50. Letter, F. H. Craddock to Leon Jourolmon, Jr., May 9, 1950, President's Water Resources Policy Commission, Commission Deliberation, 1950-51, Committee on Power Policy as Related to Water Resources Statements . . . by Committee Members folder, PWRPC Records.

51. Memorandum, Acting Director, Branch of Power Utilization, to Director, Branch of Project Planning, May 12, 1950, File 122, President's Water Resources Policy Commission, RG 115.

52. Letter, Monrad C. Wallgren to Cooke, September 27, 1950, File 1-310, Administrative General, Power Development, RG 48; see also The Arkansas-White River Basin Report for the President's Water Resources Policy Commission, prepared by the Southwest Field Committee, Department of Interior, August 1950, File 122, President's Water Resources Policy Commission, RG 115.

53. *A Water Policy for the American People*, 1: 245-46.

54. *Ibid.*, 303.

55. *New York Times*, December 18, 1950, 25; *Electrical World*, December 18, 1950, 71.

56. *Electrical World*, December 18, 1950, 71.

57. *A Water Policy for the American People*, 1: 10-11, 49.

58. *Ibid.*, 49; letter, Truman to Cooke, January 3, 1950, President's Water Resources Policy Commission, Administrative, 1950-51, Establishment of Commission folder, PWRPC Records.

59. *Public Papers, 1951*, 85; letter to Elmer B. Staats from Leland Olds, January 5, 1951, Commission Report and Recommendations, 1950-51, Final Report of Commission, Legislative Recommendations, Proposed Language for State-of-the Union Message folder, PWRPC Records.

60. Memorandum, Cooke to Truman, February 12, 1951, Proposed Water Resources Act of 1951, President's Water Resources Policy Commission, Commission Report an Recommendations, 1950-51, Recommendations of Commission folder, PWRPC Records; see also Press Release, President's Water Resources Policy Commission, February 11, 1951, Administrative, 1950-51, Press Releases, *ibid*.

61. Press Releases, February 25, 1951 and February 26, 1951, President's Water Resources Policy Commission, Administrative, 1950-51, Press Releases, PWRPC Records.

62. Letter to Department and Agency Heads on the Report of the Water Resources Policy Commission, March 14, 1951, *Public Papers, 1951*, 185.

63. *Public Papers, 1951*, 185; letter, Truman to F. J. Lawton, March 14, 1951; letter, Chapman to Truman, March 27, 1951, memorandum, Lawton to Truman, April 4, 1951, OF 2393A, HST Papers; letter, Vernon D. Northrop to Warne, May 29, 1951, File 1-318, Administrative General, River Valley Authorities, RG 48.

64. Memorandum, M. D. Scheidt to Elmer B. Staats, February 12, 1952, Division of Fiscal Analysis, 1939-52, Unit 943, Bureau of the Budget, RG 51.

65. Memoranda, E. C. Weitzell to Claude R. Wickard, William C. Wise and Riggs Sheppard, September 13, 1951, Subcommittee on Power Policy to Inter-Agency Water Policy Review Committee, August 30, 1951, Office Files of William C. Wise, Deputy Administrator, Rural Electrification Administration, RG 221.

66. Memorandum, Weitzell to Wickard, Wise and Sheppard, September 13, 1951, *ibid*.

67. Memorandum, Subcommittee on Power Policy to Inter-Agency Water Policy Review Committee, August 30, 1951, *ibid*.

68. *Ibid*.

69. *Ibid*.

70. For a more detailed treatment of this episode as it relates to the struggle over river basin organizational machinery, see Chapter 3, above.

71. Memorandum, Lawton to Truman, May 21, 1952, OF 2393A, HST Papers.

72. Memorandum, Elmer B. Staats to Thomas C. Buchanan, May 29, 1952, Federal Power Commission Files, Water Resources Policy Act, 1952 folder, Doty Papers; Special Message to the Congress on the Nation's Land and Water Resources, January 19, 1953, *Public Papers, 1953-53*, 1214, 1208.

73. Letter to William S. Paley on Creation of the President's Materials Policy Commission, January 22, 1951, *Public Papers, 1951*, 118; Craufurd D. Goodwin, "The Truman Administration," in *Energy Policy in Perspective*, ed. Craufurd D. Goodwin, 52-53. William Roy Hamilton, a student of political science, has studied this commission as a means of analyzing the purposes of *ad hoc* presidential commissions generally; see "The President's Materials Policy Commission" (Ph.D. diss., University of Maryland, 1962). Hamilton concludes that these commissions can never be merely fact finding or completely objective; they also must be viewed as political instruments.

74. Memorandum, Secretary of Interior to Heads of Bureaus and Offices, March 8, 1951, Reading File, Chapman Papers; The President's Materials Policy Commission, *Resources for Freedom, 1: Foundations for Growth and Security*, ii.

75. Letter to William S. Paley on Creation of the President's Materials Policy Commission, January 22, 1951, *Public Papers, 1951*, 118.

76. Memorandum, Secretary of Interior to Heads of Bureaus and Offices, March 8, 1951, Reading File, Chapman Papers; memorandum, Lyle E. Craine, Acting Director, Program Staff to Heads of Bureaus and Offices, August 15, 1951, File 1222, Administration and Planning, Planning Board, President's Materials Policy Commission, RG 115; *Electrical World*, August 4, 1952, 8-9; *Resources for Freedom*, 1: ii.

77. Drafts of Report, Electrical Energy Drafts I, Overall, Energy Draft III, Energy Resources Section, President's Materials Policy Commission Records (hereafter cited as PMPC Records), HSTL.

78. *Ibid*.

79. Letter, Arthur A. Maass to Phil Coombs, Staff Director, March 21, 1952, Executive Secretary, Comments on Drafts of Reports, Energy (Electric-Petroleum Oil #1) PMPC Records.

80. *Ibid*.

81. Letters, Rolande C. Widgery to William C. Ackerman, February 29, 1952, Eugene C. Ayres to Ackerman, February 28, 1952, C. H. Giroux, Special Assistant, Department of the Army to Ackerman, March 4, 1952, *ibid*.

82. Letter, Francis L. Adams to Ackerman, February 4, 1952; memorandum, E. W. Morehouse to President's Materials Policy Commission, March 3, 1952, *ibid*.

83. *Electrical World*, August 4, 1952, 8; Letter in Response to Report of the President's Materials Policy Commission, June 23, 1952, *Public Papers, 1952-53*, 438-39; *Resources for Freedom*, 1: 118.

84. *Resources for Freedom*, 1: 118.

85. *Ibid.*, 121.

86. Letter to the President of the Senate and to the Speaker of the House Transmitting Report of the President's Materials Policy Commission, July 1, 1952, *Public Papers, 1952-53*, 455-56.

87. National Security Resources Board, *The Objectives of United States Materials Resources Policy and Suggested Initial Steps in Their Accomplishment*, 114, 149.

Chapter 9. Victory or Defeat: Tallying Up

1. Special Message to the National Rural Electric Cooperative Association, March 13, 1952, *Public Papers: Truman, 1952-53*, 200-01.

2. *Ibid*.

3. Speech, "The Need for More Electric Power," delivered in Washington, D.C., April 11, 1949; for examples of Truman's use of similar rhetoric, see *Public Papers, 1949*, 5, 80, *Public Papers, 1950*, 86, 279, 306, 350, 365-66, 478; *Public Papers, 1951*, 89; *Public Papers, 1952*, 92, 202-03, 333, 458, 973, 981, 1149. For instances of Krug's statements in this vein, see Speech and Article File, Krug Papers; for examples by Chapman, see Reading File of Oscar L. Chapman, 1952, Miscellaneous Records, Chapman Papers and File No. 1-3, Interviews with Secretary, General, 1937-1953, RG 48; for comments by Warne, see speech, November 30, 1950, File 1-310, Administrative General, Power Development, Public Statements by Department Officials, RG 48.

4. For examples of expressions of this view, see William Warne to William L. Anglin, Jr., November 1, 1951, File 1-310, Administrative General, Power Development, RG 48, and Oscar Chapman Radio interview, March 245, 1950, Capitol Cloak Room, Chapman Papers. Chapman told his radio audience, "I'm one of those who feel that public power can develop and make progress for the best interests of the people along with and integrated with private power."

5. Notes of Meeting on Cooperatives Having Contracts with SPA, May 18, 1953, Files of Riggs Sheppard, REA, RG 221.

6. *Annual Report of the Federal Power Commission, 1945*, 16, 63; *ibid., 1946*, 82; *ibid., 1952*, 177; *ibid., 1953*, 177, 339, 346; *Annual Report of the Tennessee Valley Authority, 1945*, 60; *ibid., 1953*, 17.

7. *Electrical World*, January 25, 1954, 167, 177.

8. *Ibid.* At the end of the Truman presidency, generating capacity of these public bodies consisted of 9.8 percent of the nation's total and their production 6.1 percent. At the outset of the Truman years, these figures stood at 9.3 and 5.9 respectively.

9. December 1, 1952, Longhand Notes, 1953 folder, PSF.

10. Harold Seidman, *Politics, Position and Power, the Dynamics of Federal Organization* (New York, 1970), 23-24; see also David B. Truman, *The Governmental Process*, 435-36.

11. In a speech to the National Rural Electric Cooperative Association, for example, he denounced private power's "vicious propaganda barrage" that he said was intended to restore "the unlimited right of private monopoly to exploit this nation's water power resources." *New York Times*, March 14, 1952, 1.

12. *Electrical World*, July 14, 1952, 114.

13. Memorandum, Krug to Heads of Bureaus and Offices, November 30, 1948, File 110, Administration, Authorization and Policies, July 1, 1945-December 31, 1948, RG 115.

14. Richardson, *Dams, Parks & Politics*, 55; *The Nation*, March 1949, 267-68. In an 1988 interview, William Warne said Chapman operated as though his job was more of a public relations than an administrative one; see Warne oral history, 46-47.

15. Park Service Director Newton Drury made the point about Chapman's political skills being related to deviousness in a 1961 interview. Drury, who thought little of Chapman's intellectual or administrative abilities, commented that with Chapman at the helm, the Bureau of Reclamation was "like the state of Prussia in the German empire, where everything was weighted in its favor." Quoted in Richardson, *Dams, Parks & Politics*, 55.

16. Richardson, *Dams, Parks & Politics*, 55; Oscar L. Chapman oral history, 471-72, HSTL; newspaper clipping, January 1, 1951, Department of the Interior Subject File-Oscar Chapman, Doty Papers; Warne oral history, 45.

17. Straus had been working against a Columbia Valley Authority since becoming commissioner in 1945. Chapman was assistant secretary at the time and was under secretary when Straus defied Davidson's order to support departmental policy on the Columbia Valley Authority.

18. Besides the secretary of agriculture, mainly through the Rural Electrification Administration, and the secretary of the army, through the Corps of Engineers, the secretary of commerce was involved but in only a minor way, primarily insofar as power policies were related to the economic and business development of an area.

19. Davidson, the senior assistant secretary, and Warne were joined by Dale E. Doty and Vernon D. Northrop, government service career men, in June 1950, when Chapman appointed them assistant secretaries under a presidential reorganization plan that allowed him to strengthen his staff. Chapman did not fill the vacant post of under-secretary until April 1951. Richard D. Searles, an Arizona rancher, served in that post until August 1952, and Northrop was named to succeed him. Davidson resigned in late 1950, and Warne left the department in late 1951.

20. Memorandum, Raver to Chapman, January 31, 1952, File 1-310, Administrative General, Power Development-Pacific Northwest, RG 48.

21. Newspaper clippings, *Oregon Daily Journal*, December 19, 1952, *Longview Daily News* (Longview, Washington), December 17, 1952, *ibid.*; *Electrical World*, December 29, 1952, 52, January 19, 1953, 5.

22. Robert H. Ferrell, *Harry S. Truman*, 186.

23. See Hamby, *Liberalism and Its Challengers*, 70.

24. Alonzo L. Hamby, "Harry S. Truman: Insecurity and Responsibility," in *Leadership in the Modern Presidency*, Fred I. Greenstein, ed., 69.

25. Truman had vetoed the anti-labor Taft-Hartley bill, but he also had broken a Kansas City Teamsters strike when he was a county judge, and in his first term as president had used the injunction against striking miners and had proposed drafting striking railroad workers.

26. *Public Utilities Fortnightly*, March 13, 1952, 375.

27. "Collection of Scare Words on Electric Power," Electric Power folder, David D. Lloyd Papers, HSTL.

28. Richardson, *Dams, Parks & Politics*, 35-36; press conference, September 7, 1950, *Public Papers, 1950*, 621; *New York Times*, September 7, 1950, 35, September 8, 1952, 12; September 11, 1950, 18; September 29, 1950, 21.

29. Telephone call, John N. Spencer, Supervisor, Region 7, Bureau of Reclamation, to Gordon H. Storm, Manager, Pathfinder Irrigation District, May 2, 1952; memorandum, Straus to Chapman, May 6, 1953; memorandum, Administrative Assistant Northrop to Chapman, June 20, 1952; letter, Chapman to Representative John R. Murdock, Chairman, Committee on Interior and

Insular Affairs, June 20, 1952; memorandum, Straus to Chapman, May 6, 1952, all in File 1-310, Administrative General, Power Development-Administrative, RG 48.

30. Speech to Statewide Electric Cooperative Annual Convention, Oklahoma City," March 29-30, 1951, *ibid.*; see also Speech to NRECA Annual Meeting, Region X, October 27, 1950, and Address to Laclede Electric Cooperative Annual Meeting, Lebanon, Missouri, June 29, 1951, File 1-310, Administrative General Power Development-Public Statements by Departmental Officials, RG 48.

31. Memorandum, Otis Beasley, Director, Division of Budget and Finance, to Northrop, March 14, 1951; letter, Chapman to Edwin T. Gibson, Acting Administrator, Defense Production Administration, May 9, 1950, File 1-310, Administrative General, Power Development-Administrative, RG 48; memorandum, Oscar Chapman to Truman, April 12, 1951, Secretary of the Interior, Miscellaneous File, Box 158, PSF.

32. *Public Papers of the Presidents: Dwight D. Eisenhower, 1953* (Washington, D.C., 1957), 26-27.

33. Federal Power Commission Daily News Digest, August 19, 1953, FPC Files, Subject File: Power, Doty Papers. See also Frank Smith, *The Politics of Conservation*, 278-81; *Congress and the Nation*, 833-966; Richardson, *Dams, Parks & Politics*, Chapter 6.

Bibliography

Manuscripts

Bell, David E. Papers. Harry S. Truman Library, Independence, Mo.
Bessey, Roy F. Papers. Harry S. Truman Library.
Chapman, Oscar L. Papers. Harry S. Truman Library.
Davidson, C. Girard. Papers. Harry S. Truman Library.
Democratic National Committee. Records. Harry S. Truman Library.
Doty, Dale E. Papers. Harry S. Truman Library.
Gardner, Warner W. Papers. Harry S. Truman Library.
Krug, Julius A. Papers. Library of Congress, Washington, D.C.
Lawton, Frederick J. Papers. Harry S. Truman Library.
Lloyd, David D. Papers. Harry S. Truman Library.
Missouri Basin Survey Commission. Records. Harry S. Truman Library.
Murphy, Charles S. Papers, Harry S. Truman Library.
President's Materials Policy Commission. Records. Harry S. Truman Library.
President's Water Resources Policy Commission. Records. Harry S. Truman
    Library.
Rosenman, Samuel I. Papers. Harry S. Truman Library.
Spingarn, Stephen J. Papers. Harry S. Truman Library.
Truman, Harry S. Papers. Harry S. Truman Library.
U.S. Agriculture Department, Records of the Office of the Secretary. Record
    Group 16. National Archives, Washington, D.C.
U.S. Army Corps of Engineers, Records of the Office of the Chief of Engi-
    neers. Record Group 77. National Archives, Washington D.C.
U.S. Bureau of the Budget, Records. Record Group 51. National Archives,
    Washington, D.C.
U.S. Bureau of Reclamation, Records. Record Group 115. National Archives,
    Washington, D.C.
U.S. Commerce Department, Records. Record Group 40. National Archives,
    Washington, D.C.
U.S. Federal Power Commission, Files. Federal Power Commission, Washing-
    ton, D.C.
U.S. Interior Department, Records of the Office of the Secretary, Central
    Classified Files. Record Group 48. National Archives, Washington, D.C.

U.S. Rural Electrification Administration, Records. Record Group 221. National
    Archives, Washington, D.C.
Wallgren, Monrad C. Papers. Harry S. Truman Library.
Webb, James E. Papers. Harry S. Truman Library.
Wolfsohn, Joel D. Papers. Harry S. Truman Library.
Wright, Douglas. Papers. Harry S. Truman Library.

Oral Histories

All are deposited in the Harry S. Truman Library.

Chapman, Oscar L., by Jerry N. Hess, 1972-73
Clifford, Clark, by Jerry N. Hess. 1971-73.
Murphy, Charles S., by Jerry N. Hess. 1963-69.
_____; Neustadt, Richard; Stowe, David; and Webb, James, by Hugh Heclo
    and Anna Nelson. 1980.
Warne, William E., by Niel M. Johnson. 1988.

United States Public Documents

Congress:

Conference Report 888. 82d Cong., 1st sess. Washington, D.C., 1950.
    Congressional Record. Vol. 36 (1903), Vols. 92-98 (1946-1953).
House of Representatives. *House Document 473.* 81st Cong., 2d sess. 2 vols.
    Washington, D.C., 1950.
_____. *House Document 531.* 81st Cong., 2d sess. Washington, D.C., 1950.
_____. *House Report 1797.* 81st Cong., 2d sess. Washington, D.C., 1950.
_____. Committee on Agriculture. *Activities of the Department of Agriculture.*
    Hearings before the Committee on Agriculture, 82d Cong., 1st sess.
    Washington, D.C., 1951.
_____. Committee on Appropriations. *Interior Department Appropriations Bill
    for 1948. Hearings before a Subcommittee of the Committee on Appropria-
    tions,* 80th Cong., 1st sess. Washington, D.C., 1947.
_____. Committee on Appropriations. *Interior Department Appropriations Bill
    for 1949. Hearings before a Subcommittee of the Committee on Appropria-
    tions,* 80th Cong., 2d sess. Washington, D.C., 1948.
_____. Committee on Appropriations. *Interior Department Appropriations Bill
    for 1950. Hearings before a Subcommittee of the Committee on Appropria-
    tions,* 81st Cong., 1st sess. Washington, D.C., 1949.

_____. Committee on Appropriations. *Interior Department Appropriations Bill for 1951. Hearings before a Subcommittee of the Committee on Appropriations*, 81st Cong., 2d sess. Washington, D.C., 1950.

_____. Committee on Appropriations. *Interior Department Appropriations Bill for 1952. Hearings before a Subcommittee of the Committee on Appropriations*, 82d Cong., 1st sess. Washington, D.C., 1951.

_____. Committee on Interior and Insular Affairs. *Hearings on H.R. 5743 before the Subcommittee on Irrigation and Reclamation of the Committee on Interior and Insular Affairs*, 82d Cong., 2d sess. Washington, D.C., 1952.

_____. Committee on Interior and Insular Affairs. *An Interpretation of the Recommendations of the President's Water Resources Policy Commission. Hearings before the Subcommittee on Irrigation and Reclamation of the Committee on Interior and Insular Affairs*, 82d Cong., 1st sess. Washington, D.C., 1951.

_____. Committee on Public Works. *Bills to Reorganize and Consolidate Certain Federal Functions and Thereby Secure More Effective Administration by Establishing a Columbia Valley Administration to Assist in the Achievement of Unified Water Control and Resource Conservation and Development of the Columbia River, Its Tributaries, and the Surrounding Lands. Hearings before the Committee on Public Works*, 81st Cong., 1st sess. Washington, D.C., 1949.

Senate. *Appropriations, Budget Estimates, Etc., Senate Document 125*, 81st Cong., 1st sess. Washington, D.C. 1949.

_____. *Appropriations, Budget Estimates, Etc., Senate Document 239*, 82d Cong., 2d sess. Washington, D.C. 1950.

_____. *Appropriations, Budget Estimates, Etc., Senate Document 88*, 82d Cong., 1st sess. Washington, D.C. 1951.

_____. *Appropriations, Budget Estimates, Etc., Senate Document 169*, 82d Cong., 2d sess. Washington, D.C. 1952.

_____. Committee on Appropriations. *Agriculture Department Appropriations Bill for 1951. Hearings before a Subcommittee of the Committee on Appropriations*, 81st Cong., 2d sess. Washington, D.C., 1950.

_____. Committee on Appropriations. Agriculture Department Appropriations Bill for 1952. *Hearings before a Subcommittee of the Committee on Appropriations*, 82d Cong., 2d sess. Washington, D.C., 1951.

_____. Committee on Appropriations. *Hearings before the Subcommittee of the Committee on Appropriations on H.R. 3734 (Civil Functions) for Fiscal 1950*, 81st Cong., 1st sess. Washington, D.C., 1949.

_____. Committee on Appropriations. *Hearings before the Subcommittee of the Committee on Appropriations Making Appropriations for the Civil Functions*

Administered by the Department of the Army for the Fiscal Year 1951, 81st
Cong., 2d sess. Washington, D.C., 1950.

———. Committee on Appropriations. *Interior Department Appropriations Bill
for 1948. Hearings before a Subcommittee of the Committee on Appropriations*, 80th Cong., 1st sess. Washington, D.C., 1947.

———. Committee on Appropriations. *Interior Department Appropriations Bill
for 1949. Hearings before a Subcommittee of the Committee on Appropriations*, 80th Cong., 2d sess. Washington, D.C., 1948.

———. Committee on Appropriations. *Interior Department Appropriations Bill
for 1950. Hearings before a Subcommittee of the Committee on Appropriations*, 81st Cong., 1st sess. Washington, D.C., 1949.

———. Committee on Appropriations. *Interior Department Appropriations Bill
for 1951. Hearings before a Subcommittee of the Committee on Appropriations*, 81st Cong., 2d sess. Washington, D.C., 1950.

———. Committee on Appropriations. *Interior Department on Supplemental
Appropriations Bill for 1951. Hearings before a Subcommittee of the
Committee on Appropriations*, 81st Cong., 2d sess. Washington, D.C.,
1950.

———. Committee on Appropriations. *Interior Department Appropriations Bill
for 1952. Hearings before a Subcommittee of the Committee on Appropriations*, 82d Cong., 1st sess. Washington, D.C., 1951.

———. Committee on Appropriations. *Interior Department Appropriations Bill
for 1953. Hearings before a Subcommittee of the Committee on Appropriations*, 82d Cong., 2d sess. Washington, D.C., 1952.

———. Committee on Public Works. *Bills Dealing with the Development of the
Water Resources of the Columbia River Basin and the Establishment of a
Columbia Valley Administration, and for other Purposes. Hearings before
the Committee on Public Works*, 81st Cong., 1st sess. Washington, D.C.,
1949.

———. Committee on Public Works. *Project for Redevelopment of Niagara
Falls. Hearings before the Committee on Public Works*, 82d Cong., 1st
sess. Washington, D.C., 1951.

Executive Department:

Department of Agriculture. *Annual Report of the Administrator of the Rural
Electrification Administration for the Fiscal Year Ended June 30*, 1949.
Washington, D.C., 1950.

———. *Annual Report of the Administrator of the Rural Electrification
Administration for the Fiscal Year Ended June 30*, 1950. Washington,
D.C., 1951.

_____. *Annual Report of the Administrator of the Rural Electrification Adminis-tration for the Fiscal Year Ended June 30*, 1951. Washington, D.C., 1952.

_____. *Annual Report of the Administrator of the Rural Electrification Administration for the Fiscal Year Ended June 30*, 1952. Washington, D.C., 1953.

_____. Rural Electrification Administration. *Rural Lines, U.S.A.: The Story of the Rural Electrification Administration's First Twenty-five Years, 1935.* Washington, D.C., 1960.

Department of the Interior. *Annual Report of the Secretary of the Interior for the Fiscal Year Ended June 30, 1946,*Washington, D.C., 1947.

_____. *Annual Report of the Secretary of the Interior for the Fiscal Year Ended June 30, 1947.* Washington, D.C., 1948.

Department of State. *United States Treaties and Other International Agreements.* Vol. 1, *1950.* Washington, D.C., 1952.

Federal Power Commission. *Annual Report of the Federal Power Commission for the Fiscal Year Ended June 30, 1945.* Washington, D.C., 1946.

_____. *Annual Report of the Federal Power Commission for the Fiscal Year Ended June 30, 1946.* Washington, D.C., 1947.

_____. *Annual Report of the Federal Power Commission for the Fiscal Year Ended June 30, 1947.* Washington, D.C, 1948.

_____. *Annual Report of the Federal Power Commission for the Fiscal Year Ended June 30, 1951.* Washington, D.C, 1952.

_____. *Annual Report of the Federal Power Commission for the Fiscal Year Ended June 30, 1952.* Washington, D.C, 1953.

Tennessee Valley Authority. *Annual Report of the Tennessee Valley Authority for the Fiscal Year Ended 1945.* Washington, D.C., 1946.

_____. *Annual Report of the Tennessee Valley Authority for the Fiscal Year Ended 1953.* Washington, D.C., 1954.

Presidential and Other Special Commissions:

The Hoover Commission Report on Organization of the Executive Branch of the Government. Westport, Conn., 1970 [1949].

Missouri Basin Survey Commission. *Missouri: Land and Water.* Washington, D.C., 1953.

The Objectives of United States Materials Resources Policy and Suggested Initial Steps in their Accomplishment, a Report by the Chairman of the National Security Resources Board Based on the Report of the President's Materials Policy Commission and Federal Agency Comments Thereon. Washington, D.C., 1952.

The President's Materials Policy Commission. *Resources for Freedom.* Vol. 1: *Foundations for Growth and Security.* Vol. 2: *The Outlook for Energy Sources.* Washington, D.C., 1952.

The President's Water Resources Policy Commission. *A Water Policy for the American People: The Report of the President's Water Resources Policy Commission*, Vol. 1. Washington, D.C., 1950.

Statutes:

Statutes at Large 26 (1889-91); 30 (1897-99); 34 Part 1 (1905-07); 50, Part 1 (1937); 58, Part 1 (1944); 65 (1951); 66 (1952).

Supreme Court:

United States Reports 345 (October Term, 1952). Washington, D.C., 1953.

Newspapers and Periodicals

Arkansas Gazette, July 14, 1950.
Charlotte Observer, May 10, 1951.
Christian Science Monitor, March 21, 1950.
Congressional Quarterly Almanac, 1947-1952.
Daily Oklahoman, July 14, 1950.
Edison Electric Institute Bulletin, August 1945.
Electrical World, 1949-1952.
The Nation, 1949-1952.
New Republic, March 17, 1952.
News and Courier, Charleston, S.C., June 2, 1950.
New York Times, 1949-1952.
Public Utilities Fortnightly, 1949-1952.
Richmond Times Dispatch, December 20, 1950.
San Francisco Chronicle, March 23, 1950.
Tulsa World, May 4, 1950, July 14, 1950.

Books

Abrams, Ernest R. *Power in Transition.* New York: Scribner, 1940.
Anderson, Clinton P. *Outsider in the Senate: Senator Clinton P. Anderson's Memoirs.* Garden City, N.Y.: World Publishing, 1968.

Bailey, Stephen K., and Samuel, Howard D. *Congress at Work*. New York: Henry Holt, 1952.

Bauer, John, and Gold, Nathaniel. *The Electric Power Industry: Development, Organization and Public Policies*. New York: Harper, 1939.

Berman, William C. *The Politics of Civil Rights in the Truman Administration*. Columbus: Ohio State University Press, 1970.

Bernstein, Barton J., ed. *Politics and Policies of the Truman Administration*. Chicago: Quandrangle, 1970.

_____. *Towards a New Past: Dissenting Essays in American History*. New York: Vintage, 1969.

Bonbright, James C. *Public Utilities and the National Power Policies*. New York: Columbia University Press, 1940.

Burns, James MacGregor. *The Crosswinds of Freedom*. New York: Vintage, 1990.

Burns, Richard Dean. *Harry S. Truman: A Bibliography of His Times and Presidency*. Wilmington, Del.: Scholarly Resources, 1984.

Childs, M.S. *The Farmer Takes a Hand: The Electric Power Revolution in Rural America*. Garden City, N.Y.: Doubleday, 1952.

Clapp, Gordon R. *The TVA: An Approach to the Development of a Region*. Chicago: University of Chicago Press, 1955.

Clifford, Clark. *Counsel to the President*. New York: Random House, 1991.

Cochran, Bert. *Harry Truman and the Crisis Presidency*. New York: Funk & Wagnalls, 1973.

Coleman, Charles M. *P.G. and E. of California, The Centennial Story of Pacific Gas and Electric Company, 1852-1952*. New York: McGraw-Hill, 1952.

Congress and the Nation: A Review of Government and Politics in the Postwar Years. Vol. 1: *1945-1964*. Washington, D.C.: Congressional Quarterly, 1965.

Conkin, Paul. *The New Deal*. 2d. ed., Arlington Heights, Ill.: Thomas Y. Crowell, 1975.

Daniels, Jonathan. *The Man of Independence*. Philadelphia: Lippincott, 1950.

Davis, David Howard. *Energy Politics*. 2d ed. New York: St. Martin's Press, 1978.

Donovan, Robert J. *Tumultuous Years: The Presidency of Harry S. Truman, 1949-1953*. New York: Norton, 1982.

Einaudi, Mario. *The Roosevelt Revolution*. New York: Harcourt, Brace, 1959.

Electric Power and Government Policy, a Survey of the Relations Between the Government and the Electric Power Industry. New York: Twentieth Century Fund, 1948.

Ferrell. Robert H. *Harry S. Truman: A Life*. Columbia: University of Missouri Press, 1994.

_____. *Harry S. Truman and the Modern Presidency*. Boston: Little, Brown, 1983.

_____, ed. *The Autobiography of Harry S. Truman*. Boulder: Colorado Associated University Press, 1980.

_____, ed. *Dear Bess: The Letters from Harry to Bess Truman, 1910-1959*. New York: Norton, 1983.

_____, ed. *Off the Record: The Private Papers of Harry S. Truman*. New York: Harper and Row, 1980.

Fox, William F., Jr. *Federal Regulation of Energy*. Colorado Springs, Colo.: Shepard's/McGraw-Hill, 1974.

Galbraith, John K. *American Capitalism: The Concept of Countervailing Power*. Boston: Houghton, 1952.

Glaeser, Martin G. *Public Utilities in American Capitalism*. New York: Macmillan, 1957.

Goldman, Eric. *The Crucial Decade—And After: America, 1945-1960*. New York: Random House, 1966.

Golzé, Alfred R. *Reclamation in the United States*. Caldwell, Idaho: Caxton Printers, 1961.

Gosnell, Harold F. *Truman's Crises*. Westport, Conn.: Greenwood, 1980.

Hamby, Alonzo L. *Beyond the New Deal: Harry S. Truman and American Liberalism*. New York: Columbia University Press, 1973.

_____. *Harry S. Truman and the Fair Deal*. Lexington, Mass.: Heath, 1974.

_____. *Liberalism and Its Challengers: F.D.R. to Reagan*. New York: Oxford University Press, 1985.

_____. *Man of the People: A Life of Harry S. Truman*. New York: Oxford University Press, 1995.

Harris, Seymour E. *Saving American Capitalism, A Liberal Economic Program*. New York: Knopf, 1948.

Hartmann, Susan M. *Truman and the 80th Congress*. Columbia: University of Missouri Press, 1971.

Hartz, Louis B. *The Liberal Tradition in America*. New York: Harcourt, Brace, 1955.

Hawley, Ellis W. The New Deal and the Problem of Monopoly: A Study in Economic Ambivalence. Princeton, N.J.: Princeton University Press, 1966.

Hays, Samuel P. *Conservation and the Gospel of Efficiency: The Progressive Conservation Movement, 1890-1920*. Cambridge, Mass.: Harvard University Press, 1959.

_____. *The Response to Industrialism*. Chicago: University of Chicago Press, 1957.

Hechler, Ken. *Working with Truman: A Personal Memoir of the White House Years*. New York: Putnam, 1982.

Heller, Francis. *The Truman White House: The Administration of the Presidency, 1945-1953.* Lawrence: Regents Press of Kansas, 1980.

Hicks, John D. *Republican Ascendancy, 1921-1933.* New York: Harper, 1963.

Hofstadter, Richard. *The Age of Reform: From Bryan to F.D.R.* New York: Vintage, 1955.

_____. *The American Political Tradition and the Men Who Made It.* New York: Vintage, 1949.

Hubbard, Preston, J. *Origins of the TVA: The Muscle Shoals Controversy, 1920-1932.* Nashville: Vanderbilt University Press, 1961.

Hunt, Edward Eyre, ed. *The Power Industry and the Public Interest: A Summary of the Results of a Survey of the Relations Between the Government and the Electric Power Industry.* New York: Twentieth Century Fund, 1944.

Ickes, Harold L. *Secret Diary.* Vol. 2: *The Inside Struggle, 1936-1939.* Vol. 3: *The Lowering Clouds, 1939-1941.* New York: Simon and Schuster, 1954, 1955.

Kerwin, Jerome G. *Federal Water-Power Legislation.* New York: Columbia University Press, 1926.

King, Judson. *The Conservation Fight.* Washington, D.C.: Public Affairs Press, 1959.

Kirkendall, Richard S., ed. *The Truman Period as a Research Field: A Reappraisal.* Rev. ed. Columbia, Mo.: University of Missouri Press, 1974.

Kohlmeier, Louis M., Jr. *The Regulators.* New York: Harper and Row, 1969.

Kolko, Gabriel. *The Triumph of Conservatism, A Reinterpretation of American History, 1900-1916.* New York: Free Press, 1977.

Lawson, R. Alan. *The Failure of Independent Liberalism, 1930-1941.* New York: Putnam, 1971.

Leuctenburg, William E. *Franklin D. Roosevelt and the New Deal, 1932-1940.* New York: Harper and Row, 1963.

_____. *In the Shadow of FDR: From Harry Truman to Ronald Reagan.* Rev. ed. Ithaca, N.Y.: Cornell University Press, 1993.

Lief, Alfred. *Democracy's Norris: The Biography of a Lonely Crusader.* New York: Stackpole, 1939.

Lilienthal, David E. *The Journals of David E. Lilienthal.* Vol. 1: *The TVA Years, 1939-45.* Vol. 2: *The Atomic Energy Years.* New York: Harper and Row, 1964.

_____. *TVA: Democracy on the March.* Twentieth anniversary ed. New York: Harper and Row, 1953.

Lowitt, Richard. *George W. Norris, The Persistence of a Progressive, 1913-1933.* Urbana: University of Illinois Press, 1971.

Lubell, Samuel. *The Future of American Politics.* 3d ed., rev. New York: Harper and Row, 1965.

MacIver, R. M. *The Ramparts We Guard.* New York: Macmillan, 1950.

McConnell, Grant. *Private Power and American Democracy*. New York: Knopf, 1966.

McCoy, Donald R. *The Presidency of Harry S. Truman*. Lawrence: University of Kansas Press, 1984.

McCraw, Thomas K. *TVA and the Power Fight, 1933-1939*. Philadelphia: Lippincott, 1971.

McCullough, David. *Truman*. New York: Simon and Schuster, 1992.

McGeary, M. Nelson. *Gifford Pinchot, Forester, Politician*. Princeton, N.J.: Princeton University Press, 1960.

Maass, Arthur. *Muddy Waters: The Army Engineers and the Nation's Rivers*. Cambridge, Mass.: Harvard University Press, 1951.

Markowitz, Norman D. *The Rise and Fall of the People's Century: Henry A. Wallace and American Liberalism*. New York: Free Press, 1973.

Martin, John Frederick. *Civil Rights and the Crisis of Liberalism: The Democratic Party, 1945-1976*. Boulder, Colo.: Westview Press, 1979.

Mayer, George H. *The Republican Party, 1854-1964*. New York: Oxford University Press, 1964.

Mayhew, David R. *Party Loyalty among Congressmen: The Difference between Democrats and Republicans, 1947-1962*. Cambridge, Mass.: Harvard University Press, 1966.

Metcalf, Lee, and Reinemer, Vic. *Overcharge*. New York: David McKay, 1967.

Neustadt, Richard. *Presidential Power: The Politics of Leadership*. New York: Wiley, 1960.

Norris, George W. *Fighting Liberal: The Autobiography of George W. Norris*. New York: Macmillan, 1945.

Patterson, James T. *The New Deal and the States: Federalism in Transition*. Princeton, N.J.: Princeton University Press, 1969.

Pemberton, William E., *Bureaucratic Politics: Executive Reorganization during the Truman Administration*. Columbia: University of Missouri Press, 1979.

_____. *Harry S. Truman: Fair Dealer and Cold Warrior*. Boston: Twayne, 1989.

Peterson, F. Ross. *Prophet Without Honor: Glen H. Taylor and the Fight for American Liberalism*. Lexington: University Press of Kentucky, 1974.

Phillips, Cabell. *The Truman Presidency*, New York: Macmillan, 1966.

Pinchot, Gifford. *Breaking New Ground*. New York: Harcourt, Brace, 1947.

Poen, Monte M., ed. *Strictly Personal and Confidential: The Letters Harry Truman Never Mailed*. Boston: Little, Brown, 1982.

Porter, David L. *Congress and the Waning of the New Deal*. Port Washington, N.Y.: Kennikat Press, 1980.

Porter, Kirk H., and Johnson, Donald Bruce, comps. *National Party Platforms, 1840-1956*. Urbana: University of Illinois Press, 1956.

Pritchett, C. Herman. *The Tennessee Valley Authority: A Study in Public Administration.* Chapel Hill: University of North Carolina Press, 1943.

Public Papers of the Presidents: Harry S. Truman, 1945-1953. 8 vols. Washington, D.C.: Government Printing Office, 1961-1966.

Raushenbush, H.S., and Laidler, Harry W. *Power Control.* New York: New Republic, 1928.

Reichard, Gary W. *Politics as Usual: The Age of Truman and Eisenhower.* Arlington, Ill.: Davidson, 1988.

Richardson, Elmo. *Dams, Parks & Politics: Resource Development and Preservation in the Truman-Eisenhower Era.* Lexington: University of Kentucky Press, 1973.

Robbins, Roy M. *Our Landed Heritage: The Public Domain, 1776-1936.* Princeton, N.J.: Princeton University Press, 1942.

Rosenman, Samuel I., ed. *The Public Papers and Addresses of Franklin D. Roosevelt.* Vol. 2: *The Year of Crisis, 1933.* New York: Harper, 1938.

_____. *The Public Papers and Addresses of Franklin D. Roosevelt.* Vol. 12: *The Tide Turns, 1943.* New York: Random House, 1950.

Ross, Irwin. *The Loneliest Campaign: The Truman Victory of 1948.* New York: New American Library, 1968.

Rossiter, Clinton. *The American Presidency.* New York: Harcourt, Brace, 1956.

_____. *Conservatism in America.* London: Heinemann, 1955.

Schapiro, J. Salwyn. *Liberalism: Its Meaning and History.* Princeton, N.J.: van Nostrand, 1958.

Schlesinger, Arthur M., Jr. *The Age of Roosevelt.* 3 vols. Boston: Houghton Mifflin, 1957-1960.

_____. *The Vital Center: The Politics of Freedom.* 2d. ed. Boston: Houghton Mifflin, 1962.

Smith, Frank E. *The Politics of Conservation.* New York: Pantheon, 1966.

Stein, Harold, ed. *Public Administration and Policy Development.* New York: Harcourt Brace, 1952.

Sundborg, George. *Hail Columbia: The Thirty-Year Struggle for Grand Coulee Dam.* New York: Macmillan, 1954.

Thompson, Carl D. *Confessions of the Power Trust.* New York: Dutton, 1932.

_____. *Public Ownership.* New York: Crowell, 1925.

Trombley, Kenneth E. *The Life and Times of a Happy Liberal: A Biography of Morris Llewellyn Cook.* New York: Harper, 1954.

Truman, David B. *The Congressional Party: A Case Study.* New York: Wiley, 1959.

_____. *The Governmental Process: Political Interests and Public Opinion.* New York: Knopf, 1951.

Truman, Harry S. *Memoirs.* Vol. 1: *Year of Decision.* Vol. 2: *Years of Trial and Hope.* Garden City, N.Y.: Doubleday, 1955, 1956.

Truman, Margaret. *Harry S. Truman.* New York: Morrow, 1973.

_____, ed. *Where the Buck Stops: The Personal and Private Writings of Harry S. Truman.* New York: Warner, 1989.

Underhill, Robert. *The Truman Persuasion.* Ames: Iowa State University Press, 1981.

Vennard, Edwin. *Government in the Power Business.* New York: McGraw-Hill, 1968.

Warne, William. *The Bureau of Reclamation.* New York: Praeger, 1973.

Weibe, Robert H. *The Search for Order, 1877-1920.* New York: Hill and Wang, 1967.

Willoughby, William R. *The St. Lawrence Waterway, A Study in Politics and Diplomacy.* Madison: University of Wisconsin Press, 1961.

Woll, Peter. *American Bureaucracy.* 2nd ed. New York: Norton, 1977.

Yarnell, Allen. *Democrats and Progressives: The 1948 Election as a Test of Postwar Liberalism.* Berkeley: University of California Press, 1974.

Zinn, Howard, ed. *New Deal Thought.* New York: Bobbs, Merrill, 1966.

Articles

Bendiner, Robert. "Politics and People." *The Nation,* March 26, 1949, 349-50.

Bernstein, Barton J. "The Presidency Under Truman." *Yale Political Review* 4 (Fall 1964): 8-9, 24.

Bessey, Roy F. "The Political Issues of the Hells Canyon Controversy." *Western Political Quarterly* 9 (September 1956): 676-90.

Clifford, Clark. "Annals of Government: Serving the President." *The New Yorker,* March 1, 1991, 40-68.

_____. "Annals of Government: The Truman Years." *The New Yorker,* April 1, 1991, 36-40.

Cooke, Morris. "Early Days of Rural Electrification." *American Political Science Review* 42 (1948): 431-47.

de Roos, Robert and Maass, Arthur A. "The Lobby That Can't Be Licked." *Harper's Magazine* 199 (July-December 1949): 21-30.

DeVane, Dozier A. "Highlights of Legislative History of the Federal Power Act of 1935 and the Natural Gas Act of 1938." *The George Washington Law Review* 14 (December 1945): 30-41.

Ferrell, John R. "Water in the Missouri Valley: The Inter-Agency River Committee Concept at Mid-Century." *Journal of the West* 7 (January 1968): 96-104.

_____. "Truman's Place in History." *Reviews in American History* 18 (March 1990): 1-9.

Goodwin, Craufurd D. "Policies toward Particular Energy Sources." In *Energy Policy in Perspective: Today's Problems, Yesterday's Solutions*. Edited by Craufurd D. Goodwin, 63-203. Washington, D.C.: Brookings Institution, 1981.

_____. "The Truman Administration: Toward a National Energy Policy." In *Energy Policy in Perspective: Today's Problems, Yesterday's Solutions*. Edited by Craufurd D. Goodwin, 1-62. Washington, D.C.: Brookings Institution, 1981.

Griffith, Robert. "Forging America's Postwar Order: Domestic Politics and Political Economy in the Age of Truman." In *The Truman Presidency*. Edited by Michael J. Lacey, 57-88. New York: Cambridge University Press, 1989.

_____. "Truman and the Historians: The Reconstruction of Postwar American History." *Wisconsin Magazine of History* 59 (autumn 1975): 20-50.

Hamby, Alonzo L. "An American Democrat: A Reevaluation of the Personality of Harry S. Truman." *Political Science Quarterly* 106 (1991), 33-55.

_____. "The Mind and Character of Harry S. Truman." In *The Truman Presidency*. Edited by Michael J. Lacey, 19-53. New York: Cambridge University Press, 1989.

_____. "Harry S. Truman: Insecurity and Responsibility." In *Leadership in the Modern Presidency*. Edited by Fred I. Greenstein, 41-75. Cambridge, Mass.: Harvard University Press, 1988.

Hays, Samuel P. "The Politics of Reform in Municipal Government in the Progressive Era." *Pacific Northwest Quarterly* 55 (October 1964): 157-69.

Lacey, Michael J. "Introduction and Summary: The Truman Era in Retrospect." In *The Truman Presidency*. Edited by Michael J. Lacey, 1-18. New York: Cambridge University Press, 1988.

Leuchtenburg, William E. "Roosevelt, Morris and the 'Seven Little TVA's.'" *The Journal of Politics* 24 (1952): 418-41.

Livingston, John. "Liberalism and the Role of Reason." *Western Political Quarterly* 9 (September 1956): 641-57.

Mann, Arthur. "The Progressive Tradition." In *The Reconstruction of American History*. Edited by John Higham, 157-79. New York: Harper and Row, 1962.

Mitchell, Franklin D. "Harry S Truman and the Verdict of History." *South Atlantic Quarterly* 85 (summer 1986): 261-69.

Neustadt, Richard E. "Congress and the Fair Deal: A Legislative Balance Sheet." *Public Policy* 5 (1954): 366-67.

Person, H. D. "The Rural Electrification Administration in Perspective." *Agricultural History* 24 (1950): 70-89.

Pinchot, Gifford. "The Long Struggle for Effective Federal Water Power Legislation." *The George Washington Law Review* 14 (December 1945): 9-20.

Polenberg, Richard. "The Great Conservation Contest." *Forest History* 10 (January 1967): 13-23.

_____. "Historians and the Liberal Presidency: Recent Appraisals of Roosevelt and Truman." *South Atlantic Quarterly* 75 (winter 1976): 20-25.

Rhyne, Charles S. "Municipal Interest in the Work of the Federal Power Commission." *The George Washington Law Review* 14 (December 1945): 247-60.

Theoharis, Athan. "The Truman Presidency: Trial and Error." *Wisconsin Magazine of History* (autumn 1971), 49-58.

Wheeler, Burton K. "The Federal Power Commission as an Agency of Congress." *The George Washington Law Review* 14 (December 1945): 1-4.

Williams, R.J. "Harry S. Truman and the American Presidency." *Journal of American Studies* 13 (1979): 393-408.

Dissertations and Theses

Hamilton, William Roy. "The President's Materials Policy Commission: A History and Analytical Inquiry into Policy Formation by a Presidential Commission." Ph.D. dissertation, University of Maryland, 1962.

Hinchey, Mary H. "The Frustration of the New Deal Revival, 1944-46." Ph.D. dissertation, University of Missouri, 1965.

Kathka, David Arlin. "The Bureau of Reclamation in the Truman Administration: Personnel, Politics and Policy." Ph.D. dissertation, University of Missouri, 1976.

Peterson, Gale E. "President Harry S. Truman and the Independent Regulatory Commissions, 1945-1952." Ph.D. dissertation, University of Maryland, 1973.

Waltrip, John R. "Public Power During the Truman Administration." Ph.D. dissertation, University of Missouri, 1965.

Whiteside, Larry Allen. "Harry S. Truman and James E. Murray: The Missouri Valley Authority Proposal." M.A. thesis, Central Missouri State College, 1970.

Index

Phyllis Komarek de Luna received her Ph.D. from the University of Alberta. She has taught American history there as well as at the University of Victoria, Portland Community College (Oregon), and Central Michigan University. Her articles have appeared in various professional journals.

Modern American History
The United States since 1865

Frank Ninkovich
General Editor

This series welcomes manuscripts in American History since 1865. The series will consider and publish monographs from any and all fields of historical research—political, social, cultural, economic, intellectual, or diplomatic—that deal with particular aspects of America's development into a modern nation and society.

For additional information about this series or for the submission of manuscripts, please contact:

Frank Ninkovich
Department of History
St. John's University
8000 Utopia Parkway
Jamaica, NY 11439